UNITED NATIONS CONFERENCE ON TRADE AND DEVELOPMENT

UNCTAD

INFORMATION ECONOMY REPORT 2013

The Cloud Economy and Developing Countries

UNITED NATIONS
New York and Geneva 2013

NOTE

Within the UNCTAD Division on Technology and Logistics, the ICT Analysis Section carries out policy-oriented analytical work on the development implications of information and communication technologies (ICTs). It is responsible for the preparation of the *Information Economy Report*. The ICT Analysis Section promotes international dialogue on issues related to ICTs for development, and contributes to building developing countries' capacities to measure the information economy and to design and implement relevant policies and legal frameworks.

In this Report, the terms country/economy refer, as appropriate, to territories or areas. The designations employed and the presentation of the material do not imply the expression of any opinion whatsoever on the part of the Secretariat of the United Nations concerning the legal status of any country, territory, city or area or of its authorities, or concerning the delimitation of its frontiers or boundaries. In addition, the designations of country groups are intended solely for statistical or analytical convenience and do not necessarily express a judgement about the stage of development reached by a particular country or area in the development process. The major country groupings used in this Report follow the classification of the United Nations Statistical Office. These are:

Developed countries: the member countries of the Organization for Economic Cooperation and Development (OECD) (other than Chile, Mexico, the Republic of Korea and Turkey), plus the new European Union member countries that are not OECD members (Bulgaria, Cyprus, Latvia, Lithuania, Malta and Romania), plus Andorra, Liechtenstein, Monaco and San Marino. Countries with economies in transition: South-East Europe and the Commonwealth of Independent States. Developing economies: in general, all the economies that are not specified above. For statistical purposes, the data for China do not include those for Hong Kong Special Administrative Region (Hong Kong, China), Macao Special Administrative Region (Macao, China), or Taiwan Province of China.

Reference to companies and their activities should not be construed as an endorsement by UNCTAD of those companies or their activities.

The following symbols have been used in the tables:

Two dots (..) indicate that data are not available or are not separately reported. Rows in tables have been omitted in those cases where no data are available for any of the elements in the row;

A dash (-) indicates that the item is equal to zero or its value is negligible;

A blank in a table indicates that the item is not applicable, unless otherwise indicated;

A slash (/) between dates representing years, for example, 1994/95, indicates a financial year;

Use of an en dash (–) between dates representing years, for example, 1994–1995, signifies the full period involved, including the beginning and end years;

Reference to "dollars" ($) means United States of America dollars, unless otherwise indicated;

Annual rates of growth or change, unless otherwise stated, refer to annual compound rates;

Details and percentages in tables do not necessarily add up to the totals because of rounding.

The material contained in this study may be freely quoted with appropriate acknowledgement.

UNITED NATIONS PUBLICATION

UNCTAD/IER/2013

Sales No. E.13.II.D.6

ISSN 2075-4396

ISBN 978-92-1-112869-7

e-ISBN 978-92-1-054154-1

Copyright © United Nations, 2013

All rights reserved. Printed in Switzerland

PREFACE

Innovation in the realm of information technology continues its rapid pace, with cloud computing representing one of the latest advances. Significant improvements in the capacity to process, transmit and store data are making cloud computing increasingly important in the delivery of public and private services. This has considerable potential for economic and social development, in particular our efforts to achieve the Millennium Development Goals and define a bold agenda for a prosperous, sustainable and equitable future.

The *Information Economy Report 2013* marks the first time the United Nations is examining the economic potential of cloud computing for low- and middle-income countries, where rates of adoption are currently low. With governments, businesses and other organizations in the developing world considering whether to migrate some or all of their data and activities to the cloud, this publication is especially timely. I commend its information and analysis to all those interested in learning more about the benefits and risks of the cloud economy.

BAN Ki-moon
Secretary-General
United Nations

ACKNOWLEDGEMENTS

The *Information Economy Report 2013* was prepared by a team comprising Torbjörn Fredriksson (team leader), Cécile Barayre, Shubhangi Denblyden, Scarlett Fondeur Gil, Suwan Jang, Diana Korka, Smita Lakhe and Marie Sicat under the direction of Anne Miroux, Director of the Division on Technology and Logistics.

The report benefited from major substantive inputs provided by Michael Minges, David Souter, Ian Walden and Shazna Zuhyle. Research ICT Africa provided original research for five country case studies. Additional inputs were contributed by Tiziana Bonapace, Axel Daiber, Nir Kshetri, Rémi Lang and Howard Williams.

Comments on the initial outline of the report were provided by experts attending a brainstorming meeting organized in Geneva in February 2013, including Jamil Chawki, Alison Gillwald, Abi Jagun, Martin Labbé, Juuso Moisander, Jason Munyan, Jorge Navarro, Thao Nguyen, Marta Pérez Cusó and Lucas von Zallinger. Valuable feedback on various parts of the text was also given by experts attending a peer review meeting organized in Geneva in July 2013, including Chris Connolly, Bernd Friedrich, Alison Gillwald, Angel González-Sanz, Nir Kshetri, Matthias Langenegger, Mpho Moyo, Tansuğ Ok, Daniel Ramos and Carlos Razo.

Additional comments were received at various stages of the production of the report from Dimo Calovski, Padmashree Gehl Sampath, Esperanza Magpantay, Markie Muryawan and Marco Obiso. Ngozi Onodugo provided helpful assistance and inputs during her internship with UNCTAD.

UNCTAD is grateful for the sharing of data by national statistical offices and responses received to UNCTAD's annual survey questionnaire on ICT usage by enterprises and on the ICT sector. The sharing of data for this report by the International Telecommunication Union, LIRNEasia, Research ICT Africa and TeleGeography is highly appreciated.

The cover was done by Sophie Combette. Desktop publishing was done by Nathalie Loriot, graphics were carried out by Stephane Porzi and Christian Rosé and the *Information Economy Report 2013* was edited by Maritza Ascencios, Lucy Annette Deleze-Black and John Rogers.

Financial support from the Government of Finland and the Republic of Korea is gratefully acknowledged.

CONTENTS

Boxes

Tables

Box table and figure

Figures

LIST OF ABBREVIATIONS

3G	third generation (refers to mobile phones)
ACP	The African, Caribbean and Pacific Group of States
ADSL	asymmetric digital subscriber line
API	application programming interface
BPaaS	business process as a service
BPO	business process outsourcing
bps	bits per second
BRICS	Brazil, the Russian Federation, India, China and South Africa
CaaS	communication as a service
CERT	computer emergency response team
CIO	chief information officer
CPC	Central Product Classification
CPU	central processing unit
CRM	client customer relationship management
ERP	enterprise resource planning
GATS	General Agreement on Trade in Services
GB	gigabyte
Gbit/s, Gbps	gigabits per second
GDP	gross domestic product
IaaS	infrastructure as a service
ICT	information and communication technology
IDC	International Data Corporation
IP	Internet protocol
ISO	International Organization for Standardization
ISP	Internet service provider
IT	information technology
ITU	International Telecommunication Union
ITU-T	ITU Telecommunication Standardization Sector
IXP	Internet exchange point
kbit/s, kbps	kilobits per second
LDC	least developed country
LTE	long-term evolution
m2m	mothers-2-mothers organization
Mbit/s, Mbps	megabits per second
ms	millisecond
NCIA	National Computing and Information Agency (Republic of Korea)
NDC	national data centre
NGO	non-governmental organization
NIST	National Institute of Standards and Technology

NTT	Nippon Telegraph and Telephone Corporation
OECD	Organization for Economic Cooperation and Development
PaaS	platform as a service
PC	personal computer
PPP	public–private partnership
PUE	power usage effectiveness
QoS	quality of service
RTT	round-trip time
SaaS	software as a service
SLA	service level agreement
SME	small and medium-sized enterprise
SMS	short message service
Tbps	terabits per second
TDF	transborder data flow
TNC	transnational corporation
UNCTAD	United Nations Conference on Trade and Development
WTO	World Trade Organization
XaaS	x as a service

OVERVIEW

Cloud computing accentuates the quality dimension of the digital divide.

The differential between countries in access to and use of information and communication technologies (ICTs) – the digital divide – has long been a significant concern of Governments and the international community. Over time, its nature has changed. The gap in access to basic telephone services, once very substantial, is now significantly diminished and expected to shrink further in the next few years. In its place has come a gap in access to the Internet and, particularly, in access to broadband services. The digital divide in broadband capacity and quality leads in turn to a divide between countries and regions in the extent to which individuals, businesses, economies and societies are able to take advantage of new ICT innovations and applications.

Cloud computing is a recent manifestation of this evolving ICT landscape. Given its potential, it is becoming increasingly important for Governments and enterprises. In simple terms, cloud computing enables users, through the Internet or other digital networks, to access a scalable and elastic pool of data storage and computing resources, as and when required. Some predict that cloud technology will be among the most significant disruptive technologies over the next two decades, with major implications for markets, economies and societies. Against this background, the *Information Economy Report 2013* provides an objective analysis of the possible implications for developing countries of the evolving cloud economy.

Massive improvements in storage, processing and transmission capacity have paved the way for the cloud economy.

The metaphor of the "cloud" can be misleading. Rather than representing an amorphous phenomenon in the sky, cloud computing is well anchored on the ground by the combination of physical hardware, networks, storage, services and interfaces that are needed to deliver computing as a service. A key feature of cloud computing is that it often involves transferring data to a server controlled by a third party.

The shift that is taking place towards the cloud represents a step change in the relationship between telecommunications, business and society, and has been enabled by massively enhanced processing power, data storage and higher transmission speeds. For example, Intel's 22-nanometre central processing unit is 4,000 times faster than that which the same company introduced in 1971, and between 1986 and 2007 the world's "technological memory" roughly doubled every three years. Meanwhile, the fastest theoretical speed of a dial-up connection in 1993, the year the Internet browser was introduced, was 56 kilobits per second (kbit/s); as of 2013, consumer broadband packages of 2 gigabits per second (Gbit/s) are available, almost 36,000 times faster than dial-up. Major cloud service providers today have hundreds of thousands of servers located in massive data centres in different parts of the world.

According to definitions proposed in April 2013 by the International Telecommunication Union (ITU) and the International Organization for Standardization (ISO), cloud computing is a paradigm for enabling network access to a scalable and elastic pool of shareable physical or virtual resources with on-demand self-service provisioning and administration. Cloud services are defined as services that are provided and used by clients on demand at any time, through any access network, using any connected devices that use cloud computing technologies. The implications of cloud computing and cloud services on wider economic development are discussed in this report in the context of the cloud economy.

The cloud economy comprises various cloud service categories and deployments.

However, the "cloud" and "cloud services" are not homogenous products but come in different shapes and configurations. Three categories of cloud services – infrastructure as a service (IaaS), platform as a service (PaaS) and software as a service (SaaS) – are commonly used to encompass the whole range of cloud service categories that are currently available. The defining characteristic of each of these variations of the cloud is the type of computing or information technology (IT) facilities that is made available remotely to a cloud service customer, on a rental or subscription basis, by a cloud service provider:

In the case of IaaS, the cloud provider's processing, storage, networks and other fundamental computing resources allow the cloud customer to deploy and run software. The elasticity of IaaS allows an organization or enterprise to access computing infrastructure in a flexible and timely manner.

In the case of PaaS, the cloud customer deploys its own applications and data on platform tools, including programming tools, belonging to and managed by the cloud provider.

With SaaS, the cloud customer takes advantage of software running on the cloud-provider's infrastructure rather than on the customer's own hardware. The applications required are accessible from various client devices through either a thin client interface, such as a web browser (for example, web-based email), or a program interface.

Cloud services can also be deployed to users in a variety of ways, the most significant of which are summarized below:

- **Public clouds:** open resources that offer services over a network that is open for public use. Many mass market services widely used by individuals, such as webmail, online storage and social media are public cloud services.

- **Private clouds:** proprietary resources provided for a single organization (for example, a Government or large enterprise), managed and hosted internally or by a third-party.

- **Community clouds:** resources/services provided for and shared between a limited range of clients/ users, managed and hosted internally or by a third-party.

- **Hybrid clouds:** a mix of the deployment models described above, for example, public and private cloud provision.

Different cloud configurations offer both opportunities and risks for potential cloud service customers.

As a basis for the analysis, the *Information Economy Report 2013* uses the concept of the cloud economy ecosystem, which highlights the deployment and impacts of cloud computing and cloud services within the wider information economy and, thereby, their relevance to national economic development. The cloud economy ecosystem includes a complex set of relationships between technology and business, governance and innovation, production and consumption. It is how this ecosystem evolves, rather than the potential of the technology alone, that will determine the outcomes for developing countries.

As Governments, enterprises and other organizations in the developing world consider whether to migrate some or all of their data and activities to the cloud, they need to assess the potential advantages and risks of such a move.

Potential advantages include:

- Reduced costs for rented IT hardware and software compared to in-house equipment and IT management;

- Enhanced elasticity of storage/processing capacity as required by demand;

- Greater flexibility and mobility of access to data and services;

- Immediate and cost-free upgrading of software;

- Enhanced reliability/security of data management and services.

Potential risks or disadvantages include:

- Increased costs of communications (to telecommunication operators/Internet service providers (ISPs));

- Increased costs for migration and integration;

- Reduced control over data and applications;

- Data security and privacy concerns;

- Risk of services being inaccessible, for example, due to inadequate ICT or power infrastructure;

- Risk of lock-in (limited interoperability and data portability) with providers in uncompetitive cloud markets.

The cloud's potential to improve efficiency is a strong incentive for organizations in the private and public sectors to transfer activities to the cloud. At the same time, there are important trade-offs to be made, for example, between cost savings on the one hand and considerations related to data security and privacy on the other. Various cloud customers will assess the opportunities and risks associated with the cloud differently, therefore opting for different solutions. Some businesses, Governments and other organizations are better positioned to reap the benefits of a shift to the cloud, or can gain greater advantage than others because of the nature of their activities or business model. This is the case, for example, for those that have high fixed costs in maintaining in-house IT departments, recurrently need IT software and hardware, face large or unpredictable variations in demand for IT resources or can gain substantial added value from more efficient exploitation of data and market opportunities.

The cloud economy is expanding fast but is still small.

There are various estimates of the size of the market for cloud services. Fee-generated revenues from public provision of IaaS, PaaS and SaaS have been forecast to reach somewhere between $43 billion and $94 billion by 2015. To this can be added the revenue generated through advertising on cloud-enabled web applications that are available at no cost to the user. Such revenue is currently considerably larger than the fees generated from public cloud provision. Estimates of the value of private cloud services also vary greatly – from about $5 billion to about $50 billion. Discrepancies in projections reflect different methodologies, but most forecasts agree that cloud adoption will continue to expand rapidly over the next few years.

This is still very small compared with the revenue of the global ICT sector, which was estimated at about $4 trillion in 2011. However, most segments of the ICT sector are in some way affected by cloud computing. The demand for bandwidth will drive telecommunication services revenue, although revenues from voice services could be affected as more people switch to cloud-based voice over Internet protocol applications. Demand for equipment and computer hardware, particularly data servers and network equipment, will rise as more services move to the cloud.

The shift to the cloud is generating considerable growth in data traffic. During an average minute in 2012, Google received two million search requests, Facebook users shared around 700,000 content items and Twitter sent out 100,000 tweets. In 2012, 60 per cent of such cloud traffic on the Internet emanated from Europe and North America. Asia–Pacific was responsible for another third while Latin America and the Middle East and Africa together accounted for only 5 per cent. However, the highest growth rates in the next few years are expected in the Middle East and Africa.

On the supply side, the cloud economy is currently dominated by a few very large cloud service providers, almost all headquartered in the United States. Their early entry into cloud computing gave them first-mover advantages, not least in terms of building large networks of users and massive data storage and processing capacity. The absolute levels of investment required for major cloud-computing estates are very high; it can cost more than half a billion dollars for a cluster of data centres.

While the cloud service provider market is likely to continue to be dominated by a small number of global IT businesses, some factors may favour national or regional players. Some Governments and enterprises are required (by law or corporate policy) to locate their data within national jurisdictions, or prefer to do so for security or geopolitical reasons. Large corporations and Governments have hitherto shown a preference for private over public clouds, eschewing some cost saving to ensure a greater sense of security and control over their data and services. Recent international publicity concerning data surveillance may have reinforced such a preference.

Cloud adoption in developing countries has potential implications for both the supply and the user side of the cloud economy.

The most significant activities and potential supply opportunities for enterprises in developing countries are concerned with: (a) data-centre and related cloud provision; (b) the development and provision of local cloud services for groups of customers, including local businesses and individual citizens; (c) cloud aggregation, system integration, brokerage and related services. In addition to these explicitly cloud-based areas of activity, opportunities exist for national communications businesses (telecommunications operators and ISPs) which can gain from increased data traffic using their networks. Despite the advantages of global cloud service providers, there are some factors that offer scope for local or regional data centres to expand in developing countries, such as growing demand for private cloud solutions, national data-protection laws or corporate policies requiring data to be kept within national jurisdictions, and high costs of or unreliable international broadband connectivity.

There has been extensive adoption by individuals in developing countries of free cloud services such as webmail and online social networks. This is true in almost all countries, in particular those with higher levels of Internet use and cloud readiness. The most popular cloud-based applications are generally those provided at a global level. In low-income countries at a nascent stage of cloud readiness, IaaS is often the first category of cloud services to emerge. As the infrastructure situation improves and if the SME sector expands, the market for SaaS in developing countries will become more important and eventually dominant as it already is in developed countries.

Foreign affiliates in developing countries make extensive use of the cloud as part of their parent companies' global networks. With some wariness, Governments in developing countries are also moving towards the cloud. Some are developing systematic cloud strategies, as part of broader ICT strategies or sometimes alongside these. Where government departments and larger corporations are concerned, there is so far a general preference for private over public cloud approaches. There is planned adoption of the cloud in domestic enterprises, although less extensive than anticipated by cloud advocates.

Experience of cloud computing in developing countries is too recent for there to be a strongly established evidence base on which to assess impacts. Businesses, Governments and other organizations should carefully examine the potential for cloud services to improve their management and service delivery. They should only migrate data and services to the cloud when they are confident that the cloud offers significant benefits and that attendant risks can be appropriately mitigated. Both public and private cloud solutions should be considered in this context, taking into account implications for data security and privacy.

Infrastructure deficiencies seriously hamper the uptake of and benefits from cloud computing in many developing countries.

For several reasons, the options for cloud adoption available in low- and middle-income countries look different from those in more advanced economies. Critical factors relate, among other things, to the availability and quality of cloud-related infrastructure, cost considerations and inadequate legal and regulatory frameworks to address data protection and privacy concerns.

As regards access to and availability of cloud-related infrastructure, and despite significant improvements in broadband connectivity in many developing economies, the gap between developed and developing countries keeps widening. Average fixed broadband penetration is now more than 28 subscriptions per 100 people in developed economies, 6 in developing countries and only 0.2 in the least developed countries (LDCs). In the case of mobile broadband, the gap is also significant. The average number of subscriptions in 2012 was about 67 per 100 people in developed countries, 14 in developing countries and below 2 in the LDCs.

In addition, in most low-income countries, mobile broadband networks are characterized by low speed and high latency and are therefore currently not ideal for cloud service provision, especially of the more advanced kinds. The net value of cloud-based solutions will be lower in countries with a heightened risk of communication- and power-network outages. The lack of supporting infrastructure, such as Internet exchange points (IXPs), reliable and inexpensive electricity and robust fibre-optic backbones also affect the deployment of national data centres. Indeed, as much as 85 per cent of data centres offering co-location services are in developed economies. This "data centre divide" is reflected in the availability of servers; whereas there were in 2011 more than 1,000 secure data servers per million inhabitants in high-income economies, there was only one such server per million inhabitants in LDCs.

The cost of communication remains another critical obstacle for adoption of cloud services in many developing countries. The fees paid to cloud service providers and for broadband access and usage, charges by the ISP and the hardware and software costs incurred are likely to form a much higher proportion of the total costs of cloud provisioning than in advanced economies. The combination of few national data centres and high costs of international broadband communications further weighs on the net value of relying on cloud solutions.

The cloud raises legal and regulatory challenges, especially concerning data protection and privacy.

The rapid emergence of cloud computing has raised concerns about its legal and regulatory implications. Issues of data protection and security are among the concerns most frequently mentioned by potential cloud customers in both developed and developing countries. Such concerns have intensified following the disclosure in 2013 of national surveillance programmes and reports on access by law-enforcement agencies to data hosted by global cloud service providers. Governments need to protect national interests and their citizens; service providers require a stable framework to facilitate innovation and investment; and users require assurance and trust to encourage the take-up of such services. Policy responses may range from a do-nothing attitude to the adoption of cloud-specific laws.

Public law is essential to secure the basic rights of end users. While there is no imperative to develop specific laws or regulations on cloud computing, areas requiring reform are relatively clear: privacy, data protection, information security and cybercrime. For Governments of developing countries, it is essential that appropriate laws and regulations are adopted and enforced in these areas. As of 2013, there were 99 countries with data-privacy laws. As far as is known, Mexico is the only country which has adopted cloud-specific provisions in relation to data protection. There is no international harmonized privacy framework regulating data transfers across borders, but developing countries could benefit from implementing strong domestic-privacy regimes.

In addition to public law, contractual agreements between cloud service providers and cloud service customers also greatly impact on the operation and effects of the cloud economy. In some circumstances, regulatory intervention in the freedom to contract may be necessary to protect the public interest. The placement of data in the cloud may require regulatory intervention to address concerns related to personal privacy, commercial secrecy or national security. For example, within data protection laws, imposing minimum responsibilities on the cloud service providers – to ensure the security of customer data and to notify its customers if there is a security breach – could help to provide greater transparency about vulnerabilities and to enable mitigation in a timely manner.

Where there are apprehensions on relying heavily on cloud services offered by providers based in a foreign jurisdiction, it may be difficult to address this market reality through regulatory intervention. An alternative policy response may be to encourage the establishment of domestic cloud services, either by offering foreign investors a favorable environment to invest in the building of local infrastructure (such as data centres) or encouraging domestic enterprises to enter the supply side of the cloud economy. Whereas such measures may involve regulatory components, such as imposing "localization" requirements, they would be designed to facilitate the provision of cloud services rather than to constrain them. Several Governments of developing countries are building government clouds to serve the needs of the Government itself and sometimes others. In Europe, there have been calls for the development of a secure European cloud and some national cloud initiatives have been launched to offer an alternative source of cloud service provision.

Governments should facilitate benefits from the cloud economy but be aware of pitfalls.

Although cloud adoption is still at a nascent stage in developing countries, policymakers should waste no time in enhancing their understanding of how it may affect their economies and societies, in order to be

able to make informed policy decisions. Government policies should be based on an assessment of the pros and cons of cloud solutions and be rooted in a thorough understanding of existing ICT and cloud use within countries. Governments need to recognize the diversity of business models and services within the cloud, the multiplicity of customers of cloud services, and the complexity of the cloud economy ecosystem. In view of its relevance for both public service delivery and business competitiveness, it is important to integrate any cloud strategy in the overall national development plan, and to plan for its execution, monitoring and evaluation. Policy approaches should be tailored to the circumstances of individual economies, and be consistent with the overall strategic framework for national economic development and for leveraging ICTs.

On the whole, Governments should broadly welcome and support the development of a cloud economy and the adoption of cloud services. In principle, there is no general case for government policy and regulation to discourage migration towards the cloud. Rather, policies and regulatory approaches should seek to create an enabling framework that supports firms and organizations that wish to migrate data and services to the cloud so that they may do so easily and safely. However, this does not mean that cloud-based solutions are always preferable to alternative approaches. In addition, there are multiple ways of making use of cloud technology – using public, private or hybrid clouds at national, regional or global levels. Governments should seek to facilitate those approaches that seem most likely to deliver wider economic benefits in their particular context.

A number of steps could be considered by Governments that wish to translate the potential of the cloud into tangible development gains. In terms of scope, at the national level policymaking would be advised to consider measures related to the following areas:

- **Assess the cloud readiness of the country.** Governments should start by carefully assessing the current situation in their countries, to identify bottlenecks and weaknesses that need to be addressed if the cloud is to be effectively exploited, and clarify what kind of cloud solutions are most propitious.
- **Develop a national cloud strategy.** Based on the readiness assessment, a national cloud strategy could be drafted either as a stand-alone

policy document or as an integral part of the national ICT strategy.

- **Address the infrastructure challenge**. This would involve measures to improve the provision of reliable and affordable broadband infrastructure and to monitor regularly the quality of broadband services. Effective communications regulations are here of the essence. Attention should also be given to the role of IXPs and the provision of electricity.

- **Address relevant legal and regulatory issues related to cloud adoption to ensure that cloud service users' interests are properly protected**. Key areas include the location of data, e-transactions and cybercrime. Efforts should be made to reflect international best practice in the development of new legislation.

- **Map opportunities in the supply side of the cloud economy**. Three key areas deserve particular attention: the development of national data centres, the potential for cloud aggregation services, and the development of new cloud services.

- **Address the need for human resources**. Skill areas that are likely to become increasingly important include those related to the IT and software skills needed to manage the migration and integration of cloud services; management and organizational skills to handle the reorganization and re-engineering of business processes; and legal and procurement skills.

- **Government use of cloud services**. Given their important role in the information economy in many developing countries, the role of Governments should be explored with regard to the establishment of national data centres, e-government systems and related public procurement.

Development partners should work with Governments in responding to the cloud economy.

Addressing the many challenges that developing countries face in seeking to benefit from the evolving cloud economy will require both expertise in various fields and financial resources. Development partners could help in that respect, by ensuring that cloud-related development challenges are incorporated in their agendas to reduce the risk that the move towards the cloud economy may result in a widening of the digital divide. They may also provide support at the country level in contributing to financing broadband infrastructure, establishing appropriate legal and regulatory frameworks, and building capacity in relevant areas.

International agencies could facilitate this assistance through some of their existing activities. UNCTAD and other international organizations can, for example, facilitate an exchange of experiences with regard to the policy challenges that developing countries face to derive benefits from the cloud economy and avoid pitfalls.

Another key area in which development partners can play a role concerns international standards for cloud services, which are essential to facilitate interoperability and to help customers understand what they are purchasing. Standardization forums should consider how to engage developing countries and their users to ensure that their specific needs and requirements are addressed. More research is also needed in a number of areas to allow for a more comprehensive assessment of the impact of different forms of cloud adoption. As the evidence base expands, it will become feasible to assess macroeconomic implications for economic growth, employment, productivity and trade.

As with other ICT areas, the pace of change in cloud technology and markets is rapid. The experiences described in this report relate to present circumstances. The nature of cloud services and of the cloud economy will continue to develop fast, and may be very different in five years' time. Governments, businesses and development partners need to bear these changes in mind, and to re-evaluate their policies and strategies concerning the cloud regularly to ensure that they continue to maximize potential benefits and minimize potential risks to their citizens, businesses and customers.

Mukhisa Kituyi
Secretary-General, UNCTAD

THE CLOUD
ECONOMY ECOSYSTEM

1

Improvements in processing power, storage capabilities and communication transmission speeds have together facilitated the emergence of what has come to be known as cloud computing. This phenomenon is likely to influence, in various ways, both the production and use of services delivered through ICTs over coming years. As with other new technological developments, it is difficult to predict the full implications of cloud computing. While it offers significant potential benefits to those who are able to leverage them, it also raises concerns for users, not least with regard to data protection and privacy. Moreover, the spread of cloud computing may widen the digital divide between those – countries, businesses and individuals – that are and those that are not well placed to benefit from it.

Although cloud adoption is still at a nascent stage in developing countries, policymakers should waste no time in improving their understanding of how it may affect their economies and societies, in order to be able to make informed policy decisions. The *Information Economy Report 2013* seeks to assist in this context, by stimulating a nuanced discussion of the potential role and value of the "cloud economy". This first chapter explains the evolution towards the cloud, defines key terms, outlines the most important drivers and barriers of cloud adoption, and presents an overall framework for analysing the cloud economy ecosystem. It thereby provides a road map for the following chapters of this report.

A. EVOLUTION TO THE CLOUD

Cloud computing and the emergence of a cloud economy based upon it are becoming increasingly important considerations for Governments and enterprises. A recent study has described cloud technology as one of the most significant disruptive technologies which will develop over the next two decades, with major implications for markets, economies and societies (Manyika et al., 2013). It predicts that, by 2025, most information technology (IT) and web applications and services could be cloud delivered or cloud enabled, and that most enterprises might be using cloud facilities and services. While it is always difficult, even risky, to predict the development of IT so far ahead, policymakers and business leaders should start examining the opportunities and potential risks of this growing phenomenon.

In simple terms, cloud computing enables users, through the Internet or another digital network, to access a scalable and elastic pool of data storage and computing resources, as and when they are required (see also section I.B). The metaphor of the "cloud" can be misleading here. Rather than representing something amorphous or in the sky, cloud computing is enabled by the combination of the physical hardware, networks, storage, services and interfaces that are needed to deliver computing as a service. A key feature of cloud computing is that it often involves transferring data and computing to a server controlled by a third party.

The shift towards cloud computing that is currently taking place can be seen as a step change in the relationship between telecommunications, business and society, enabled by greatly enhanced processing power, data storage and higher transmission speeds, accompanied by sharp price reductions (box I.1).

In one sense, the cloud has taken the relationship between user and computer back towards an earlier era (table I.1). Computing began in the 1950s and 1960s with access to large "mainframe" computers through "dumb terminals", typewriter-like devices with

---

Box I.1. The expansion of computing and communication power

A few examples can help to illustrate the dramatic evolution of processing, storage and transmission capacity.

- Processing power. The first transistor, precursor to the central processing unit (CPU) that forms the "brain" of a computer, was built by hand in 1947. Gordon Moore, one of the founders of microprocessor manufacturer Intel, predicted in 1965 that the number of transistors on a chip will double roughly every year ("Moore's Law"). Intel introduced its first CPU (the 4004) in 1971; Intel's current 22 nanometre CPU is 4,000 times faster, uses only 0.02 per cent of the energy and costs 50,000 times less (Intel, 2011).

- Digital storage capabilities. The world's "technological memory" roughly doubled every three years between 1986 and 2007, about the time that cloud computing began to take off. It grew in this period from 2.5 optimally compressed exabytes[a] (1 per cent digitized) to around 300 (94 per cent digitized) (Hilbert and López, 2011). The first IBM personal computor (PC), which was introduced in 1981, cost $3,000 and could only accept diskettes of 160 kilobytes storage.[b] By 2010, for $600 it was possible to buy a hard disk that could store all the world's recorded music.[c]

- Transmission speeds. At both user and backbone levels these have increased dramatically. The fastest theoretical speed of a dial-up connection in 1993, the year the Internet browser was introduced, was 56 kbps. As of 2013, consumer broadband packages of 2 Giga bit per second (Gbps) are available, almost 36,000 times faster than dial-up (see also section II.B). The first transatlantic fibre optic cable, TAT-8, was introduced in 1988 with a speed of 280 Mbps.[d] In 2011 the Hibernia Atlantic Submarine Cable System reached speeds of 100 Gbps, some 350 times faster.[e]

Source: UNCTAD.

[a] The byte (8 bits) is the unit used for expressing digital information. One exabyte is equal to one quintillion bytes.

[b] See http://www-03.ibm.com/ibm/history/exhibits/pc25/pc25_press.html (accessed 2 October 2013) and http://www-03.ibm.com/ibm/history/exhibits/pc25/pc25_fact.html (accessed 2 October 2013).

[c] Kevin Kelly, Web 2.0 Expo and Conference, March 29, 2011. Video available at www.web2expo.com/webexsf2011/public/schedule/proceedings (accessed 2 October 2013).

[d] See http://atlantic-cable.com/Cables/speed.htm (accessed 2 October 2013).

[e] See http://www.submarinenetworks.com/systems/trans-atlantic/hibernia-atlantic/hibernia-atlantic-trials-100g-transatlantic (accessed 2 October 2013).

no intelligence of their own. The "personal" computer appeared in the 1980s, providing users with their own processing power and storage independent of these earlier mainframe devices. When there was a need to obtain remotely stored information in this new paradigm the user's client computer accessed a server (client/server computing). The introduction of the Internet initially allowed only slow telephone dial-up access, first for email and file downloads, later to access websites. As telecommunications networks have developed they have enabled ever faster access to more sophisticated applications.

While the evolution of computing towards the cloud has been gradual, it is only in the past few years that the economics of cloud computing have triggered a move away from processing and storing data on client hardware to using cloud-based data centres. As stated in a recent review of cloud computing (Crémer et al., 2012):

> The seeds of cloud computing were deposited as soon as the Internet began developing and…recent evolutions have been questions of degrees, not of nature. But when there are enough degrees of difference, the nature of the beast becomes totally different.

Although there are similarities between the mainframe model and today's cloud paradigm, there are also crucial differences. The mainframe model was designed to manage scarce and expensive data storage and processing resources, rationing their availability to a limited set of users within an organization. By contrast, cloud computing is being deployed in an era of abundant data storage and processing resources. Cloud providers aim to ensure that the much wider availability, greater diversity of applications and lower costs that result from this abundance are made widely available to the growing numbers of Internet and cloud users. Cloud computing's success depends explicitly on the conjunction between great computing capacity (data storage and processing power) and reliable high-speed communications (which enable users to access that computing capacity in real or near-to-real time).

As will be discussed below, this new paradigm has the capacity to reduce capital expenditure on IT, improve operational efficiency (by introducing new administrative and service-delivery models), enable new applications, and improve customer service. A general shift in business and government data and data handling to the cloud, it has been argued, could thereby stimulate efficiency, productivity and economic growth. At the same time, there is nothing automatic about these potential gains, which are likely to be unevenly distributed, geographically, within societies, and over time. Cloud adoption in developing countries faces several significant constraints which are discussed later in this report, including inadequacies in infrastructure and legal and regulatory frameworks. As in other countries there are also concerns about security, data protection, privacy and reliability. Moreover, since the early stages in the development of the cloud, some experts have cautioned against the risk of surrendering control over the software used by relying on third-party servers and without being able to study the source code used. These are complex aspects of the cloud economy with important implications not just for individuals, businesses and Governments, but for economic and social development in general.

Cloud computing is already having an impact on the ways in which Governments, businesses and citizens interact online. Consumer-oriented services such as webmail, online social networks and file-sharing applications are among the most popular applications currently used on the Internet. All are fundamentally cloud based. Enterprises and Governments, particularly in developed countries, are increasingly transferring data to the cloud and making use of cloud services rather than relying on their own hardware and

Table I.1. From mainframes to the cloud						
Characteristics	1960 1970 1980 Mainframe computing >>>>			1990 2000 Client/server computing		2010 >>>>>> >>>> Cloud computing
Technology	Centralized computation & storage; thin clients			Optimized for efficiency because of high cost		High up-front costs for hardware and software
Economic	PCs and servers for distributed computation, storage, etc.			Optimized for agility because of the low cost		Perpetual licence for operating system and application software
Business model	Large data centres, ability to scale, commodity hardware, devices			Efficiency and agility an order of magnitude better		Ability to pay as you go, and only for what you use

Source: UNCTAD, adapted from (Microsoft, 2010).

software. For some, the use of the cloud has already become the norm, at least for data storage, with new services set to follow. There have been warnings of a hype cycle, reminiscent of the earlier dot.com boom, with regard to cloud computing, with overly optimistic expectations over the next few years (Renda, 2012: 25). For example, high prices are being paid by major cloud providers for the acquisition of smaller businesses that have developed new cloud services and applications.[2]

The remainder of this chapter is structured as follows. Section B provides definitions of cloud computing, cloud services and other relevant terms. Section C briefly summarizes the main advantages and concerns that are attributed to cloud adoption from the perspectives of different users. Section D identifies the principal stakeholders in the cloud economy and draws these together into a descriptive model of the cloud economy ecosystem. Finally, section E outlines the main research questions that are addressed in the report and provides a roadmap to subsequent chapters.

B. DEFINITIONS OF KEY TERMS CONCERNED WITH CLOUD COMPUTING

In order to understand the implications of the emerging cloud economy – the interactions between cloud service providers and cloud service customers in different parts of society – it is important first to clarify exactly what is meant by cloud computing, to describe what it does and to summarize how it works. This section of the chapter provides core definitions which underpin the understanding of cloud computing and the cloud economy in the remainder of the report.

1. Cloud computing and cloud services

The concept of cloud computing is still evolving. What cloud computing offers today differs from what it offered five years ago and from what it will offer five years hence. Different definitions therefore emphasize different aspects of the cloud: its technology, its economics or how it is experienced.

Cloud computing is a way of delivering applications, services or content remotely to end users, rather than requiring them to hold data, software or applications on their own devices, a process known as "virtualization". The automation of infrastructure and application processes (including configuration, provisioning, auto-scaling and failure recovery) enables cloud providers to hold data and run applications/services on behalf of cloud customers. Data and applications are managed through application programming interfaces (APIs) between cloud software and cloud customers' own IT systems. Virtualization also allows resources such as servers and storage devices to be shared between many different users, an arrangement known as "multi-tenancy" that maximizes the operational efficiency of data centres and enables sharing of overhead costs among numerous cloud customers, so further reducing the total costs of usage.

Cloud computing can be described as a rental or pay-as-you-go model for the exploitation of IT assets and resources, by contrast with the ownership model (for both hardware and software) which has become prevalent during the client/server era of computing. It exploits the storage capacity of very large-scale data centres and the communications capabilities of broadband infrastructure, where these are both available, to achieve economies of scale and scope that can be passed on as lower costs for end users. The legal and economic terms of such arrangements are contractually agreed between cloud providers and cloud customers, and governed by service-level agreements (SLAs) reached between them (European Telecommunications Network Operators' Association, 2011).

One widely used definition of cloud computing, which draws on these descriptions, is that put forward by the National Institute of Standards and Technology (NIST) of the United States of America, as follows (National Institute of Standards and Technology, 2011):

> Cloud computing is a model for enabling ubiquitous, convenient, on-demand network access to a shared pool of configurable computing resources (e.g., networks, servers, storage, applications, and services) that can be rapidly provisioned and released with minimal management effort or service provider interaction.

An alternative definition has been proposed more recently (April 2013) by the International Telecommunication Union (ITU) and the International Organization for Standardization (ISO):[3]

Cloud computing is a paradigm for enabling network access to a scalable and elastic pool of shareable physical or virtual resources with on-demand self-service provisioning and administration.

Both of these definitions establish the fundamental nature of the concept. Following on from them, "cloud services" have been defined as services that are provided and used by clients "on demand at any time, through any access network, using any connected devices [that use] cloud computing technologies" (ITU, 2012a). A further distinction can be made between cloud services that can be accessed via a web browser without having to install any software on the user's device, and "cloud-based services" which require software installation in order to make use of cloud resources. For the sake of simplicity, the term "cloud services" will be used in this report to represent both kinds of services.

2. Cloud service categories

A number of different cloud service categories are consistent with these characteristics. These are generally described using the formula "X as a service" (XaaS), where X represents the kind of facility made available, on the terms described above, by the cloud service provider to the cloud service customer (see ecosystem diagram in figure I.2). A number of different formulations of XaaS are described in the literature, depending on the granularity with which they seek to describe the services that are being offered. Three categories of cloud services – infrastructure, platform and software as a service (IaaS, PaaS and SaaS) – are commonly used to encompass the whole range of cloud service categories that are currently available.

These are compared in table I.2 with one another and with traditional IT systems.

- **IaaS.** In this category, the cloud provider's processing, storage, networks and other fundamental computing resources allow the cloud customer to deploy and run software, which can include operating systems and applications. The cloud customer does not manage or control the underlying infrastructure but has control over operating systems, storage and deployed applications, and may have limited control of select networking components (for example, host firewalls). Making use of the elasticity of IaaS for data storage and processing capacity allows an organization or enterprise to access computing infrastructure in a flexible and timely manner, for example when demand is uncertain or unpredictable.

- **PaaS.** In this category, the cloud customers deploy their own applications and data on platform tools, including programming tools, belonging to and managed by the cloud provider. Application developers working on mobile applications commonly use cloud-based platforms to develop and launch their services. The cloud customer does not manage or control the underlying cloud infrastructure such as network, servers, operating systems, or storage, but has control over the deployed applications and perhaps over configuration settings for the application-hosting environment. For example, a developer working on Android applications can use PaaS to ensure that an application can automatically take advantage of changes implemented in, and follow the look and feel of, new releases of the Android operating system as they appear.

Table I.2. Different computing categories

Traditional IT		IaaS		PaaS		SaaS
Applications		Applications		Applications		Applications
Data		Data		Data		Data
Runtime		Runtime		Runtime		Runtime
Middleware		Middleware		Middleware		Middleware
Operating system		Operating system		Operating system		Operating system
Virtualization		Virtualization		Virtualization		Virtualization
Servers		Servers		Servers		Servers
Storage		Storage		Storage		Storage
Networking		Networking		Networking		Networking

Source: Microsoft, 2010.

- **SaaS.** In this category, the cloud customer takes advantage of software running on the cloud provider's infrastructure rather than on the customer's own hardware. The applications required are accessible from various client devices through either a thin client interface, such as a web browser (for example, web-based email), or a program interface. In SaaS services, the customer has no control over the underlying cloud infrastructure, accessing applications through a web browser or separate programme interface.[4] Another formulation of XaaS that might broadly be included in SaaS is CaaS (communications as a service), which includes cloud services for messaging and voice-over Internet protocol (IP).[5]

The defining characteristic of each of these variations of the cloud is the type of computing or IT facilities that are made available remotely to a cloud service customer, on a rental or subscription basis, by a cloud service provider. Globally, the most widespread of these service models today is SaaS, followed by IaaS and PaaS (Chapter II). However, as will be illustrated in subsequent chapters, the degrees of prevalence differ considerably between countries, depending on their level of development in terms of broadband infrastructure and regulatory framework.

3. Cloud deployment models

As well as different service categories, cloud services can be deployed to users in a variety of ways, the most significant of which can be summarized as follows:

- **Public clouds** are an open resource that offers services over a network that is open for public use. Examples of public clouds include Amazon Elastic Compute Cloud (EC2), IBM's Blue Cloud, Sun Cloud, Google AppEngine and Windows Azure Services Platform. Many mass market services widely used by individuals, such as webmail and online storage, are public cloud services.

- **Private clouds**, by contrast, are a proprietary resource provided for a single organization (for example, a Government or large business customer). It can be managed internally or by a third party, and hosted internally or externally.

- **Community clouds** are a resource/service provided for and shared between a limited range of clients/users. It can be managed internally or by a third party and hosted internally or externally. It might be considered halfway between public and private cloud provisioning.

Box I.2.   Economies of scale and the cloud

The scale of computing power involved in the very large data centres that are at the heart of major cloud provider businesses has markedly different economic impacts from earlier models of data centre provisioning. A traditional data centre comprises a collection of corporate IT resources. It typically houses hardware that can support a variety of applications (and software architectures), and therefore has to manage complex workloads. This requires multiple management tools and incurs high maintenance costs. As a result, traditional data centres have typically maintained substantial surplus capacity and been relatively expensive to run. The differences in costs between traditional data centres and the very large-scale data centres characteristic of cloud computing are illustrated in box table I.1. While costs vary in absolute terms and in relation to one another, this underscores the significant potential for cost reduction that becomes available through the cloud.

Box table I.1.   Cost implications of scale economies in data centre operations

	Cost in medium-sized data centre	Cost in very large data centre	Ratio
Network	$95 per Mbps/month	$13 Mbps/month	7.1
Storage	$2.2 per Gbyte/month	$0.40 per Gbyte/month	5.7
Administration	Approx. 140 servers/administrator	<1000 servers/administrator	7.1

Source: Armbrust et al., 2009.

Economies of scale grow even more important through the agglomerations of data centres that form the cloud. Major cloud providers do not necessarily warehouse data from an individual customer in any particular data centre but may distribute the data across several large data centres, often in diverse jurisdictions. Indeed, the ability to do this forms a significant part of their competitive advantage. By creating interconnected agglomerations, cloud providers can offer much more powerful computational outcomes. The ability to reap optimal benefits from such accumulation of computing power usually requires cross-border data flows – the source of some policy and regulatory challenges associated with the cloud.

Source: UNCTAD.

- **Hybrid clouds** expand deployment options for cloud services by mixing the deployment models described above, for example, public and private cloud provision. This may be valuable, for example, where the data and applications involved require different levels of security or are subject to different regulatory requirements.

In practice, major cloud providers often use the same data centres when offering both public and private services. Governments and individual businesses may make use of more than one cloud and more than one cloud service provider for different purposes. Interoperability between clouds and service providers is therefore important in providing flexibility and competition in service provision, not least in enabling customers to switch between providers.

Different cloud users have different needs and are therefore likely to prefer different deployment models. At present, individual users and small and medium-sized enterprises (SMEs) make widespread use of public clouds, either consciously (for example,

through cloud storage services), or in many cases without realizing that they are doing so (such as when using social networks or webmail services). Many public cloud services with mass markets are either offered free of charge to customers and funded by advertising revenue, or are available at low cost. Such business models are made possible by the massive economies of scale that can be achieved by cloud computing data centres handling very large quantities of information (box I.2). In spite of such economies of scale, however, major enterprise and government customers have so far generally preferred to procure private cloud provision, which can be more easily tailored to individual requirements and which is perceived to have security and data protection advantages.

The diverse aspects of cloud computing defined above are drawn together in figure I.1, which also highlights certain characteristics that give cloud computing a comparative advantage over other models of handling data (National Institute of Standards and Technology, 2011). These can be summarized as:

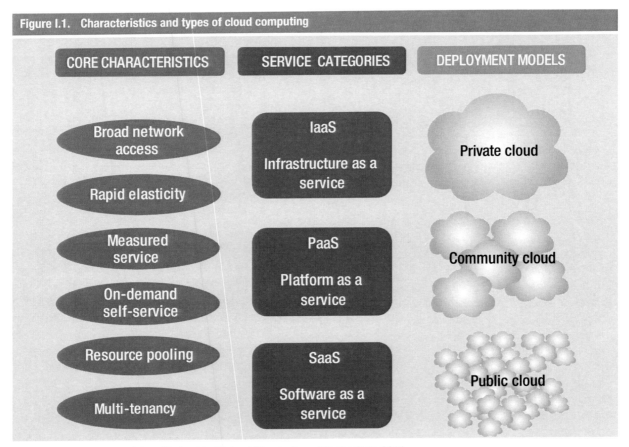

Figure I.1. Characteristics and types of cloud computing

CORE CHARACTERISTICS	SERVICE CATEGORIES	DEPLOYMENT MODELS
Broad network access	IaaS Infrastructure as a service	Private cloud
Rapid elasticity		
Measured service	PaaS Platform as a service	Community cloud
On-demand self-service		
Resource pooling	SaaS Software as a service	Public cloud
Multi-tenancy		

Source: UNCTAD, adapted from National Institute of Standards and Technology, 2011.

- **Broad network access.** Capabilities can be accessed over the network using standard terminal devices such as PCs, laptops, tablets and smartphones;
- **Rapid elasticity.** The capability for rapid scaling, up or down, of the access or services provided in accordance with user requirements;
- **Measured service.** The business model that data access or service provided is monitored and charged by usage (on a pay-as-you-go basis);
- **On-demand self-service.** Based on the principle that users can provision relevant resources as and when required, on their own initiative, without having to negotiate access terms at the time of need;
- **Resource pooling.** The resources supplied by a cloud provider serve multiple users rather than being dedicated to a single user, and they are assigned as required by user demand, resulting in them being less costly per unit than they would be if provided for a single user;
- **Multi-tenancy.** Physical and virtual resources are allocated in such a way that multiple tenants and their computations and data are isolated from, and inaccessible to one another.

C. DRIVERS AND BARRIERS RELATED TO CLOUD COMPUTING

A transition to the cloud involves both potential advantages and potential risks and costs. This makes it important for Governments and organizations in the public and private sectors to analyse carefully how they might be affected by such a transition and how to respond.

The cost-effectiveness of the cloud model with its large economies of scale would suggest that it could become the norm, rather than the exception, for data storage and service provisioning. This is already the case for globally provided mass market applications, such as webmail and online social networks. In developed countries, almost all listed companies and other large private companies make significant use of the cloud, though cloud adoption among SMEs is more limited. While developing countries do not yet exhibit such high adoption rates, enterprises are starting to explore cloud provisioning, and their economies will be impacted by its growing prevalence (chapter III).

There is a burgeoning literature on the potential advantages of cloud computing. Much of this consists of studies conducted or sponsored by the cloud industry rather than reflecting independent empirical research. Experience of cloud computing, particularly in developing countries, is too recent for there to be a strongly established evidence base on which to assess impacts on individual firms, organizations or national economies. There is, however, a consensus on the principal potential benefits that can be derived. These can be summarized in the following three points, which will be discussed in greater detail in chapter III:

1. **Cost savings.** Hardware and software in conventional business environments are rarely used to, or approaching, full capacity. Aggregation of demand in the cloud means that cloud service providers' equipment is used more efficiently than their customers' equipment would be, enabling benefits from economies of scale to be passed on to users. These factors may result in cost savings in three main areas:

(a) Hardware requirements for devices that primarily use the cloud can be much lower, with lower specifications and less frequent need for hardware upgrades;

(b) Latest versions of software can be accessed as and when required, rather than purchased (or pirated) and uploaded to all hardware on which they might be required;

(c) There is less need for in-house IT maintenance and support staff (though staff dealing with IT management, procurement, and the like, need to be as highly skilled in cloud as in conventional environments).

Overall, transition to the cloud can permit firms to divert significant resources from capital to operational expenditure, enabling earlier return on investment. The potential for reaping benefits from these economies of scale is greater in public and community clouds, where there is more aggregation of demand. Nonetheless, many Governments and enterprises prefer private cloud solutions, balancing these advantages against other issues such as control over data management and security.

2. **Flexible access to facilities on demand, with a high degree of elasticity.** Cloud procurement enables businesses to implement new administrative or customer service approaches more quickly than would be possible through the

acquisition, development and implementation of bespoke applications. Cloud service customers can also more or less instantly increase or decrease the services/resources they require from the cloud in response to fluctuations in demand. This makes it easier for cloud service customers to manage peak workloads, and to downsize when necessary.

3. Improved system management, reliability and IT security. Cloud providers claim that their services enable businesses to access new administrative and service delivery models which are more agile and responsive to changes in consumer behaviour and demand, as well as enabling smooth migration of data and services between software generations. For organizations that lack the necessary in-house IT staff to protect and secure their systems, cloud-based solutions may also offer more effective and systematic backup of data, and access to the specialized IT expertise of the cloud service provider.

However, as stressed above, such potential gains cannot be guaranteed merely by migrating data or applications to the cloud. Businesses with highly variable data-management requirements, or with complex customer relationships requiring frequent interaction, can be expected to benefit more than others from the inherent flexibility of cloud provisioning. SMEs in manufacturing and non-ICT services, which are generally too small to maintain skilled IT personnel, may gain by reducing their direct IT costs and relying on services rented from the cloud.

At the same time, the cost of additional services and facilities procured from cloud providers may undercut some of the cost savings that would otherwise be achieved. In most cases, there will be some initial costs in cloud migration which must be factored into cost–benefit assessments, and which may inhibit smaller firms from taking the plunge.

As is generally the case with new technology, potential benefits such as those described above can only be fully realized if and when management and operational systems are re-engineered and staff retrained to take advantage of them. Legacy administrative processes need to be overhauled and realigned in ways that optimize the capabilities of cloud applications and communications costs. Legacy hardware and software may need to be written off. In-house IT departments will need to be restructured – a matter of ensuring the continued availability of essential skills as well as shedding those that are no longer needed.

The need for reorganization and re-engineering of business processes can involve significant migration costs that businesses and other organizations need to juxtapose against financial benefits when assessing the net benefits.

Another important aspect in this context is the development of industry standards. Cloud computing is relatively new and changing rapidly, with new services and modalities of provisioning continuously becoming available. Different cloud service providers offer different approaches, based on different business models, different capabilities and different customer profiles. Each seeks to secure advantage in a growing marketplace by differentiating its service from its competitors, often using proprietary systems. From the perspective of cloud service customers, however, standards are critical to facilitate more competition between different cloud service providers. Customers can only make effective use of multiple cloud providers if those providers' services are interoperable, and they can only migrate data and applications located in the cloud operated by one provider to another, to take advantage of lower prices or better provisioning, if they are not locked into proprietary standards. The limited degree of standardization at present contributes to the reservations that some businesses have about migration.[6]

In addition to cost implications, two particularly important concerns for potential cloud service customers are related to data security/privacy and to management control of data transferred to the cloud. A shift towards cloud computing can imply a loss of control over applications and data when the computing is conducting on a server that is not owned by the user. It may not be possible, for example, for cloud service customers to know where data are processed and stored, to ensure that data are not shared or manipulated in ways that lie outside their cloud agreements, or to see the software source code related to the services that they have bought. Governments and enterprises are wary of the risk of becoming dependent on large cloud service providers, especially if their headquarters and facilities lie in another jurisdiction. Concerns related to data protection and privacy are compounded by the possibility that third parties (including foreign Governments) could gain access to sensitive national, business or personal data. Such aspects have received increased attention as a result of revelations that some Governments may have with cloud providers to access data passing through their servers.[7] There is furthermore the risk that cloud service providers may exercise market power to lock clients into relationships which might become progressively less satisfactory and more costly to them.

The feasibility of cloud computing depends to a great extent on the availability of reliable, affordable, high-quality communications networks. In practice, this means broadband networks that link all parties in the supply chains described in the following section on the cloud economy ecosystem. Variations in access to such networks, and in their quality, in different countries fundamentally affect the ability of firms and other organizations to participate successfully in the cloud economy. Many low-income countries suffer from limited or inadequate access to high-quality and affordable broadband infrastructure, as well as from a shortage of relevant IT skills (chapter II). Against this background, it is essential to place any discussion of the cloud alongside broader considerations of how to strengthen ICT readiness. Existing bottlenecks in

traditional areas of ICT deployment can act as an effective barrier to cloud adoption.

From a supply-side perspective, developing countries will also take into account to what extent their local enterprises can play an active role in the cloud economy, either by offering their own related services or by adding value to existing cloud services. The advent of the cloud may influence the growth and trajectory of local IT sectors, enabling some enterprises (including new start-ups) to flourish while undercutting the business models of others.

D. THE CLOUD ECONOMY ECOSYSTEM

The "cloud economy ecosystem" encompasses the deployment and impacts of cloud computing and cloud services within the wider information economy and, thereby, their relevance to national economic

Figure I.2. Main stakeholders and market relationships in the cloud economy

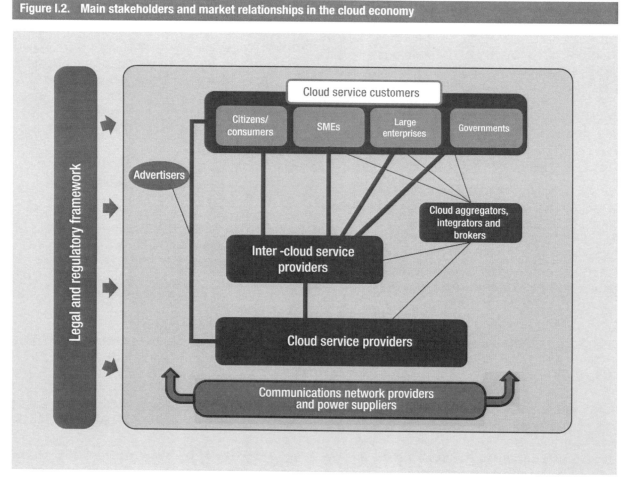

Source: UNCTAD.

development. The cloud economy is more than cloud computing, just as the information economy is more than ICTs. Its ecosystem includes a complex set of relationships, synergies and interactions between technology and business, governance and innovation, and production and consumption, which involve different stakeholders and which contribute in different ways to economic and social development. It is how this ecosystem evolves, rather than the potential of the technology alone, that will determine outcomes for developing countries.

At the heart of the cloud economy lies the interface between a rapidly evolving technology and those – in business, Government and other organizations – that seek to use it to achieve administrative and commercial goals with greater efficiency and at lower cost. A number of attempts have been made to develop models of the cloud economy ecosystem, which are valuable for different explorations of the cloud and its impact on society and economy.[8] The model proposed in this report is primarily concerned with the relationships between leading stakeholders in the cloud economy and how those relationships can influence the cloud's potential in developing countries.

As with all market ecosystems, the principal relationships revolve around the supply and demand. Figure I.2 illustrates schematically the various relationships that connect cloud service providers with cloud service customers and other entities in the cloud economy.

Cloud service providers in this ecosystem are those businesses that own the cloud computing centres and other infrastructure that form the cloud, and make services, platforms and/or infrastructure available through them to cloud service customers and users. Some providers specialize in one or other provisioning relationship – IaaS, PaaS or SaaS – while many of the larger providers offer customers all three. As will be elaborated in chapter II, cloud service provision is currently dominated by a few large IT corporations, mostly based in the United States, companies which can offer cloud service customers the benefits of lower costs arising from economies of scope and scale which are derived from global operations in the cloud and other IT sectors.

Inter-cloud service providers act as intermediaries and rely on one or more other cloud service providers to offer IaaS, PaaS or SaaS services to cloud service customers. Where this is the case, a cloud service customer will have a contractual relationship with an inter-cloud service provider, which in turn will have a contractual relationship with another cloud service provider. An example of an inter-cloud service provider of this kind is Salesforce.com, a provider of customer relations management and other cloud applications with over 100,000 customers worldwide, and which runs its products from data centres managed by co-location companies, such as Equinox.

Cloud service customers as defined here, include all those that acquire cloud services directly from cloud service providers and inter-cloud service providers. Cloud service customers are diverse – including citizens, consumers, enterprises and Governments – and have varying requirements and objectives in making use of the cloud. A variety of different relationships results between cloud providers, cloud service customers and end users of cloud services, depending on the type of customer involved and the characteristics of the applications.

Cloud service customers obtain cloud services in diverse ways:

(a) Customers – not just individual citizens but also SMEs, larger businesses, Governments and other organizations – may access some services free of charge directly from cloud and inter-cloud service providers. This applies particularly to consumer-oriented, mass-market services, such as search facilities, webmail and online social networks that are often financed by advertising revenue (indicated to the left of figure I.2). The user interface for these services provides an ideal platform for advertising placement, while data mining of the accumulated information that service providers hold about many millions of end users enables much more precise targeting of advertising than is possible in print and broadcast media. Advertisers are, therefore, also significant stakeholders in the cloud economy.

(b) Other cloud services (IaaS, PaaS or SaaS) are provided on a fee-paying basis, whereby end users pay either a flat-rate subscription or a variable fee dependent on the level or extent of service use. Such services may be acquired directly from different service providers. Larger businesses, government agencies and other organizations, however, also procure a wider range of services that are specifically adapted to their commercial or administrative needs.

These more tailored services may also come from cloud service or inter-cloud service providers.

As cloud markets become more diverse and competitive, cloud service customers – especially enterprises and Governments – are likely to make use of aggregators, systems integrators and brokers (sometimes referred to as cloud service partners) that can help them to identify the best solutions and integrate services from different cloud and inter-cloud service providers. This presents a significant opportunity for new business development at a national level (chapter III).

The relationships between the various actors in this cloud economy ecosystem depend at a fundamental level on some key infrastructure providers. The most significant of these are the communications network operators that provide the infrastructure of the Internet. These businesses – principally telecommunications operators and Internet Service Providers (ISPs) – gain from the increased volume of data traffic that results from cloud adoption. They may also see opportunities themselves for diversifying into cloud provisioning and become a cloud service provider (or inter-cloud service provider) in their own right. Another important set of stakeholders are the power suppliers. Access to reliable and affordable electricity is particularly essential for running large data centres, as well as being necessary for users to enjoy reliable cloud services.

The development of the cloud economy is influenced by stakeholders that fall outside these core commercial relationships. Governments are important actors in the cloud economy in several ways. Some Governments not only buy services from the market (acting as cloud service customers), but also act as cloud service providers to their own private clouds or even to third parties (see chapter III). More generally, through their policies and actions, they shape the legal and regulatory frameworks that can foster or constrain the migration to the cloud by businesses and other organizations within their jurisdictions. For example, data protection and other legislation set limits around the extent to which data can be shared or stored outside national boundaries.

Government departments can set benchmarks through their own adoption of the cloud, their confidence or otherwise in it encouraging or discouraging that of others. Governments which develop their own cloud strategies across the whole of government show

that they are taking the opportunities and challenges of the cloud seriously. Development partners may also play a part in encouraging them to do so. The roles of government and development partners in relation to the cloud economy are discussed, with recommendations, in chapters IV and V.

Finally, it is worth noting that the impact of the cloud on end users does not stop at those who make direct use of cloud services. Many people and organizations that do not directly use cloud services are still affected indirectly by the use of them by Governments and businesses to manage public and commercial services that are important to them.

E. IMPLICATIONS FOR DEVELOPING COUNTRIES

There is currently a general debate on the significance, value and risks of cloud computing. This is particularly the case for developing countries. On the one hand, it can be seen as a major opportunity, representing the next major step in the Internet's evolution into the most important driver of the world economy. This view rests upon a belief in the power of technology as a principal driver of social and economic outcomes. On the other hand, there are important factors that suggest caution with regard to the cloud's potential value for developing countries, including privacy-related concerns. Processes of adoption and diffusion are shaped by many complex human as well as technical factors, and past predictions of rapid growth in IT and services – in areas such as e-commerce – have not always fulfilled their expectations.

Nevertheless, cloud computing is becoming increasingly important in the delivery of public and private services around the world. Even where the cloud has not yet been adopted substantially by Governments and businesses, widespread use of mass-market cloud services by citizens has established the significance of a cloud economy that will become more important over the next few years.

Governments and businesses in middle-income and low-income countries should, therefore, actively seek to assess the relevance and potential of the cloud for their particular context. At a practical level, they need to develop a realistic understanding of the opportunities and risks associated with cloud provisioning of internal administration and service delivery before making commitments that might be beneficial but also costly and difficult to reverse. At a policy level, they need to understand the implications of cloud computing for national economic outcomes in order to consider appropriate policy and regulatory changes. This Report offers a frame of reference to help them in considering these issues.

These are still early days for the cloud economy in developing countries. Most of the literature about cloud computing is concerned with its perceived potential rather than with what actually has happened or is happening. Moreover, most of the literature that has considered cloud computing in developing countries has focused on emerging markets, particularly larger countries with growing economies and relatively large installed IT. It is important in assessing the potential of cloud computing for developing countries, not to consider only those that are best equipped to take advantage of the cloud economy, but also the wider diversity of developing countries, their economies and capabilities, including least developed countries (LDCs) and other low-income countries.

The analysis in this report draws on the limited evidence that has been published about cloud adoption in developing countries and on selected individual case studies. There is, however, a need for more research into current experience on the ground, including changing attitudes and perceptions, and into new thinking about the cloud's potential in developmental contexts. This should include the needs of developing-country SMEs, the potential value and impact of the cloud for local ICT sectors, and the ability of Governments to provide e-services.

Potential applications of the cloud differ according to customer needs. It is equally important, therefore, to pay attention to the diversity of businesses within developing countries, from transnational corporations (TNCs) to SMEs, and to both users and producers of cloud services. While proponents of the cloud argue that its most efficient use requires full freedom of location and free movement of information – that the economies of scale achievable make global corporations the most cost-effective and efficient cloud providers – other approaches, extending beyond mere efficiency, may be appropriate or better suited to particular circumstances. Migration to the cloud may incur new costs and there is little empirical evidence to

date on the total cost of paying as you go for software and other applications. In addition, the cost dimension needs to be weighed against other considerations, for example, those related to data protection and privacy.

Three sets of research questions emerge from this context, and form the basis for the investigation in this Report:

(a) **The current status of the cloud economy in developing countries.** How far are cloud-based approaches being adopted, which service and deployment models are proving attractive and/or effective, and what specific drivers and barriers stimulate or constrain development and adoption? This is addressed in chapters II and III.

(b) **The potential impacts of the cloud economy for different stakeholders in developing countries, in the short, medium and longer term.** Which developing countries and developing-country businesses are best equipped to take advantage of the opportunities presented by the cloud economy? What opportunities and challenges do cloud models pose for Governments, enterprises of different size and for local ICT sectors? Chapter III examines the available evidence in this context.

(c) **The policy and regulatory approaches which will facilitate the adoption and effective utilization of the cloud, to maximize its value and minimize negative impacts.** How should Governments in developing countries assess the cloud economy in their specific national contexts? What investments and policy interventions should they undertake, and how might these be supported by international agencies, including UNCTAD? Chapters IV and V are devoted to this set of questions.

The *Information Economy Report 2013* seeks to address the challenges of evidence and interpretation described above and to respond, at least tentatively, to these research questions. While it is too early to draw many firm conclusions, it hopes to contribute to a nuanced discussion of the potential role and value of the cloud economy among policymakers and business leaders across developing countries.

NOTES

[1] See, for example, "Cloud computing is a trap, warns GNU founder Richard Stallman", The Guardian, 29 September 2008, available at http://www.theguardian.com/technology/2008/sep/29/cloud.computing.richard.stallman (accessed 2 October 2013).

[2] See, for example, "The cloud builds up steam", The Financial Times, 6 June 2013, available at http://www.ft.com/cms/s/0/e2b826a2-ce20-11e2-8313-00144feab7de.html#axzz2chNG8oKc (accessed 2 October 2013).

[3] This definition was agreed by the Collaborative Team between ITU Telecommunication Standardization Sector (ITU-T) and ISO on cloud computing vocabulary. It was expected to be finally approved in September 2013.

[4] For example, by providing software applications as a service, users can access only those that they need as and when required, rather than buying a full package of software applications and installing all on a particular computer.

[5] Special reference is sometimes also made to Business Process as a Service (BPaaS), which builds on the other three categories of cloud services. It can be seen as a cloud-based variation of more traditional business process outsourcing (BPO) and is expected to grow in the future.

[6] At present, the challenges of standardization are being addressed by a large number of organizations, including industry associations, ISO, ITU and the Distributed Management Task Force. See, for example, http://cloud-standards.org/wiki/index.php?title=Main_Page (accessed 3 October 2013).

[7] See also chapter IV.

[8] One such model is built around three layers of "technical architecture" – provision of cloud services based on data centres, provision of networks based on communications infrastructure, and the manufacture and supply of terminal devices (Kushida et al., 2012). This is particularly useful for exploring the relationship of the cloud to the global ICT industry, and for analysing the strategies of major cloud providers.

TRENDS IN THE CLOUD ECONOMY AND RELATED INFRASTRUCTURE

2

The market for cloud services is growing rapidly, but is still small in developing countries. While the supply side of the cloud economy is dominated by global cloud service providers headquartered in the United States, various regional and local players are also emerging in different parts of the world. The ability to leverage the opportunities created by cloud computing – on the supply as well as demand side – is greatly influenced by the quality of ICT infrastructure. As the shift towards the cloud continues, the digital divide becomes less a question of basic access and more about the quality of use.

This chapter examines recent developments in the cloud economy and related trends in the infrastructure needed for cloud services. Leading cloud providers and other stakeholders in the cloud economy are identified. The performance of different countries with regard to their readiness to benefit from the cloud economy is discussed, with special emphasis on broadband infrastructure for effective usage of cloud services of varying degrees of sophistication. The analysis furthermore considers the cost of broadband access and the spread of data centres and Internet exchange points (IXPs). The chapter concludes with a summary of the main findings.

A. TRENDS IN THE CLOUD ECONOMY

This section reviews various estimates of the size and growth of the cloud computing market, noting the importance of advertising revenues generated in connection with the provision of public cloud services in addition to fees charged for the direct use of cloud services. It finds that the markets for both public and private clouds are expected to grow considerably in the next few years. This is followed by a discussion on the leading global cloud providers and other relevant actors in the cloud economy ecosystem, and on the link between cloud computing and international trade statistics.

1. Cloud markets and traffic

Cloud market classifications are highly fluid with varying scope, depending on whether analyst definitions are applied or the wider ecosystem is considered. As noted in chapter I, there is general agreement regarding three standard categories of cloud services: IaaS, PaaS and SaaS. There are basically two main models of creating revenue from the provision of these cloud services to end users: service provision against a flat-rate or variable subscription fee dependent on the level or extent of service use, and advertising.

It is estimated that sales of worldwide public cloud services were worth $111 billion in 2012.[1] According to this source, the largest revenue segment by far was advertising, which accounted for more than $53 billion. With regard to the fee-generated revenue for the three main cloud service categories, SaaS was the largest category (about $17 billion), followed by IaaS (about $6 billion) and PaaS (about $1 billion).[2] Forecasts of the future growth of cloud computing differ significantly. For example, while one consultancy firm anticipates that the total market for public cloud deployments of IaaS, PaaS and SaaS will grow from $14 billion to $43 billion between 2010 and 2015,

another expects that the market will be twice that size by 2015 (table II.1). Discrepancies in projections may reflect different methodologies as well as difficulties in predicting the speed at which the cloud computing phenomenon will evolve. Nevertheless, most forecasts suggest that cloud adoption will continue to expand rapidly over the next few years.

Estimates of the value of private cloud services also vary. According to one private source, private cloud revenue was estimated at around only $5 billion in 2012, and expected to grow to about $24 billion by 2016.[3] According to another private source, however, private cloud provisioning generated more than €40 billion ($53 billion) in 2012, and it was expected to rise to about €75 billion ($99 billion) by 2016 (Pierre Audoin Consultants, 2013). Whereas SaaS dominates the market for public cloud services, IaaS is the dominant feature for private cloud services. There also appear to be different preferences among cloud service customers in different regions. For example, public cloud provisioning, and SaaS in particular, is most frequently used in North America and the United Kingdom, whereas French enterprises invest mainly in private clouds, preferably hosted by French companies (Pierre Audoin Consultants, 2013).

As stressed in chapter I, the cloud economy has wider implications. A broader market perspective would encompass activities such as access, support and usage of web-enabled services. This includes, for example, IT equipment purchased by cloud providers in order to offer their services and connectivity purchased by businesses, Governments and households to access cloud services and user purchases of services delivered from the cloud.[4] Such a broader view would generate a considerably higher estimate of the value and potential of the cloud economy.

The value of the global ICT sector in 2011 has been estimated at €2.9 trillion ($4 trillion), a figure forecast to rise to €3.2 trillion ($4.5 trillion) by 2014 (IDATE Foundation, 2012).[5] Telecommunication services

Table II.1.	Estimates and forecasts of cloud revenue, 2010 and 2015 (Billions of dollars)							
	2010				2015			
	SaaS	*Paas*	*Iaas*	*Total*	*SaaS*	*Paas*	*Iaas*	*Total*
Gartner	10 (70.9%)	1.3 (9.2%)	2.8 (19.9%)	14.1 (100%)	21.3 (49.2%)	2.4 (5.5%)	19.6 (45.3%)	43.3 (100%)
Forrester	13.4 (91.1%)	0.3 (2.2%)	1 (6.7%)	14.7 (100%)	78.4 (83.5%)	9.8 (10.4%)	5.8 (6.1%)	94.1 (100%)

Source: Berry and Reisman, 2012.
Note: This table only includes revenue from the services shown.

Figure II.1. Global cloud data centre traffic (2011–2016) and distribution by region (2012)

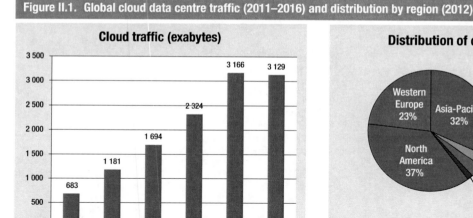

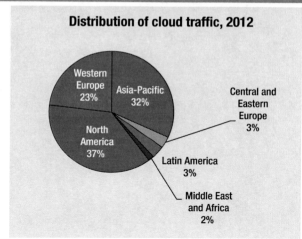

Source: Cisco Analysis, 2012.
Note: Data for 2012–2016 are estimates.

accounted for 36 per cent of this, making it the largest segment, followed by software and computer services. All segments are in some way affected by cloud computing. For example, the demand for higher bandwidth will drive telecommunication services revenue, although revenues from voice services could be affected as more people switch to cloud-based Voice over Internet Protocol (VoIP) applications. Demand for equipment and computer hardware, particularly data servers and network equipment, will rise as more services move to the cloud. Television services will be affected by increasing demand for video streaming.

The shift to the cloud is generating considerable growth in data traffic, requiring further investment in broadband capacity. Consider that during an average minute in 2012, Google received two million search requests, Facebook users shared around 700,000 content items and Twitter sent out 100,000 tweets.[6] According to some estimates, cloud traffic crossed the zettabyte[7] milestone in 2012 (figure II.1, left). The same source predicts an annual growth rate of over 40 per cent between 2011 and 2016 (Cisco Analysis, 2012). Some 40 per cent of all traffic reflects storage requests (retrieving or sending data from/to the cloud). By 2016, cloud traffic is expected to represent as much as 64 per cent of all data centre traffic.[8]

In 2012, the majority of such traffic emanated from the Europe and North America, which together accounted for 60 per cent of the total (figure II.1, right). Asia-Pacific was responsible for another third, while Latin America

and the Middle East and Africa together accounted for only 5 per cent. Asia-Pacific is forecast to overtake North America as the top cloud traffic region by 2014. Meanwhile, the highest growth rates are expected in the Middle East and Africa between 2011 and 2016, albeit from a low base.

2. Leading corporate players in the cloud economy

Cloud service providers include businesses that own cloud computing centres and other cloud infrastructure, and those that provide cloud services, platforms and/or storage capacity available to cloud service customers. Identifying the leading cloud service providers is far from straightforward. In terms of financial size, some companies do not separate their cloud activities from other revenues;[9] and some providers might be significant in a particular niche but small in terms of overall market revenue. There is furthermore no consensus about whether cloud revenues should be related only to the cloud service model categories or to the wider cloud ecosystem. In terms of the number or size of clients, there is scarce information. Against this background, this subsection uses various alternative metrics, such as number of data servers or geographical client reach, as well as information from qualitative rankings to identify the top corporate actors in the cloud economy.[10] The pattern that emerges is one of a concentrated industry with most of the major providers coming from the United States.

Table II.2. Top 10 companies by estimated number of servers, 2012			
Company	Estimated number of servers	Estimated cloud revenue (billion dollars)	Comments
Google (United States)	900 000	50	The Google Cloud Platform includes software applications and data storage. It has six data centres in the United States and three in Europe; four more are under construction (three in Asia and one in South America). Over 90 per cent of revenue stems from advertising on the web.
Microsoft (United States)	300 000	n.d.	Offers both commercial and consumer cloud services. Cloud revenue is earned primarily from usage fees and advertising. Products include cloud-based versions of Office (365), Skype, Xbox and Azure. Data centres throughout the Americas, Europe and Asia.
Amazon Web Services (United States)	250 000	2.1	Launched by Amazon in 2006, providing infrastructure services to hundreds of thousands of enterprises, Governments and start-ups in 190 countries around the world. AWS offers over 30 different services. Data centre locations in the United States, Brazil, Europe, Japan, Singapore and Australia.
Facebook (United States)	180 000	5.1	Social network company data centres in the United States and Sweden. Generates most revenue from advertising and fees from purchase of virtual and digital goods from platform developers. One billion users (at least once a month) at December 2012.
Akamai (United States)	127 000	1.4	Data servers located in 81 countries. Provides content delivery and cloud infrastructure services, including delivery of conventional content on websites, tools supporting delivery and operation of cloud-based applications, and live and on-demand streaming video.
OVH (France)	120 000	n.d.	Has eight data centres. Is the leading webhosting company in Europe with more than 400,000 customers.
Softlayer (United States)	100 000	n.d.	Employs a unified global infrastructure platform to provide on-demand, hour-to-hour or month-to-month billing through one portal and one API. Has 13 data centres in the United States, Asia, and Europe. Has 100,000 devices under management, claiming it is the largest privately held IaaS provider in the world.
Rackspace (United States)	79 805 (2011)	1	Offers traditional hosting as well as PaaS. Served 172,510 customers in 2012. Has nine data centres located in the United States, the United Kingdom, Hong Kong, China and Australia.
Intel (United States)	75 000	n.d.	The microprocessor giant has 69 worldwide data centres. Offers on-demand applications for staff, partners and private cloud clients, and online netbook applications such as services to help validate applications and software.
1&1 (United States)	70 000	n.d.	Web-hosting provider with around 12 million customer contracts served through five data centres in Europe and the United States.

Source: UNCTAD, based on information from company reports and other sources.
Note: n.d. = cloud revenue not disclosed and no reliable estimate exists.

[a] http://huanliu.wordpress.com/2012/03/13/amazon-data-center-size/ (accessed 2 October 2013).

[b] http://online.wsj.com/article/SB10001424127887324442304578236000008569908.html (accessed 2 October 2013).

[c] http://perspectives.mvdirona.com/2012/08/13/FunWithEnergyConsumptionData.aspx (accessed 2 October 2013).

[d] http://www.akamai.com/html/about/facts_figures.html (accessed 2 October 2013).

[e] http://www.ovh.co.uk/aboutus/ (accessed 2 October 2013).

[f] http://cdn.softlayer.com/PS_DataCenterOverview.pdf (accessed 2 October 2013).

[g] http://www.intel.com/content/www/us/en/it-management/intel-it/intel-it-data-center-solutions.html (accessed 2 October 2013).

[h] http://www.1and1.com/Facts?__lf=Order-Tariff (accessed 2 October 2013).

Given that the provision of cloud services requires storage of applications and data in dispersed data centres, a practical comparable metric is the number of data servers. Although such information is often considered commercially confidential, estimates made by market analysts can serve as a basis. Table II.2 identifies the top 10 companies ranked according to the number of worldwide data servers.[11] Almost all operate globally and their headquarters are largely concentrated in the United States. Some are giants, such as Amazon, Microsoft and Intel, for which cloud computing comprises only a relatively small portion of total revenue. Some (e.g. Google or Facebook) are large Internet-based companies that derive a significant share of their revenue from cloud advertising. Others specialize in specific cloud services, mainly hosting but also software and application integration for clients. In terms of revenue, Google is by far the largest, generating most of its some $50 billion of revenues in 2012 from its overall web-based services, almost all from advertising.

At the same time, several inter-cloud service providers have few or no servers and instead lease capacity to offer their services to cloud service customers. For example, the top 10 SaaS providers among the world's 100 largest software firms, based on 2011 revenue, are shown in table II.3. Some of the listed SaaS companies are also active in other cloud services, such as PaaS (Salesforce.com, Microsoft) or have a significant number of data servers (Microsoft, Google). Again, apart from DATEV (Germany), all firms included in the list are based in the United States.

To broaden the perspective to the cloud economy, additional companies should be considered. This includes, for example, major vendors of IT equipment and software used for the cloud, such as Cisco, EMC, IBM, VMware and HP (all from the United States) and major telecom operators that provide the communication networks, such as AT&T, Level 3 and Verizon (all three from the United States), BT (United Kingdom) and Nippon Telegraph and Telephone Corporation (NTT) (Japan).

Though global cloud service providers operate across different regions, there is scope for regional players to compete by providing more localized and personalized niche services. Regional cloud provision trends have been marked by alliances between telecommunication operators and IT companies. This match unites the operator's direct contact with the customer with companies that have specific cloud

Table II.3.	Top 10 generators of SaaS revenue among the global 100 software firms, 2011			
Company	Country headquarters	2011 SaaS revenue (million dollars)	2011 software revenue (million dollars)	SaaS revenue as share of software revenue (percentage)
Salesforce.com	United States	1 848	2 008.7	92
Intuit	United States	950	2 456.5	38.7
Cisco	United States	831	1 796.9	46.3
Microsoft	United States	788	57 668.4	1.4
Symantec	United States	572	6 330.3	9
Google Inc.	United States	462	575.6	80.3
Oracle	United States	446	26 175.9	1.7
Adobe	United States	410	4 154.1	9.9
Blackboard	United States	396	411.7	96.2
DATEV	Germany	395	974.2	40.5
Total		7 098	102 552.2	6.9

Source: PWC. See http://www.pwc.com/us/en/technology/publications/global-100-software-us-rankings.jhtml (accessed 3 October 2013).

expertise. Outright purchases of cloud service firms by telecommunication operators is one model, but this has mainly been limited to the North American market (e.g. Verizon's acquisition of cloud company Terremark for $1.4 billion). In other regions, links between telecommunication operators and cloud providers have with some exceptions been established primarily through partnerships.[13]

- In Africa, Vodacom, a South African telecommunication operator, has partnered with Novell, an IT provider, to offer cloud services.[14] Vodacom operates across a number of African countries. MTN, another South African-based operator with subsidiaries in several African countries, provides e-mail and other cloud services to customers in Cameroon, Ghana, Nigeria and South Africa. Seacom, the company behind the undersea cable of the same name, has launched a new company, called Pamoja, to offer SMEs the ability to provide cloud computing-based services to their customers without the capital outlay such services usually require. France Télécom has appointed a regional director for cloud computing in Africa and the Middle East.

- In Latin America, Telefonica (Spain) has partnered with NEC Corporation (Japan) to offer cloud services.[15] Products include an SaaS called Aplicateca featuring an app store aimed at businesses.[16] According to Pyramid Research, the market for cloud services in Latin America was $4.8 billion in 2012 (Ramos, 2012). The same company reckons that cloud revenues from serving SMEs may reach $12.7 billion by 2017.

- In Asia, Telkom (Indonesia) offers its cloud offering through the IT company TelkomSigma, while Indosat has partnered with Dimension Data to launch an enterprise-class public cloud service.[17] India's Tata Communications is another telecommunication operator that is expanding into cloud services. It has developed its own pay-as-you-go IaaS called InstaCompute.[18] Around 1,000 companies are trialling InstaCompute, and some 300 are commercial clients.[19]

Global cloud services can generally be accessed directly online by users from any place in the world. At first glance, it may appear difficult for purely local providers to compete with regional or global suppliers of cloud services. However, that presumes that potential domestic customers are aware of these global or regional sources or how to use them. Furthermore, factors such as security, localization and latency may create a role for local software companies to create domestic cloud solutions and for brokers and aggregators to interface between the local market and regional and global cloud providers (see also chapter III). In China, for example, Microsoft has entered the cloud market by partnering with 21Vianet, a Chinese carrier-neutral provider of data centre services in 33 cities.[20] This allows Microsoft to offer its services with customers using a Chinese company that guarantees that the data used will remain in China.

Local telecommunication operators have an important strength through their direct relationship to the customer. Cloud services need to get to the customer over the networks operated by the telecommunications firms. As noted above, many network operators are forging partnerships with cloud service companies and this is flowing down to the local level in some countries through subsidiaries. Individual domestic telecommunication operators could be at a disadvantage in terms of cloud expertise. Moreover, cloud adoption may be slower in countries without a certain level of competition, where operators are not part of a global consortium and may lack expertise.

3. Can cloud computing trends be seen in trade statistics?

The expansion of cloud computing has various implications for the development of international trade in both ICT services and ICT goods. The cloud business model rests in large part on the possibility to locate large data centres (hardware) in the most cost-effective location and then to send and receive data (services), often across borders, between the storage location and the cloud customers as well as between different data centres.

However, measuring international trade related to cloud computing is challenging. Official data only give a partial impression of related developments. International classifications do not allow for separate identification of trade in cloud services (see box II.1), and it is difficult to determine how much of the trade in data servers and other communication equipment that is linked specifically to the provision of cloud computing. Most analysis on the topic thus also relies on estimates from specialized market research firms and industry associations.

(a) Trade in services

In the United States, attempts have been made to measure the value of trade in cloud services. A first conservative estimate of the value of that country's exports of public cloud computing services in 2010,

---

Box II.1.   Cloud computing services in international classifications

Even though it does not have a subclass or group of products corresponding directly to cloud computing services, Central Product Classification (CPC) Version 2 is the most amenable international classification for identifying computer-related services linked to cloud computing. The subclasses of CPC Version 2[21] mentioned below can be identified as most relevant. However, international trade in services data are not yet available at this level of disaggregation.

     83151 Website hosting services

     83152 Application service provisioning

     83159 Other hosting and IT infrastructure provisioning services

Source: UNCTAD, based on information provided by the United Nations Statistics Division.

arrived at $1.5 billion for cross-border transactions (or 3.4 per cent of United States exports of services likely to involve cloud computing)[22] and $1.4 billion for sales of majority-owned foreign affiliates (0.5 per cent of their total sales in 2009) (Berry and Reisman, 2012). The estimates are conservative in that they do not take into account private cloud computing services, typically developed in-house by individual companies. Neither do they take into account sales of businesses whose main activity falls outside the computer and data processing services and royalties and license fees sectors but that may nevertheless offer cloud services.[23] In India, for example, many firms use cloud computing platforms located in Singapore due to lower bandwidth costs and more robust infrastructure.[24]

Moreover, these estimates do not fully capture the value of trade in cloud services financed through advertising revenue or that are based on other secondary-content-supported business models. In these cases, the value created by Internet data exchange is not closely associated with the financial transaction and is therefore difficult to seize in trade statistics.[25]

Examining the case of the United States is relevant in this context, as it is the home of most of the main cloud service providers. At the same time, the estimation method applied in the case of the United Sates cannot be easily extrapolated to other countries and economies that are at a less advanced stage in terms of both cloud service provision and use.

(b) Trade in goods

The impact of cloud computing on trade in ICT goods is similarly difficult to gauge. Still, preliminary information suggests that the value of trade in goods related to cloud computing may be at least of a similar magnitude with that of trade in services.

Relevant trade flows include those involving the ICT devices needed for using cloud services such as computers and smartphones. In 2012, the value of world imports of portable computers amounted to $136 billion. In the same year, world imports of cellular telephones of all types amounted to $186 billion.[26] A certain portion of these devices (computers and smartphones) is likely to be used for cloud services, but it is difficult determine its magnitude. Estimates from market consultancy firms suggest that the number of smartphones – which are more suited for accessing cloud services – sold globally is now higher than that of feature phones.[27]

From a cloud service production perspective, relevant trade flows involve ICT goods needed to set up and run cloud computing services, notably computer servers and related communication equipment. Common components of a cloud computing hardware architecture include the following:[28]

- Server computers, such as application servers, chat servers, database servers, e-mail servers, file servers, gateway servers, load balancers, media servers, office servers, presentation servers, print servers, security servers, telephone servers, web accelerators, web servers and wireless gateway servers.
- Storage devices, such as disk drives, disk library, tape drives, and tape library.
- Support hardware, such as air conditioners, fire suppression, physical security devices, and uninterruptable power supply.
- Network components such as extranets, grid networks, the Internet, intranets, local area networks, mesh networks, metropolitan area networks, peer-to-peer networks, ring networks, star networks, storage area networks and wide area networks.
- Network connectivity devices, such as access adapters, bridges, cables, caches, connectors, firewalls, gateways, hubs, modems, multiplexers, network interface cards, optical amplifiers, receivers, repeaters, routers, switches and transmitters.
- Network connections, such as coaxial cables, fibre optic cables, infrared radiation and twisted wire cables.

Consider the example of computer servers. This broad term denotes many types of automated data processing machines that can be sold in a variety of configurations. Depending on the product specifics, computer servers can be imported under any of the following three HS 2007 classification subheadings: 847141, 847149 and 847150.[29] For simplicity this section uses the example of data reported only under category HS 847150, which covers computer servers without keyboard and monitor. This category includes servers that are more likely to be used in data centres, as well as some server computers used for other purposes.[30] World exports of this product category reached $42 billion in 2012, reflecting a modest 4 percentage point increase from 2008 to 2012 (table II.4). China was responsible for 31 per cent of the global export value, developed countries for 46 per cent and the remaining 23 per cent came from other developing and transition economies. Large exporters with high growth rates over recent years include China, Hong Kong, China,[31] Malaysia, Mexico and Singapore.[32]

In terms of import market shares, the United States accounted for more than one third (36 per cent) of the global value in 2012, which is considerably higher than that country's share of total ICT goods imports (15 per cent). The United States also displayed some of the highest import growth rates during the past five years. This may reflect its prominent role in the cloud economy. Other developed countries accounted for another 40 per cent, leaving the remaining 24 per cent for developing and transition economies.

Market estimates of global sales of computer servers indicate faster growth for servers that are the most relevant for the production of cloud services.

According to International Data Corporation (IDC), the worldwide server systems factory, revenue reached $51.3 billion[33] in 2012, up a modest 6 per cent per year from 2009.[34] This overall number masks diverging trends for different kinds of servers. Those that are most used in cloud infrastructure deployments appear to have grown faster. For example, the share of Linux servers rose from 17 per cent of all server revenue in 2010 to 20 per cent in the first quarter of 2013.[35] In addition, two types of modular data servers that are used extensively by cloud computing providers – blade servers, used mostly in private cloud data centres, and density optimized servers, used in large public cloud data centres – saw rapid growth. The market share of blade servers increased from 13 per cent in 2010 to almost 18 per cent in the first quarter of 2013. Density-optimized servers, which represent about 7 per cent of the server market, registered strong growth in 2013.

Table II.4.	Top importing and exporting economies of computer servers of the type described under HS 847150, 2008–2012						
Top 15 importers				**Top 15 exporters**			
Economy	2012 (million dollars)	2012 market share (percentage)	Annual growth rate 2008–2012 (percentage)	Economy	2012 (million dollars)	2012 market share (percentage)	Annual growth rate, 2008–2012 (percentage)
United States	15 199	36.4	22	China	11 471	31.0	13
Japan	2 927	7.0	-4	United States	6 302	17.0	0
United Kingdom	2 223	5.3	-9	Mexico	4 328	11.7	17
Canada	1 983	4.7	0	Czech Republic	3 603	9.7	2
Germany	1 977	4.7	-11	Germany	1 862	5.0	-9
China	1 919	4.6	18	Singapore	1 771	4.8	35
France	1 565	3.7	-10	Hong Kong, China	1 574	4.3	95
Netherlands	1 496	3.6	2	Netherlands	1 445	3.9	-13
Italy	1 045	2.5	-0	Hungary	731	2.0	-11
Hong Kong, China	993	2.4	33	France	624	1.7	-14
Republic of Korea	903	2.2	6	Ireland	540	1.5	-22
Mexico	875	2.1	-12	United Kingdom	396	1.1	-18
Australia	796	1.9	11	Canada	338	0.9	-4
India	688	1.6	26	Japan	337	0.9	2
Switzerland	676	1.6	-5	Malaysia	177	0.5	31
Other economies	6 532	15.6	3	Other economies	1 478	4.0	-1
World	41 798	100.0	1	World	36 978	100.0	-1

Source: United Nations Commodity Trade Statistics Database.
Note: Discrepancies between world exports and imports can be due to a variety of factors, such as different valuation, differences in the time of recording, misclassification on importer or exporter side, exchange rates and markups during consignment.

Computer servers are only one of the identified components of the typical cloud computing hardware architecture. To get a more complete picture, it would be necessary to also analyse trade in goods such as storage devices, network connectivity devices and network components of the type closely associated with providing cloud computing.

(c) Final observations

It is difficult to identify cloud computing trends in international trade statistics. Conservative estimates for the United States suggest that cloud services may today represent about 3–4 per cent of all exports of computer and data processing services. Given the dominance of United States cloud service providers and the relatively high level of cloud adoption in that country, the share is likely to be lower in most other countries. Compared with worldwide sales of public cloud services, estimated at $111 billion (section II.A.1), the value of cloud service exports remains modest.

Meanwhile, trade in computer servers, storage devices and network components, which are needed for setting up and running cloud services, represents a non-negligible part of ICT goods trade, probably at least similar in magnitude with the value of trade in cloud services. To determine the exact value, however, it is necessary to single out those ICT goods that are used mainly for cloud computing. Aggregated data often mask diverging trends for different kinds of ICT goods within the same generic classification.

For both goods and services, estimating the cloud-related trade value is also made difficult by the evolving nature of cloud computing business models, for some of which the dollar value of transactions is decoupled from the Internet data exchange itself. More research is clearly needed to better understand the implications of cloud computing for international trade, both in goods and services, and to identify potential opportunities and niche markets for developing countries.

B. TRENDS IN CLOUD-RELATED INFRASTRUCTURE

This section reviews ICT infrastructure trends with a special focus on aspects of the broadband landscape that may affect the ability of developing countries to adopt and benefit from cloud-based applications. It

begins by reviewing the concept of "cloud readiness", highlighting the ICT network components and services considered important for the use of cloud services. This is followed by a review of broadband infrastructure, quality and pricing that impact the utilization of cloud services.

1. Factors determining the cloud readiness of countries

In order to identify factors that influence the ability of countries to benefit from the cloud economy, it is useful to consider various attempts that have been made to assess the cloud readiness of different countries and economies. Several indices available use different methodologies. Some focus on infrastructure, while others rely on a broader set of both qualitative and quantitative indicators. The geographical coverage is currently limited in available indices. Moreover, there is as yet no indicator that shows actual level of cloud adoption:

- The Enterprise Cloud Readiness Index, designed by Pyramid Research, defines enterprise cloud readiness "as the degree to which service providers in a given country can potentially leverage cloud services for the enterprise segment" (Pyramid Research, 2012). The index covers 49 countries and is purely quantitative, based on nine economic, demographic and ICT infrastructure indicators (annex table 1).

- The Global Cloud Computing Scorecard of the Business Software Alliance ranks 24 developed and developing countries in seven categories that measure "preparedness to support the growth of cloud computing" (Business Software Alliance and Galexia, 2012). The scorecard uses both qualitative and quantitative data (annex table 2).

- The Asia Cloud Computing Association Readiness Index ranks 14 economies in the Asian region across 10 categories critical to "successful deployment and use of cloud computing technology" (Asia Cloud Computing Association, 2012). It includes both qualitative and quantitative factors (annex table 3).

- The Cisco Global Cloud Readiness tool is based on only three indicators, all related to broadband: download and upload speeds and latency. These indicators are seen as reflecting a country's ability to optimally support different levels of cloud services (basic, intermediate and advanced) for both fixed or mobile broadband (Cisco Analysis,

Figure II.2. Getting to the cloud

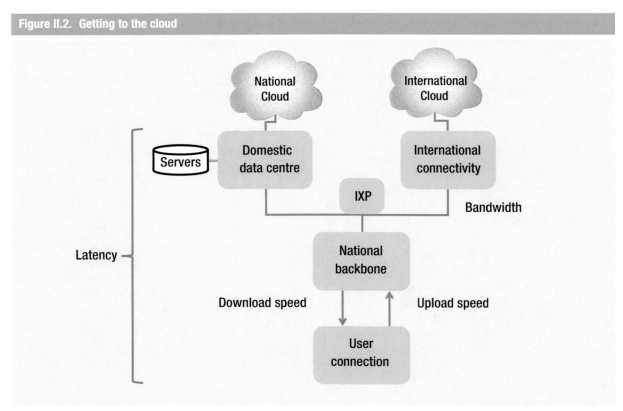

Source: UNCTAD.

Figure II.3. Incremental lit capacity of submarine cables on major routes (Tbps)

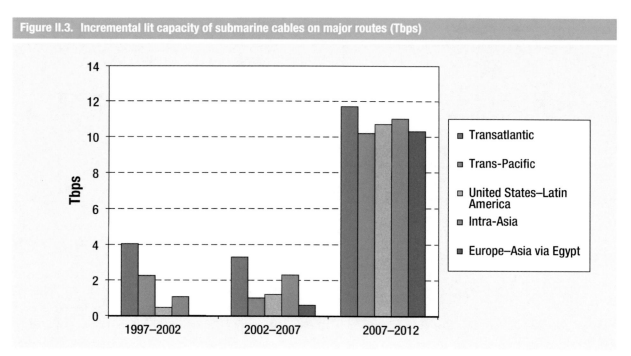

Source: TeleGeography. Available at www.telegeography.com (accessed 3 October 2013).
Note: Lit capacity is the actual traffic-carrying capability of the system today, based on what has been equipped to date.

2012). Cisco does not compute an actual index value but publishes the top 10 countries for both fixed and mobile performance based on an unspecified combination of the three indicators (annex table 4).

Given the novelty of the cloud computing phenomenon, more time is needed to refine assumptions about what drives cloud computing and to establish the best indicators for representing it. As none of the indices include statistics related to actual cloud adoption, it is difficult to develop a model to show objectively the impact and thus relevance of specific factors.[36] Considering infrastructure-related factors, broadband subscriptions are used across the first three but are not considered relevant by Cisco (annex table 4). On the other hand, broadband speed and latency are included in the Asian index and by Cisco (table II.5).

Infrastructure-related factors influencing the development of cloud computing include international and national backbones that aggregate user data for transmission back and forth to cloud services as well as end-user broadband access. These components are interrelated; if cloud services are hosted domestically, international connectivity may not be as critical (figure II.2). In the next subsections, special attention is given to international broadband connectivity, national backbone and Internet exchanges, broadband penetration, quality of service (QoS) and the affordability of broadband.

2. International broadband connectivity

International Internet bandwidth, which is critical for accessing data servers located abroad, has grown significantly in recent years. According to the telecom market research firm TeleGeography, it increased annually by 53 per cent between 2007 and 2012. Expanding demand has been met by the construction of new fibre optic networks and the upgrading of existing ones. As much as 54 terabits per second (Tbps) of capacity were added during this period (figure II.3). Demand in developing countries is rising the fastest. A key driver has been cloud services and new traffic to data centres over international connections between users and overseas locations where applications and data are located. However, this is mitigated somewhat by caching widely accessed content on national networks in efforts to improve performance and reduce international bandwidth costs (TeleGeography, 2013).[38]

Table II.5.	Infrastructure-related indicators used in different cloud readiness indices			
	ACCA	BSA	Pyramid	Cisco
Download speed	✔			✔
Upload speed	✔			✔
Latency	✔			✔
Fiber optic subscriptions			✔	
International bandwidth	✔	✔		
Wired broadband subscriptions	✔	✔	✔	
Mobile broadband subscriptions	✔	✔	✔	
Internet users		✔		
Computers		✔	✔	
Smartphones				✔

Source: ACCA = Asia Cloud Computing Association Readiness Index; BSA = Business Software Alliance's Global Cloud Computing Scorecard; Pyramid = Pyramid Research Enterprise Cloud Readiness Index; Cisco = GCI Cloud Readiness tool. Excluding compound indices and subjective indicators (e.g. opinion surveys).
Note: UNCTAD analysis.

The availability and affordability of international broadband bandwidth in Africa, which used to lag far behind in this area, have increased enormously as a result of the landing of competing submarine fibre cables on the continent's eastern and western seaboards. The principal barriers to affordable connectivity now lie in regional backbone and domestic backhaul networks, many of which are seeing upgrade investments. Significant improvements to terrestrial infrastructure, comparable to those that have occurred with submarine connectivity, could enable a step change in the adoption of cloud services by businesses, especially in Africa.

3. National backbone, Internet exchange points and data centres

National backbones, Internet exchanges and data centres are essential facilities for transmitting and processing cloud data streams. National backbones are vital for getting data to their destination. If the backbone is not robust, the users will not achieve the full speed of their local connection. There is extensive anecdotal evidence that the lack of connectivity

Figure II.4. Distribution of IXPs, by region, June 2013 (Percentage)

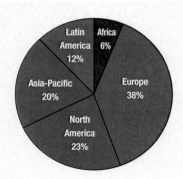

Source: Packet Clearing House, see https://prefix.pch.net/ applications/ixpdir/summary/growth-region/?sort1= bandwidth&sort2=_percent_change&order= desc (accessed 10 October 2013).

to high-speed national backbones in rural areas is a concern in many countries. However, unlike international bandwidth, globally agreed metrics and country data for quantifying and comparing national backbone capacity are lacking.[39]

As the name implies, IXPs are facilities where ISPs co-locate equipment to exchange national traffic. This reduces the cost of international bandwidth, since domestically destined traffic does not need to transit overseas. It also improves performance through lower latency (see below). The establishment of IXPs can help build national human capacity in networking skills. Once traffic reaches a certain level, IXPs can

allow content providers to cache data in the country. With growing expertise and traffic, a next step may be to locate data servers at IXPs and offer domestic cloud services.

There were in June 2013 some 397 IXPs in the world (figure II.4).[40] More than 60 per cent of them were located in Europe or North America. In Africa, which was home to only 6 per cent of the world's IXPs, such exchanges would dramatically improve the web experience through better performance. For example, a study of IXPs in Kenya and Nigeria found that they sharply improved latency, reducing it from over 200 milliseconds (ms) to less than 10 ms on average.[41]

Like public IXPs, private peering facilities similarly offer exchange of traffic but generally charge some or all participants for this privilege. Unlike most public IXPs, however, private peering facilities are profit-oriented and typically operated by a single company. They also far outnumber public IXPs; according to PeeringDB, there were some 1,221 private peering facilities around the world in July 2013.[42] Another distinction between IXPs and private peering facilities is that the latter often include centres where companies can lease or co-locate data servers. Such data centres are the concrete manifestation of the cloud, as they host the servers that store and process cloud data. This critical piece of cloud infrastructure requires special operating conditions. The most important condition is a stable energy supply to keep the servers available non-stop and to power the cooling systems so the servers do

Figure II.5. Distribution of co-location data centres, by group, 2013 and secure Internet servers per 1 million people, 2012

Co-location data centres, 2013

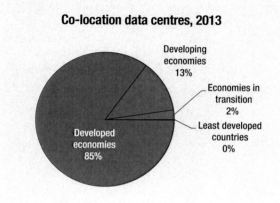

Secure Internet servers per 1 million people, 2012

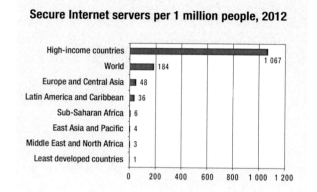

Source: See annex table 5.
Note: Regions in right-hand chart refer to developing economies only.

not overheat.[43] Other considerations include the price and the security of energy supply.

Several demanding conditions need to be met for data centres to be financially viable in a location. Risk is a factor influencing decisions by companies on where to locate their servers or build data centres, and many developing countries are perceived to pose a higher risk level.[44] The cost of energy and ensuring supply on a reliable basis can easily outweigh the demand for data centres. According to one source, as much as 85 per cent of data centres offering co-location services are in developed economies (figure II.5, left).[45] This digital divide in data centres is also reflected in the availability of servers. There were over 1,000 secure data servers per one million inhabitants in high-income economies in 2011, compared with just one per million inhabitants in LDCs (figure II.5, right). Countries without local data centres need to access overseas servers for cloud services, increasing international bandwidth costs and impacting latency-related performance. Further, some cloud service customers such as Governments require secure cloud environments that are likely best provided through national data centres.

4. Broadband infrastructure trends

There were an estimated 2.1 billion broadband subscriptions in 2012, with mobile broadband accounting for over 70 per cent of the total (figure II.6). In terms of relative importance for cloud access, the statistics should be interpreted carefully. As discussed below, fixed broadband is often of a higher and more

consistent speed, with less latency and typically shared in a household or enterprise, thus having many more users than suggested by the number of subscriptions. By contrast, mobile broadband is typically used by a single user, and so-called "active" subscriptions may sometimes include subscriptions that are "broadband capable" but may not actually be used to access data.[46]

In 2012, fixed broadband subscriptions around the world stood at 632 million (figure II.6, left). Growth has been fairly flat, with global fixed broadband penetration rising only about one per 100 people for the past few years. Although the number of subscriptions in developing economies surpassed those in developed economies in 2012, the gap in penetration keeps widening. Fixed broadband penetration in developed economies was almost five times higher than in developing regions in 2012. In LDCs, the total number of fixed broadband subscriptions was only 1.3 million – about the same as in Singapore – and average penetration was just 0.2 per 100 people. Though penetration in transition economies remained significantly below developed economies, it was higher than the world average.

The broadband user experience is greatly influenced by the kind of connection. The three main fixed broadband technologies in use around the world are digital subscriber line (DSL), cable modem and fibre optic. Although these technologies account for the vast majority of subscriptions, satellite remains important for isolated rural areas where terrestrial-based broadband is not available (box II.2). DSL delivered over copper telephone lines accounts for

Figure II.6. Global broadband subscriptions and distribution by fixed or mobile technology

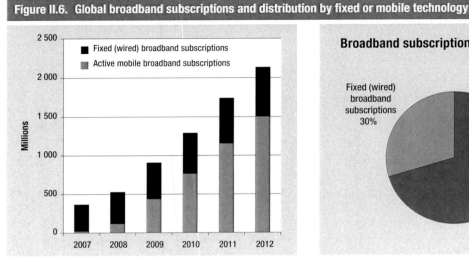

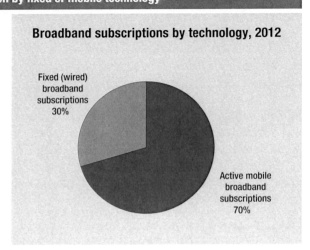

Source: ITU, World Telecommunication/ICT Indicators Database.

Figure II.7. Global fixed broadband subscriptions and per 100 people by region, 2007–2012

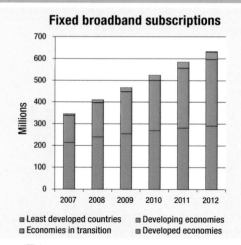

Fixed broadband subscriptions

■ Least developed countries   ■ Developing economies
■ Economies in transition   ■ Developed economies

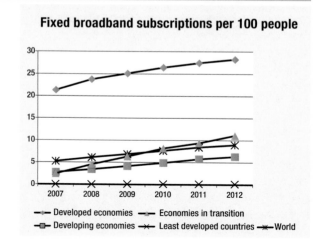

Fixed broadband subscriptions per 100 people

╼●╾ Developed economies   ╼◆╾ Economies in transition
╼■╾ Developing economies   ╼✕╾ Least developed countries ╼✳╾ World

Source: ITU.

Figure II.8. Fixed broadband market share by technology and theoretical maximum download speeds

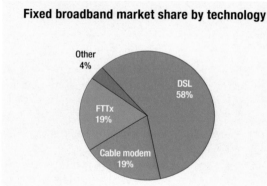

Fixed broadband market share by technology

Other 4%
DSL 58%
FTTx 19%
Cable modem 19%

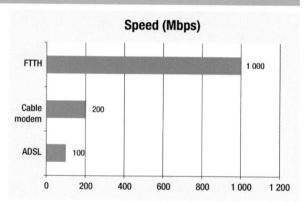

Speed (Mbps)

FTTH — 1 000
Cable modem — 200
ADSL — 100

Source: Point Topic and Broadband Strategies Toolkit, available at http://broadbandtoolkit.org/5.7 (accessed 3 October 2013).
Note: In the left-hand chart, market share information refers to the second quarter of 2012. In the right-hand chart, the cable modem refers to the EuroDOCSIS 3 standard and asymmetric digital subcriber line (ADSL) refers to VDSL2, ITU-T G.993.2 recommendation. Speeds are symmetrical.

the largest share of fixed broadband technology (figure II.8, left). These technologies offer different theoretical speeds depending on various factors, such as hardware versions used and distance of user from exchange. Maximum theoretical speeds vary between technologies, with fibre supporting the highest velocity (figure II.8, right). Further, fibre is generally available with symmetrical upload and download speeds, whereas the other technologies are predominantly asymmetric, with higher download speeds. Average speeds in most countries are far below these theoretical maximums (see annex table 5).

Fibre is the most cloud-friendly of the fixed broadband technologies since the higher the speed, the better cloud services perform.[47] Gigabit (1,000 megabits) per-

second offerings are available in several economies, primarily in East Asia. The Hong Kong Broadband Network was one of the first in the world to launch such a service in 2010.[48] Sony recently launched a 2 Gbps service to several parts of Japan.[49] In the United States, Google offers gigabit service in several cities, hoping to encourage traditional broadband operators to follow.[50] Some question whether such speeds are actually needed today, as few cloud services exploit 1 Gbps.[51] Further, even though these speeds are theoretically available to the end user, bottlenecks emerge due to the inability of backbone networks to handle such large amounts of data. However, as applications have a history of evolving to exploit available speeds, fibre offers the most future-proof fixed broadband technology.

Box II.2.   Cloud services over satellite

In many parts of the developing world that lack adequate terrestrial infrastructure or mobile broadband coverage, the only way to access the Internet or other communication networks is through satellite. Running cloud services over satellite communication, however, is difficult for two main reasons.

The first is latency. Geostationary orbit satellites are 35,786 km above the earth, and communication requires data to cover that distance twice. Therefore, there is always a latency between 500 ms and 800 ms – far above the benchmarks noted for optimal user experience of even basic cloud services. The second reason is that satellite communication is expensive. Depending on the technology used, the market price for 1 megabit per second (Mbps) and about 1 megahertz is about $3,500 plus service and one-time fees for hardware and installation. Some providers offer services at lower cost by overbooking the available capacity, but with a negative impact on end-user experience as a result.

Recent innovations may be making satellite a somewhat more attractive option. The latency problem can be partly addressed by reducing the amount of communications data that has to be transmitted between the remote site and the central data centre. This can be done using a combination of caching and intelligent data management. With regard to the cost of using satellites, the price can be reduced by sharing the bandwidth between sites and customers. A positive side effect of a reduction in data traffic that is not related to communication (handshake and communications traffic) is that less bandwidth is consumed for the transmission. This can lower the price for bandwidth by up to 70 per cent.

In South Africa, the data centre operator Business Connexion in 2011 implemented a solution to provide customers with cloud services such as central data storage and centralized software management over satellite. One of its customers is using this service to enable several subsidiaries in Zambia, Zimbabwe and the Democratic Republic of the Congo to connect with headquarters in Johannesburg, and to use applications such as customer relationship management (CRM).

In the medium term, it is likely that in many parts of developing countries it will still not be financially viable to develop terrestrial infrastructure. Making satellite communication solutions more affordable represents the main option for remote areas to obtain access to cloud services. The potential may be further enhanced by of mobile telephony operators using the global system for mobile communication connecting rural areas over satellite to their network.

Source: UNCTAD, based on information provided by the company named "meanswhat".

Asia leads in fibre subscriptions, accounting for three quarters of the global total.[52] All of the six highest-ranked fibre economies (figure II.9) are in Asia. Most economies with a high proportion of fibre have high incomes and are densely populated, making them conducive to investments in fibre to the premises.[53] Elsewhere, fibre penetration is generally low. According to one source, less than three dozen economies had a household fibre penetration of more than 1 per cent in 2012.[54] In developing countries with limited purchasing power, private operators have little incentive to invest in fibre investment beyond central business district areas. In such cases, public involvement is typically required to achieve more widespread fibre coverage. Azerbaijan offers an example of public investment in fibre optic networks. The Government of Azerbaijan recently launched a three-year fibre optic project that will increase end-user data transmission speeds to 100 Mbps in the capital Baku, to 30 Mbps in other cities and to 10 Mbps in towns and villages.[55]

In contrast to fixed broadband, mobile broadband has been growing rapidly in developing countries as well. The number of global subscriptions stood at an

Figure II.9. Economies with more than 10 per cent household penetration of fibre to the home/building plus local area networks, 2012 (Percentage)

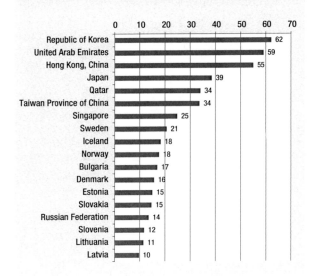

Source: ictDATA.org adapted from national regulatory authorities, the European Union and Fibre to the Home Council Europe.
Note: Data for the United Arab Emirates, Japan, Bulgaria, Estonia and Latvia refer to 2011.

Figure II.10. Global active mobile broadband subscriptions per 100 people, 2010–2012

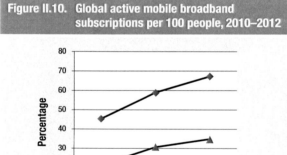

—◆— Developed economies   —▲— Economies in transition
—■— Developing economies   —✕— Least developed countries   —✱—World

Source: ITU, World Telecommunication/ICT Indicators Database.

estimated 1.5 billion in 2012, up almost 350 million or 30 per cent from the previous year.[56] The world average was estimated at 21 subscriptions per 100 people in 2012, with a large gap between developed countries at 67 and developing at 14 (figure II.10).[57] With just some 15 million active mobile broadband subscriptions in LDCs, penetration was below 2 per 100 inhabitants in 2012.

As with fixed broadband, a variety of speeds is available, depending on the technology used for the mobile broadband network (table II.6). Mobile broadband is optimally used as a single-user technology with drops in performance if the connection is shared. It generally has higher latency than fixed broadband. Furthermore, coverage is still far from ubiquitous in developing nations. Long-term evolution (LTE), fourth-generation mobile technology, offers far higher speeds than third generation (3G) networks – with a theoretical 100 Mbps for mobile use and 1 Gbps for

Table II.6. Theoretical highest mobile broadband speeds, W-CDMA family

Technology	Download speed	Upload speed
W-CDMA	384 kbps	384 kbps
HSDPA	14.4 Mbps	384 kbps
HSUPA	Specification for upload and not download	5.7 Mbps
HSPA	42 Mbps	11 Mbps

Source: World Bank, Broadband Strategies Toolkit.
Abbreviations: HSPA – high-speed packet access, HSDPA – high-speed downlink packet access, HSUPA – high-speed uplink packet access, kbps – kilobit per second, W-CDMA – wideband code division multiple access.

stationary use – and less latency. Tests carried out in Finland confirm this observation and suggest that LTE performance is comparable to some fixed line offerings (table II.7).

Table II.7. Comparison of 3G and LTE speeds and latency in Finland

	3G	LTE
Download speed	4.1 Mbps	36.1 Mbps
Latency	117ms	23ms

Source: Epitiro, 2011, LTE 'Real World' Performance Study, http://www.epitiro.com/assets/files/20-103-1006.001%20LTE-Report-World-Report.pdf (accessed 3 October 2010).

5. Quality of service of broadband networks

As connectivity in the cloud is achieved primarily via the Internet, reliable broadband access is imperative. The cloud is capable of an array of tasks, ranging from simple webmail and word processing to complicated reporting, visualization, data processing and management information systems – all of which are expected to have a quick turn-around time. As the need for reliable and fast Internet access becomes evident, so does need for higher QoS experienced by the user.

Several dimensions can be considered when assessing broadband connectivity QoS, (Gonsalves and Bharadwaj, 2009):

- Download speed is the most often cited characteristic when describing the quality of broadband services. It refers to the time taken to transfer data packets from a server to an end-user device. Usually measured in kilobits per second (kbps) or Mbps.
- Upload speed refers to the time taken to transmit data packets from an end user device to a server. Usually measured in kbps or Mbps.
- Latency or round trip time (RTT) is the time taken for a packet to reach the destination server and return to the client (the end-user device). Usually measured in ms.
- Jitter is the variation of latency or the variation in time of data packets arriving. Usually measured in ms.
- Packet loss refers to the share of packets that fail to arrive at the destination server. Usually measured as a percentage of the total number of packets transferred.

Various applications demand different performance measures in order to function within acceptable standards (table II.8). Upload and download speeds and latency affect various levels of cloud sophistication differently (figure II.11). For example, throughput is vital for streaming media, while RTT or latency is more important for networked games.[58] As a result of the nature and design of cloud services, upload speed and latency are gaining prominence for the use of broadband.

The Cisco Global Cloud Readiness tool proposes a set of thresholds with regard to QoS requirements that should be met for cloud services of different levels of sophistication (figure II.11). Low speeds and high latency do not preclude the use of cloud computing but rather the use of different cloud-based applications. For example, QoS requirements are considerably lower for basic cloud services such as webmail, web browsing and VoIP than for more advanced applications such as high-definition (HD) video streaming. A key usability factor is performance, or how immediate the interaction with the application seems.

(a) Download speed

Download speed has traditionally been a key metric of broadband performance. Prior to Web 2.0, few users generated content and most were passive consumers of downloaded information. Though social networking, blogs, wikis and video sharing have grown, users still download more than they upload. User-generated content generates more information

Table II.8. Relevance of broadband characteristics by cloud service

Service	Down-load speed (kbps)	Upload speed (kbps)	Latency (ms)	Jitter (ms)	Packet loss (per-centage)
Browsing	++	–	++	–	–
Web-based e-mail	+++	++	++	–	+
Streaming media (con-sumption)	+++	–	++	++	++
Streaming media (pro-duction)	++	+++	++	++	++
Data storage	–	+++	–	–	–
VoIP	+	+	+++	+++	+++
Gaming	++	+	+++	++	++
Data storage and analysis (real time)	+++	+++	++	–	+
Web services	+	++	+++	++	+++
Management information systems (ERP/CRM)	++	++	+++	+	++
Software development services	–	++	++	–	+++

Source: UNCTAD, based on LIRNEasia research; Gonsalves and Badarwaj, 2009.
Key: +++ Highly relevant; ++ Very relevant; + Somewhat relevant; – Irrelevant.

Figure II.11. Levels of cloud sophistication and related quality of service requirements

Basic
Download: 750 kbps
Upload: 250 kbps
Latency: 160 ms

- Single player gaming
- Text communications (E-mail, instant messaging)
- Stream basic video/music
- Web conferencing
- Web browsing
- VoIP (Internet telephony)

Intermediate
Download: 751–2 500 kbps
Upload: 251–1 000 kbps
Latency: 159–100 ms

- ERP/CRM
- HD video streaming
- Multi-player gaming
- Online shopping
- Social networking (multimedia/interactivity)
- Video conferencing

Advanced
Download: >2 500 kbps
Upload: >1 500 kbps
Latency: <100 ms

- 3D video streaming
- HD video conferencing
- Stream super HD video
- Connected education/medicine
- Group video calling
- Virtual office

Source: Adapted from http://www.cisco.com/en/US/netsol/index.html (accessed 11 October 2013).
Note: Concurrent and multiples instances of applications will require a faster network.
ERP: enterprise resource planning.

to be downloaded. The growth of broadband has also triggered more feature-rich content, especially video, with higher quality resulting in many more bits coming down to users. This is amplified by cloud services offering feature films in HD format. It has been estimated that some 1.3 billion Internet users around the world watched around 162 online videos a month in 2012.[59] This has increased the ratio of downloaded to uploaded information. A 2012 study of 5,000 users in Japan found that, on average, each one downloaded 20 times more the volume of information than they uploaded, a ratio that has doubled since 2005.[60]

(b) Upload speed

Increased use of offline storage, file sharing and back-up services require more consideration to upload speeds. Meanwhile, network operators generally promote broadband plans primarily based on download speeds with little or no mention of the upload features. As noted previously, most fixed and mobile broadband technologies other than fibre are designed so that downlinks have greater bandwidth and are faster than upstream links.[61] The concept of storage in the cloud requires users to upload data to a remotely located server. Therefore, upload speeds and data caps are critical elements when assessing the ability of a network to support cloud applications. Lack of bandwidth on the uplink can be more of an issue for home or small enterprise users than for large enterprises if the latter have access to dedicated links.

(c) Latency

The performance of applications and services is a function of the speed of which the data can be accessed and processed. For instance, data on a local hard disk can usually be accessed much faster than data located at the end of a large network. The cloud consists of multiple servers physically located around the world. The collection of these servers creates a virtual data centre. Within such a virtual environment there can be varying degrees of latency. This is in addition to the latency that exists between the end user and the server that has been queried. Therefore, unlike with traditional Internet services, different types of latencies adversely affect a user's overall experience. This aspect is sometimes overlooked as the focus tends to be on the performance and reliability of the cloud as opposed to the connectivity to the cloud, a necessity in order for it to offer a viable solution.

Less RTT means that a web page or document loads faster. Latency can be a key bottleneck for the adoption of cloud services. While a number of countries may achieve acceptable levels of download and upload speed, many do not meet the latency requirement for intermediate and advanced cloud services. In terms of fixed networks, only two economies (Hong Kong, China and Lithuania) can reportedly fully support concurrent advanced cloud services in an efficient way.[62] In the case of mobile broadband, no country can efficiently support intermediate and advanced services, due to high latency. However, as noted in table II.7, LTE is comparable to many fixed broadband offerings. There can be significant differences in terms of network latency when accessing a server within an individual ISP domain and in the international domain, respectively.

Comparing latency across countries is not straightforward. Since bits cannot travel faster than light, there will always be some element of latency.[63] As these delays increase with distance, it would be appropriate to compare countries in terms of the latency citizens experience over the same distance. Such data are not universally available for most countries.[64] At the same time, not all cloud computing servers may be accessible from within some countries. Users in these countries would then need to access overseas sites.

(d) Country comparison of broadband quality of service

With a view to presenting a crude assessment of countries' performance in this area, table II.9 uses data concerning 138 economies to illustrate whether they are able to meet the QoS benchmarks proposed by Cisco (figure II.11) for making use of basic and advanced cloud services. The table further shows in which areas (download speed, upload speed or latency) countries encounter bottlenecks.

Of the 43 economies that meet all the minimum benchmarks for advanced cloud services, 7 are from developing Asia and Oceania and 6 are transition economies. By contrast, no African or Latin American countries are represented in this group.

The largest group consists of the 61 economies that meet at least all the proposed minimum requirements for basic cloud services. It includes 9 developed economies and 7 transition economies, in addition to 6 economies from Africa, 18 from Asia and Oceania and 20 from Latin America and the Caribbean. The

Table II.9. Quality of service performance, by groups of economies

Economies that meet minimum requirements for advanced cloud services	Economies that meet minimum requirements for basic cloud services	Bottleneck			Economies that do not yet meet requirements for basic cloud services	Bottleneck		
		Download speed	Upload speed	Latency		Download speed	Upload speed	Latency
Armenia	Albania		X	X	Afghanistan	X		X
Austria	Argentina		X		Algeria	X		
Belgium	Aruba		X	X	Angola			X
Bulgaria	Australia		X		Antigua and Barbuda			X
Canada	Azerbaijan	X	X		Bangladesh	X		
China	Bahrain	X	X	X	Belize	X		X
Hong Kong	Barbados		X	X	Bolivia (Plurinational State of)	X		X
Taiwan Province	Belarus	X	X		Cayman Islands			X
Czech Republic	Bermuda			X	Côte d'Ivoire			X
Denmark	Bosnia and Herzegovina		X		Haiti			X
Estonia	Brazil		X		Iraq			X
Finland	Brunei Darussalam	X	X	X	Lebanon		X	X
France	Cambodia	X			Maldives			X
Georgia	Chile		X		Mauritius		X	
Germany	Colombia		X	X	Mozambique			X
Hungary	Costa Rica	X	X	X	Myanmar			X
Iceland	Croatia		X		Namibia			X
Japan	Cyprus		X		New Caledonia			X
Republic of Korea	Dominican Republic	X	X	X	Nigeria			X
Latvia	Ecuador	X		X	Paraguay			X
Lithuania	Egypt	X	X	X	Peru			X
Luxembourg	El Salvador	X	X	X	Samoa			X
Malaysia	Ghana		X	X	Senegal			X
Moldova	Greece		X		Sudan			X
Mongolia	Guatemala	X	X	X	Suriname	X		X
Netherlands	Honduras	X	X		Syrian Arab Republic	X		X
Norway	India	X	X	X	Tajikistan			X
Poland	Indonesia	X	X	X	Turkmenistan	X	X	X
Portugal	Iran (Islamic Republic of)	X	X	X	Uganda			X
Romania	Ireland		X		United Republic of Tanzania			X
Russian Federation	Israel		X		Uzbekistan			X
Singapore	Italy		X		Yemen			X
Slovakia	Jamaica		X	X	Zambia			X
Slovenia	Jordan	X	X	X	Zimbabwe			X
Spain	Kazakhstan			X				
Sweden	Kenya			X				
Switzerland	Kuwait	X	X	X				

Table II.9. Quality of service performance, by groups of economies *(continued)*

Economies that meet minimum requirements for advanced cloud services	Economies that meet minimum requirements for basic cloud services	Bottleneck			Economies that do not yet meet requirements for basic cloud services	Bottleneck		
		Download speed	Upload speed	Latency		Download speed	Upload speed	Latency
The former Yugoslav Republic of Macedonia	Malta		X					
Ukraine	Mexico		X					
United Arab Emirates	Montenegro		X					
United Kingdom	Morocco	X	X	X				
United States	Nepal	X	X	X				
Viet Nam	New Zealand		X					
	Nicaragua	X	X					
	Oman		X					
	Pakistan	X	X	X				
	Panama	X	X	X				
	Philippines	X	X	X				
	Puerto Rico		X					
	Qatar		X					
	Saudi Arabia		X					
	Serbia		X					
	Solomon Islands			X				
	South Africa	X	X					
	Sri Lanka	X	X	X				
	Thailand		X					
	Trinidad and Tobago		X	X				
	Tunisia	X	X	X				
	Turkey		X					
	Uruguay	X	X					
	Venezuela (Bolivarian Republic of)	X	X	X				

Source: Adapted from Cisco Analysis, 2012. See annex table 5.
Note: See figure II.11 for QoS requirements for advanced and basic cloud services.

main bottleneck impeding these economies from graduating to the next level was the benchmark for upload speeds – which more than 90 per cent of the economies failed to meet – followed by latency.

The final group comprises 34 economies that failed to meet at least one of the QoS benchmarks proposed for basic cloud services. In this case, Africa dominates with 13 entries, followed by Asia and Oceania (10), Latin America and the Caribbean (8) and transition economies (3). Latency is the most critical bottleneck for this group, faced by all but three of the economies listed.

6. Affordability of broadband services

The price of Internet access in some countries presents a key barrier to cloud adoption, potentially offsetting the cost savings from remote storage and applications. Fixed broadband prices have declined sharply in the past few years but are still high in many developing countries. While a monthly fixed broadband basket was, on average, equivalent to 40 per cent of per capita income in developing countries in 2011, it was less than 2 per cent in developed countries (figure II.12). In the case of mobile broadband, prices are lower – the world average post-paid dongle mobile broadband basket was 14 per cent of per capita income in 2011. Nevertheless, the cost of mobile broadband also remains high for developing countries (20 per cent of income for a post-paid package and 31 per cent for pre-paid) (figure II.13). Furthermore, mobile broadband plans tend to have lower usage ceilings than fixed broadband.

In Africa in particular, most broadband users rely on either ADSL or mobile broadband for last-mile connectivity. In addition to raising concerns of QoS and limited deployment, ADSL access remains relatively expensive. Recent studies confirm that at low usage, mobile broadband tends to be cheaper

than ADSL (figure II.14) (Stork et al., 2013). However, at higher usage, ADSL becomes a more competitive option. Fixed broadband tends to be packaged with higher volume limits than mobile, and this advantage increases with greater usage. This implies that in regions where mobile vastly outnumbers fixed subscriptions, cloud access will tend to be constrained by the usage limits in mobile broadband pricing structures. The data for Africa also show sharp price differences between countries that shift over the usage profile. While ADSL tends to have much bigger price divergence between countries at low usage, mobile broadband prices diverge more sharply at higher usage levels.

Figure II.12.   Fixed broadband price basket (left) and annual change (right), 2008–2011

Fixed broadband basket as percentage of gross national income per capita

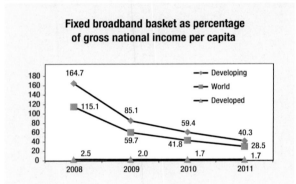

Fixed broadband basket annual change

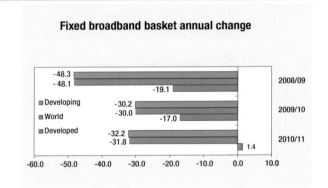

Source: ITU.
Note: Based on simple averages. For definition of regions, see http://www.itu.int/ITU-D/ict/definitions/regions/ (accessed 3 October 2013).

Figure II.13.   Mobile broadband prices as a percentage of gross national income per capita, by region and level of development, 2011

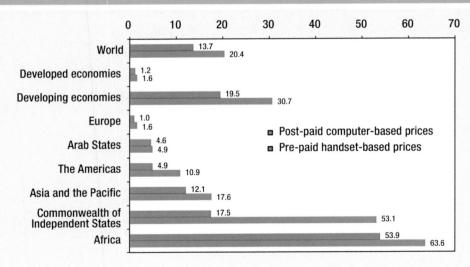

Source: ITU.
Note: Based on simple averages. For definition of regions, see http://www.itu.int/ITU-D/ict/definitions/regions/ (accessed 3 October 2013).

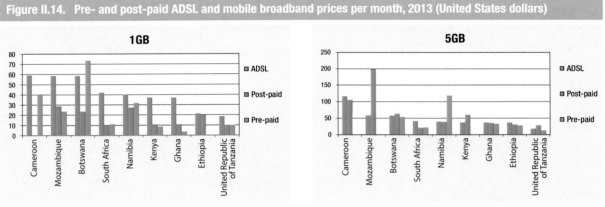

Figure II.14. Pre- and post-paid ADSL and mobile broadband prices per month, 2013 (United States dollars)

Source: Stork et al., 2013.

Note: ADSL lines were used for the fixed broadband baskets, developed in accordance with ITU broadband definitions: (a) monthly cost of 1 gigabyte (GB) use per month with at least 256 kbps connection for a period of 24 months, (b) monthly cost of 5 GB use per month with at least 256 kbps connection for a period of 24 months and (c) monthly cost of uncapped use per month with at least 256 kbps connection for a period of 24 months. For comparative purposes, the mobile broadband baskets were designed to match the fixed broadband baskets. The baskets were calculated for post- and pre-paid products.

C. CONCLUSIONS

At the global level, revenues from formal cloud service segments are small compared with the ancillary revenues from the cloud economy (equipment sales, broadband access and advertising-supported free cloud services). Various private sources give different estimates of the size of public and private cloud revenues, but all seem to agree that the cloud phenomenon is set to expand quickly in the next few years.

Metrics such as the number of data servers, revenue and estimated market shares indicate that practically all the major corporate players in the cloud economy hail from the United States. This is not a surprise, given the country's dominance of many aspects of the Internet ecosystem and its position as an early adopter of cloud computing. Their early entry into cloud computing has given them first-mover advantages, not least in terms of building large networks of users and massive data storage and processing capacity. The absolute levels of investment required for major cloud computing estates are very high; it can cost more than half a billion dollars for a cluster of data centres. Investment requirements on this scale constitute significant barriers to entry, which helps explain why the global market is dominated by a small number of providers and may raise concerns about the extent of competition in the market.

In addition, the global cloud providers are also buying up new cloud businesses, often at high valuations, before they reach the point of being able to challenge

the dominant providers. Some cloud customers are concerned about the risks of limited competition in the cloud provision market (Renda, 2012). If cloud providers can lock customers into contracts because of the way in which they store their users' data and the services they provide them with, then customers may not benefit as much as they should from the cost savings that the cloud makes possible. It may also raise questions about the scope for local cloud service providers to emerge and grow, including in developing countries (see chapter III).

At the same time, as cloud computing expands geographically, it is possible that regional and local companies will assume a greater role due to the need for localization, system integration and aggregation, combined with the need to host cloud servers close by for better performance. Telecommunication service providers are increasingly entering the cloud market through acquisitions or partnerships and in the future can be expected to play an active role due to their direct link to the end user.

The second part of this chapter focused on the infrastructure-related determinants of the ability of countries to use and benefit from cloud computing. Compared with other types of Internet use, some factors are more relevant when considering the user experience of cloud applications. Upon analysis, five main observations can be made:

- Firstly, QoS is key. In particular, both upload speed and latency become critical to ensure optimal use of cloud applications. As some degree of latency always exists, data centres should be located within countries or fairly nearby to obtain optimal performance using advanced cloud services. This has implications for the configuration of the underlying infrastructure. As documented above, there is currently a significant digital divide in terms of data centre and server availability across countries. Moreover, few operators advertise their upload speeds, making it difficult for users to compare different offerings.

- Secondly, cloud services are not homogenous. It is important to distinguish between different kinds of applications when considering the ability of countries to use and potentially benefit from the cloud economy. Most Internet users make use of some basic cloud services, such as webmail and VoIP. These types of applications require far less speed and can tolerate more latency than more advanced cloud services relevant to the business world.

- Thirdly, most mobile broadband networks are capable of supporting only basic cloud services. Although the speeds of mobile networks continue to increase, they still fall short of those achievable with fibre optic connectivity. Mobile broadband typically involves higher latency than fixed technologies. It is uncertain to what extent mobile broadband below LTE standards can be a substitute for fixed technology with respect to

efficient access to advanced cloud services. This has implications for countries that are currently relying primarily on wireless broadband, as in most low-income countries.

- Fourthly, there is a need for better, more relevant and international comparable data and definitions for measuring the potential of cloud computing. This includes official data on broadband speeds and latency as well as primary source indicators on cloud uptake such as the number of cloud servers, data centres and cloud services available.

- Lastly, in the immediate future, many developing countries, particularly in Africa, will face challenges in order to fully benefit from the cloud, especially with regard to intermediate and advanced cloud services. Although most countries have now deployed mobile broadband networks as a substitute for fixed ones, they are characterized by low speed and high latency and are therefore not ideal for cloud provision. The cost of broadband access in particular remains an obstacle for the adoption of cloud services in many developing countries. Long distances to data servers located in foreign locations increase latency, and the deployment of national data centres is affected by the lack of supporting infrastructure (IXPs, reliable and inexpensive electricity, robust fibre optic backbones) and the lack of adequate regulations (see chapter IV).

NOTES

1   That amount was forecast to would rise to $131 billion in 2013. See press release, "Gartner says worldwide public cloud services market to total $131 billion", 28 February 2013. Available at http://www.gartner.com/newsroom/id/2352816 (accessed 4 October 2013).

2   Gartner also includes a value of BPaaS, which is attributed with generated revenues of about $31 billion in 2012.

3   This figure was derived based on the forecast of $24 billion in 2016, growing at a 50 per cent annual rate from 2012. See "IDC: Private cloud-based services to see rapid growth", The Wall Street Journal, 28 February 2013. Available at http://online.wsj.com/article/BT-CO-20130228-708787.html (accessed 4 October 2013).

4   See for example Kushida et al., 2012, p. 82 .

5   It should be noted that IDATE's statistics may include an element of double counting in overlapping subsectors. Furthermore, the data are based on consumption. For certain categories, disparities with production data can be significant in cases of a high volumes of international trade (IDATE Foundation, 2012).

6   See http://www.iacpsocialmedia.org/Resources/FunFacts.aspx (accessed 4 October 2013).

7   One zettabyte is equal to 1,000 exabytes.

8   According to Cisco, most Internet traffic has originated or terminated in a data centre since 2008. Factors contributing to intra-data centre traffic include functional separation of application servers, storage and databases, which generates replication, backup and read/write traffic traversing the data centre. The ratio of traffic exiting the data centre to traffic remaining within the data centre could be expected to increase over time, mainly due to increased use of are bandwidth-heavy video files. Meanwhile, the increasing use of applications such as desktop virtualization may offset this trend (Cisco Analysis, 2012).

9   See GigaOM, "IBM says its cloud biz is growing like crazy but provides no real numbers", 23 January 2013. Available at http://gigaom.com/2013/01/23/ibm-says-ibms-cloud-biz-is-growing-like-wild-fire-but-provides-no-real-numbers/ (accessed 4 October 2013).

10 For example, one analyst firm compares 10 public cloud storage providers by various capabilities, such as accessibility, manageability, pricing, security and resiliency. See http://www.gartner.com/technology/reprints.do?id=1-1D9C6ZM&ct=121216&st=sg (accessed 4 October 2013). Another ranks the top 10 cloud providers by various features: see http://ichitect.com/best-cloud/(accessed 4 October 2013). There is also a list of the top 100 cloud services providers but no details are given on the methodology used: see http://talkincloud.com/tc100 (accessed 4 October 2013).

11 It should be noted that all servers of a particular company are not necessarily used for cloud service provision.

12 See "Verizon buys Terremark", The Wall Street Journal, 27 January 2011. Available at http://online.wsj.com/article/SB10001424052748703399204576108641018258046.html (accessed 4 October 2013).

13 One exception is NTT's (Japan) acquisition of Data Dimension (South Africa); see http://www.telegraph.co.uk/finance/newsbysector/mediatechnologyandtelecoms/telecoms/7893094/NTT-in-2.1bn-deal-to-buy-Dimension-Data.html (accessed 4 October 2013).

14 See http://www.novell.com/news/press/2010/5/vodacom-business-and-novell-partner-to-securely-manage-and-optimize-cloud-services.html (accessed 4 October 2013).

15 See http://www.nec.co.jp/press/en/1002/1803.html (accessed 4 October 2013).

16 See https://www.aplicateca.es (accessed 4 October 2013).

17 See http://www.digitalnewsasia.com/mobile-telco/special-report-telco-cloud-strategies-in-asean?page=0%2C1.

18 See http://instacompute.com (accessed 4 October 2013).

19 See http://itknowledgeexchange.techtarget.com/cloud-computing/tata-approaches-us-cloud-market-with-caution/ (accessed 4 October 2013).

20 See "Microsoft launches office, Azure services in China", Information Week, 5 November 2012. Available at http://www.informationweek.com/cloud-computing/infrastructure/microsoft-launches-office-azure-services/240044374 (accessed 4 October 2013).

21 For further information, see explanatory notes available at http://unstats.un.org/unsd/cr/registry/docs/CPCv2_explanatory_notes.pdf (accessed 4 October 2013).

22 The services sectors included were computer and data processing services and royalties and license fees for general use of computer software, amounting to a total value of $43.8 billion cross-border transactions in 2010.

23 Examples of such industries include telecommunication businesses, retail trade businesses and computer and electronic product manufacturers.

24 See "Made outside India", The Economist, 10 August 2013. Available at http://www.economist.com/news/international/21583285-growth-slows-and-reforms-falter-economic-activity-shifting-out-india-made-outside (accessed 4 October 2013).

25 Communication from the Computer and Communications Industry Association to the United States International Trade Commission regarding Digital Trade Hearing of 7 March (Investigation No. 332-531). Available at http://www.ccianet.com/libraryfiles/ccLibraryFiles/Filename/000000000764/CCIA%20Digital%20Trade%20Follow-up%20Letter.pdf (accessed 10 October 2013).

26 As reported in the UNCOMTRADE database for HS category 851712.

27 See, for example, Gartner press release, "Gartner says smartphone sales grew 46.5 percent in second quarter of 2013 and exceeded feature phone sales for first time", 14 August 2013. Available at http://www.gartner.com/newsroom/id/2573415 (accessed 10 October 2013).

28 Information provided by e-mail by TechAmerica.

29 Information provided by e-mail by the World Customs Organization.

30 The HS 847150 category is described as covering the traded value of "processing units other than those of sub-heading 8471.41/8471.49, whether/not containing in the same housing one/two of the following types of unit: storage units, input units, output units".

31 Hong Kong, China appears as a top importer and exporter in table II.4. This is partly due to high activities of re-exports through that economy to and from China.

32 Although not featured in table II.4, Taiwan Province of China also witnessed rapid growth of computer server production and exports.

33 See "Worldwide server market rebounds sharply in fourth quarter as demand for x86 servers and high-end systems leads the way, according to IDC", IDC, press release, 27 February 2013. Available at http://www.idc.com/getdoc.jsp?containerId=prUS23974913 (accessed 10 October 2013).

34 See "IDC: Q4 server revenue declines again, but shows improvement", CRN, 25 February 2010. Available at http://www.crn.com/news/components-peripherals/223100777/idc-q4-server-revenue-declines-again-but-shows-improvement.htm (accessed 10 October 2013).

35 See "Worldwide server market accelerates sharply in fourth quarter as demand for heterogeneous platforms leads the way, according to IDC", IDC, press release, 28 February 2010. Available at: http://www.idc.com/about/viewpressrelease.jsp?containerId=prUS22716111 (accessed 10 October 2013).

36 Frameworks for analysing cloud computing in developing countries have been proposed, but performance is defined in a broad sense, such as availability of cloud services, cloud awareness and diffusion of cloud for which no comparable statistics exist (Kshetri, 2010).

37 See http://www.telegeography.com/products/commsupdate/articles/2013/04/17/international-bandwidth-demand-is-decentralising/ (accessed 11 October 2013).

38   Caching refers to the process of storing previously requested Internet information (such as a web page) on a server near the user so that it can be re-used. This minimizes data traffic back to the source of the information, thereby reducing bandwidth requirements.

39   Indicators are beginning to emerge with regard to length, coverage and capacity of terrestrial networks. According to one study on terrestrial fibre backbone networks in sub-Saharan Africa, there was twice as much fibre under deployment across Africa in 2011, compared with 2009; 313 million people (36 per cent) were within reach of an operational fibre node; and cross-border networks more than doubled to 20 Gbps by the end 2010 (Hamilton, 2011).

40   Some studies suggest that a significant share of these IXPs are non-operational (Ryan and Gerson, 2012).

41   See   http://www.internetsociety.org/news/new-study-reveals-how-internet-exchange-points-ixps-spur-internet-growth-emerging-markets (accessed 14 October 2013).

42   See https://www.peeringdb.com/help/stats.php (accessed 14 October 2013).

43   The recommended temperature and relative humidity range for data centres is 18°C–27°C and between 40 per cent relative humidity (5.5°C dew point) and 60 per cent (15°C). See http://www.cisco.com/en/US/solutions/collateral/ns340/ns517/ns224/ns944/white_paper_c11-680202.pdf (accessed 14 October 2013).

44   A data centre risk index has been designed to assist companies in making strategic investment and operational decisions about where to locate their data, whether it be server rack deployments or the creation of new facilities, see (Source8 et al., 2013).

45   See http://www.datacentermap.com/datacenters.html (accessed 14 October 2013).

46   A study of mobile Internet in Europe found that the number of reported mobile broadband subscriptions was almost twice as high as the number of people who reported in surveys that they use the Internet from mobile devices over mobile networks; see http://www.ictdata.org/2013/01/mobile-internet-in-europe.html (accessed 14 October 2013).

47   See http://www.ftthcouncil.org/p/cm/ld/fid=50 (accessed 14 October 2103).

48   See "HKBN launches 1 Gbps broadband for US$26/month", press release, 14 April 2010. Available at http://uk.reuters.com/article/2010/04/14/idUS20842+14-Apr-2010+GNW20100414 (accessed 14 October 2013).

49   See "Sony ISP launches world's fastest home Internet, 2Gbps", Computer World, 15 April 2013. Available at http://www.computerworld.com/s/article/9238392/Sony_ISP_launches_world_39_s_fastest_home_Internet_2Gbps (accessed 14 October 2013).

50   See "5 reasons you want Google Fibre in your city", CNN, 12 April 2013. Available at http://edition.cnn.com/2013/04/11/tech/innovation/google-fiber-austin-cities/index.html (accessed 14 October 2013).

51   See "Fibre to the home: A highway too super", The Economist, 6 December 2012. Available at http://www.economist.com/blogs/babbage/2012/12/fibre-home (accessed 14 October 2013).

52   See http://www.ftthcouncilap.org/index.php?option=com_content&view=article&catid=6:media-releases&id=221:apac-represents-75-of-ftthb-subscribers-worldwide&Itemid=36 (accessed 14 October 2013).

53   It is cheaper to lay fibre in areas where many people live in close quarters, such as apartment buildings, and where incomes can afford the multiple services (e.g. broadband and video) fibre providers market to recoup investment.

54   See   http://www.ftthcouncil.eu/documents/Presentations/20130220PressConfLondon_Online.pdf   (accessed 14 October 2013).

55   See http://regionplus.az/en/articles/view/1983 (accessed 14 October 2013).

56   From ITU World Telecommunication/ICT Indicators Database.

57   As noted earlier, the data should be interpreted carefully for possible discrepancies between the reported and actual levels of mobile broadband usage.

[58] One study found that a one-second delay reduces customer conversation by 7 per cent, customer satisfaction by 16 per cent and page views by 11 per cent (Aberdeen Group, 2008).

[59] See http://www.comscore.com/Insights/Presentations_and_Whitepapers/2013/The_Past_Present_and_Future_of_Online_Video (accessed 13 October 2013).

[60] See http://www.iij.ad.jp/en/company/development/iir/pdf/iir_vol16_report_EN.pdf (accessed 13 October 2013).

[61] Empirical assessments confirm weaker performance with significantly slower upload than to download speeds (see LIRNEasia, 2011).

[62] See http://www.cisco.com/en/US/netsol/ns1208/networking_solutions_sub_sub_solution.html (accessed 14 October 2013).

[63] It takes around 20 ms for a packet travelling at the speed of light to cover around 3,000 km. Current fibre optic technology adds a delay, increasing latency. Recent experimental research suggests that new fibre optic design could come close to reaching the speed of light (Poletti et al., 2013).

[64] Statistics that do not use a universal latency distance thus produce misleading results. See "Use of latency in broadband ranking is silly", Digital Society, 2 October 2009. Available at http://www.digitalsociety.org/2009/10/use-of-latency-in-broadband-ranking-is-silly/ (accessed 14 October 2013).

[65] See "The billion dollar data centers", Data Center Knowledge, 29 April 2013. Available at http://www.datacenterknowledge.com/archives/2013/04/29/the-billion-dollar-data-centers/ (accessed 14 October 2013).

[66] See "The cloud builds up steam", Financial Times, 6 June 2013. Available at http://www.ft.com/intl/cms/s/0/e2b826a2-ce20-11e2-8313-00144feab7de.html#axzz2hiA0qwBY (accessed 14 October 2013) and "Cisco acquires enterprise Wi-FI startup Meraki for $1.2 billion in cash", Techcrunch.com, 18 November 2012. Available at http://techcrunch.com/2012/11/18/cisco-acquires-enterprise-wi-fi-startup-meraki-for-1-2-billion-in-cash/ (accessed 14 October 2013).

IMPLICATIONS FOR DEVELOPING COUNTRIES

3

The level of cloud adoption in most developing countries is still low. Nevertheless, this is an appropriate moment to consider what opportunities and challenges the evolving cloud economy may bring to developing countries. The picture differs between countries as well as between types of cloud service customer. The ability to seize opportunities presented by cloud computing and to avoid the pitfalls associated with it will depend substantially on the level of cloud readiness, particularly in terms of broadband connectivity (chapter II) and appropriate legal and regulatory frameworks (chapter IV).

Using the cloud economy ecosystem presented in chapter I, this chapter reviews critical drivers and barriers for cloud adoption from a developing country perspective. It draws on the still limited available evidence, which mainly consists of various surveys of prospective or existing users of cloud services. It describes opportunities for developing-country enterprises on both the supply and the demand sides of the cloud economy. The chapter recognizes that the extent to which countries, and stakeholders within countries, will be able to take advantage of the cloud economy can be influenced by proactive policies, which are considered in chapter V.

A. DRIVERS AND BARRIERS OF CLOUD ADOPTION

1. Drivers of cloud adoption

The main advantages attributed to cloud computing can be summarized in three main categories (see also chapter I):

- Cost savings in hardware, software and personnel, derived from the economies of scale that are available from the cloud;
- Flexible access to processing and storage capacity on demand, with a high degree of elasticity;
- Improved system management, reliability and IT security.

Cost savings are most frequently cited in the literature among these drivers. These are expected to result from cloud service customers paying for the use of data storage capacity and application software, rather than having to purchase otherwise the necessary hardware and software. This allows them to gain from the economies of scope and scale that are available through cloud service providers, and from their specialized management expertise. This model of provisioning effectively transfers resources from capital to operational expenditure, making it possible for companies with limited financial resources – a situation that is common in developing countries – to make use of applications that they could not otherwise afford. Savings at the cloud service customer level can also arise from reductions in IT staff costs, though companies and other organizations that make extensive use of cloud facilities will need to retain skilled personnel to manage continuing in-house IT functions, procure cloud services, oversee their relationship with cloud providers and manage cloud data and applications internally.

Flexible access to processing and storage capacity is another important driver, particularly for companies whose business activities are seasonal, whose computing requirements vary substantially at different stages of a business cycle, or which operate in sectors where demand is unpredictable. Start-up ventures often have difficulty scaling up resources if they are met with unexpected levels of demand. Cloud provisioning can enable them to respond without having to seek capital, at short notice, to invest in new equipment. Likewise, companies experiencing a business downturn benefit from the ability to reduce

software and hardware requirements without having to write off expensive IT assets. In addition, cloud provisioning enables users to apply the latest software versions as and when these become available, at limited cost, mostly associated with less need to buy and install software upgrades or replace the hardware required to run them.

Smaller businesses in developing countries often find it difficult to hire competent personnel in IT and other professional disciplines (see, for example, UNCTAD, 2011a). Cloud provisioning enables them to outsource some of the IT skills that they would otherwise have to resource internally, benefiting from the expertise that cloud service providers can offer in areas such as IT management and security. Taken to the national level, in countries with a shortage of IT skills, this could allow for a more efficient use of scarce IT expertise. From a security standpoint, the relative value of this aspect may be higher for SMEs in developing countries that may be less likely to be in a position to take measures against cyberthreats than larger enterprises or SMEs in more advanced economies (Kshetri, 2010).

Drivers such as those mentioned above apply in principle to both large and small firms, but play out differently. Larger companies, with more complex needs, are more likely to search out cloud solutions that are tailored to their specific needs. Smaller firms, with less capacity to assess different IT options, may rather rely primarily on generic, public applications. The size of an enterprise may also influence its access to the Internet, affecting the degree of sophistication of the cloud services that it can use.

Some evidence concerning the drivers of cloud adoption in non-profit sectors, where decision-makers have different priorities, can be set alongside this analysis. Although a 2011 survey of over 400 government executives in 10 developed and developing countries confirmed that cost savings were the most significant expected benefit from cloud adoption, the next most significant expected benefits were concerned with the nature of government activity (figure III.1) (KPMG, 2012). About 39 per cent of the respondents stated that they expected the use of cloud applications to change how Government interacted with citizens and 37 per cent that cloud would increase government transparency.

In a global survey of non-governmental organizations (NGOs), responses indicated that administrative advantages (such as easier software access, rapid deployment and reduced system administration)

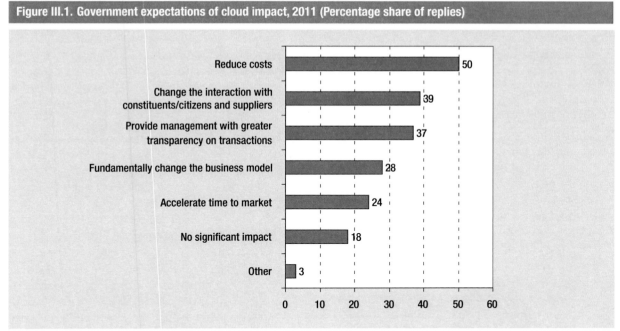

Figure III.1. Government expectations of cloud impact, 2011 (Percentage share of replies)

Note: Survey was conducted from February to May 2011 and canvassed 429 government executives in Australia, Canada, Denmark, Italy, the Netherlands, Singapore, South Africa, Spain, the United Kingdom and the United States.
Source: Adapted from (KPMG, 2012)

were considered more important than cost reductions (Tech Soup Global, 2012).[1] Nonetheless, more than 60 per cent of the respondents reported that they still considered cost reductions important. These surveys are useful reminders that different cloud users have different objectives that are related to the nature of their activities.

2. Barriers to cloud adoption

Barriers to cloud adoption in developing countries fall into two main categories: those that are internal to the potential cloud customer's business/organization, and those external barriers that relate to the wider economic and communications environment. Internal barriers to adoption include attitudes, concerns and anxieties among managers about data security in the cloud, the location of data and reliability of service. Internal barriers also relate to the customer organization's ability to adapt its own systems to use the cloud or to benefit from cloud provisioning. External barriers result from the business, legislative and communications environment in which a firm or organization operates.

(a) Internal barriers

Many of the concerns expressed by potential cloud service customers stem from reservations about the reliability and quality of contractual terms offered by

cloud service providers (see also chapter IV). Six anxieties in particular emerge from survey evidence and discussions with cloud users in developing countries, as follows:

- **Concerns related to the security and privacy of data.** In a 2010 survey of Indian enterprises, 72 per cent of respondents said that privacy and data security issues were extremely significant concerns for them (Ernst and Young, 2010). Security concerns cited by both Government and business customers of cloud services relate, among other things, to the confidentiality of company and customer data, identity management and the risk of identity theft, the risk of data being compromised or altered intentionally or inadvertently in the cloud, and to the fate of data at the end of time-limited contracts.[2] It has been argued that the security arrangements of cloud service providers are often more sophisticated and comprehensive than those that potential customers can deploy themselves (see, for example, Capgemini, 2012). Nevertheless, potential cloud service customers are likely to be reluctant to leave security in the hands of a third party, particularly if security arrangements are unclear to them. Such concerns are compounded by the possibility that third parties (including foreign Governments) could gain access to sensitive national, business or personal data.

Worryingly, data stored in the cloud can be a potential goldmine for cybercriminals. In 2009, Google reported on an attack on its infrastructure that it had found was part of a larger operation that infiltrated the infrastructures of at least 20 major companies (Information Warfare Monitor and Shadowserver Foundation, 2010). In January 2012, the Government of Kenya suffered extensive hacking, involving more than 100 official websites, as a result of attacks by an individual hacker in Indonesia.[3] Security breaches and other cybercrimes may also go unreported because of fears that information about them will negatively influence the valuation or reputation of the companies involved (Kshetri, 2010). Online payment and trading systems will become more attractive targets for cybercrime as traffic volumes and revenues on them grow, and businesses will need to pay increasing attention to security protocols throughout their IT operations as the threat and sophistication of attacks expand. The need for coherent interfaces between local and cloud security norms requires consistent application of stronger security standards throughout customers' own systems, which they may lack the expertise to deploy. Even the best cloud security can be compromised by inadequate security measures in customers' own (terrestrial) systems.

- **Concerns over the geographical location of data (including backups).** The movement of data into and out of a cloud service will often result in its falling under the rules of different jurisdictions. The cross-border transfer of data is generally opaque to the user, raising issues of control. Subsequently, questions may arise on who is responsible for the data at any given point in its cross-border movement. A cloud service customer may, for example, obtain services from an inter-cloud service provider, which in turn obtains additional cloud services from another cloud provider. Some potential users are concerned that data that are located in foreign jurisdictions could be misused or exploited by third parties. In some cases, corporate policies require data to be held within national territorial jurisdictions, barring the use of internationally provided cloud services and facilities.

In addition to legal and other concerns about security, there are other factors that may influence potential cloud customers in favour of more local provisioning. Half of the informants in a survey of 3,000 SMEs saw value in obtaining the services from a locally based provider, and for 31 per cent this was seen as critical (Microsoft, 2012). This preference for local expertise illustrates that factors other than cost savings influence cloud adoption decisions, potentially creating incentives for the expansion of local provision of data centre and other cloud services as the cloud economy evolves.

- **Concerns related to the reliability of service.** Potential cloud customers are concerned that services will be disrupted by system failures in the cloud itself, in the communications networks that connect them with the cloud, or through power cuts that make it impossible for them to access data and services when required. Such problems can result in management inefficiencies and/or poor service to their customers. In practice, there is little evidence of system failures occurring in the systems of major cloud service providers. The greater risks of unreliability are likely to be external to cloud contracts, in national communications and power networks (see external barriers, below) or in the international broadband access when data are stored abroad. Such systemic failures are much more likely to occur in countries with less complex communications networks, lower levels of redundancy and poorer power infrastructures.

- **Concerns related to the non-availability of suitable terminal devices.** Although computerization is becoming more entrenched in developing-country business environments, SMEs there tend to be less well equipped with terminal devices than their peers in other countries, and many smaller firms remain reliant on mobile phones (UNCTAD, 2011b). Although some cloud systems can work effectively with less specified in-house computer systems (or with smartphones and other recent mobile terminals), others require access to devices with sufficient computing power and capability to use them effectively.

- **Concerns related to the migration of data and upgradability.** An important consideration for users is to avoid becoming locked into contractual agreements with a particular cloud provider, thus making it difficult or too expensive to migrate to an alternative provider. Another consideration is that the services of various cloud providers will be insufficiently interoperable for the user to build a portfolio of services. Cloud proponents argue that the development of competitive markets in cloud provision should obviate these risks. At the same time, as noted in chapter II, economies of scale and first-mover advantages may lead to further concentration of the industry. The development

Box III.1. Barriers to cloud adoption in Ghana

Some of the perceived challenges to cloud computing were identified in a 2013 survey of 72 public sector managers, administrators and IT managers in Ghana (box figure III.1).

The cost of migration was the principal challenge. Respondents were concerned not only about charges made by cloud service providers, but also about surrendering the ownership and management of data to a third party. They referred to the cost of being locked-in to a particular cloud service vendor. Various costs may be incurred if the organization wanted to change a cloud service in terms of data reconfiguration to meet the requirements of the new operator or purchase new software. The risk of such future costs may deter the organization from changing its cloud service provider.

Box figure III.1. Perceived challenges of migrating to cloud service

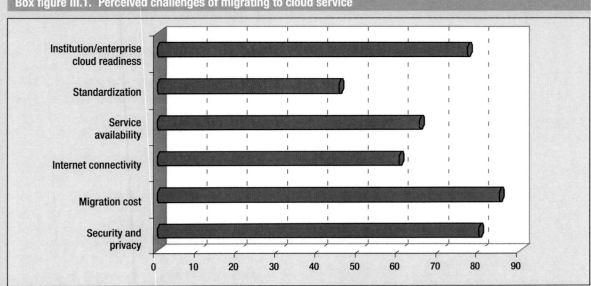

Source: Tweneboah-Koduah, 2013.

Data security and privacy was the second most important challenge identified in the survey. Institution/enterprise readiness to migrate to cloud services was in third place.

Service availability and Internet connectivity were mentioned by more than half of the respondents. The main concern here was related to the need to find appropriate last mile connections (ADSL and mobile broadband) to access services. Dependence on ADSL raised concerns over quality, limited deployment and cost.

Source: UNCTAD, based on Tweneboah-Koduah, 2013.

of common cloud standards should facilitate interoperability, although that in itself is insufficient to ensure the operation of a competitive market. The need for users to secure interoperability when considering different solutions and different providers creates opportunities for cloud brokers and aggregators (see section III.C).

- **Institutional collaboration and coordination.** Effective use of cloud computing requires a high level of organizational collaboration and coordination internally (between government departments or between business divisions). Interdepartmental coordination remains a challenge for many developing country Governments, for both institutional and technical reasons. There are

often demarcation disputes between ministries and other government agencies, which may or may not be resolved by the establishment of special bodies concerned with ICT sector development. At a technical level, in order to leverage cloud services more effectively, there may be a need to strengthen various government data networks and make them more interoperable.

The implementation of new IT systems, such as those enabled by the cloud, requires substantial organizational change – the re-engineering of management structures and business models – if the potential benefits of the cloud are to be fully realized. For a firm of any size, this requires significant investment in business restructuring and staff training, as well as the writing off of existing hardware and software assets. However, failure to implement necessary changes – for example, maintaining legacy systems which should preferably be replaced – can be even more costly as problems of integration are then likely to persist. In some developing countries, such as Ghana, the evidence suggests the cost of migration may be the most important barrier to cloud adoption, followed by security and privacy concerns (box III.1).

Developing-country businesses furthermore have to address challenges in implementing cloud services, as revealed in a global survey of managers in large corporations undertaken for Oracle in 2013 (Dynamic Markets Ltd., 2013).[4] This indicated that more than half had experienced problems with integration of cloud services, leading to staff downtime and non-use of cloud applications by parts of their businesses, and to the abandonment of some cloud applications. Poor integration, for example, with other software, had hindered innovation more in the Asia-Pacific region than elsewhere, with figures as high as 70 per cent and above among respondents in India and Singapore. Asian respondents also reported higher than average problems with customization of cloud services to company needs. Over 40 per cent had experienced usability challenges and/or security breaches with cloud applications, with a third of the respondents noting the need to call in support from their companies' IT departments in order to resolve these problems. Other problems raised by managers included poor implementation of cloud services on mobile devices. The experience reported by these managers illustrates problems at various points within the cloud economy ecosystem, in the relationship between cloud providers and corporate cloud service customers as well as within the latter.

The previously cited survey of NGO perceptions of the cloud found that lack of knowledge and skills to manage cloud resources was the most significant concern, followed by issues of cost (for example, for migration to the cloud, set-up and recurrent expenditure on both cloud providers' charges and communications) (Tech Soup Global, 2012). The latter is likely to be particularly relevant in countries with high costs for broadband connectivity. NGOs in countries with relatively low gross domestic product (GDP) per capita were more likely to identify barriers to adoption, citing foreign currency problems alongside lack of reliable Internet and electrical connectivity and government regulations concerning the location of data storage. Some expressed concerns about data

security, while others rather expected that the cloud would help to improve data security.

Lack of awareness of what cloud computing actually involves and its implications is also holding back cloud adoption. Nevertheless, organizations in developing countries with relatively advanced communications networks (for example, Egypt, Mexico and South Africa) anticipate faster deployment of the cloud within their IT systems in the next two years.[5]

In view of the above, a number of critical decisions face potential users of cloud services. Potential cloud service customers need to make judgments about whether migration of data and services to the cloud will lead, for them, to better or worse outcomes in efficiency and service delivery; about how long it will take for improvements to materialize; and about the degree of risk there is that factors related to data security, privacy, reliability and internal management and costs of the migration will negate the advantages which may otherwise arise. As well as inhibiting migration to the cloud, such reservations will likely affect choices about the kind of cloud provisioning that cloud service customers may adopt. Concerns about control over data, for example, have so far led to a preference by both Governments and businesses for private rather than public cloud solutions, in spite of the greater cost savings that could be afforded by the latter. Concerns about interoperability may also make them more cautious in their choice of cloud providers. Against this background, contractual issues will remain of central importance to the decision-making of potential cloud users (chapter IV).

(b) External barriers

External barriers fall into three main categories, as follows:

(i)   Inadequate infrastructure

As stressed in chapter II, several aspects of communications infrastructure affect the extent to which a company's migration to the cloud will yield the benefits that are generally attributed to cloud computing. Infrastructure-related deficiencies are especially critical external barriers to cloud uptake in rural areas of low-income countries. Even in Kenya, for example, where there has been a relatively good progress in ICT development, the lack of reliable power and broadband connectivity remains a major concern. Optic fibre cable vandalism occasionally results in fibre cuts that can run for a week at a time (Research ICT Africa, 2013). The lack of reliable power is a particular constraint on the building of local data centres.

(ii)   Legal and regulatory barriers

The second set of external barriers inhibiting adoption and provision of cloud services in developing countries concerns the legal and regulatory frameworks. For some sectors, cloud-related transfers and storage outside the jurisdiction of the regulated entity may imply a breach of national rules by failing to provide national authorities with "effective access" to the data (chapter IV).

Many cloud services depend on the ability of users to make secure electronic transactions. This is only possible where legislation and financial regulation give electronic transactions equivalent status to their physical counterparts, and where banks and other commercial interests are willing to treat them as equivalent. Many developing countries still lack adequate legal and regulatory frameworks for electronic commerce (chapter IV). Relevant legislation needs to cover issues such as the recognition of digital signatures and electronic transactions, data protection, evidential standards and transborder data flows. Although model legislation has been available in these areas for some years, it has been adopted only in a limited number of developing countries.[6]

Similar barriers result from weak or uncertain legislation and regulation concerning cybersecurity. The term cybersecurity is wide-ranging, including the prevention of disruption to networks and services from accidental or criminal activity, the prevention of fraud, and efforts to prevent spam and other malware from corrupting online services. As with legislation for e-commerce, many countries still need to introduce and implement necessary legislation, together with the institutions required to support cybersecurity regimes (see also chapter IV). In 2012, for example, a regional assessment by the ITU for the African, Caribbean and Pacific Group of States (ACP) indicated that only five of fifteen ACP countries in the Caribbean had legislation governing e-transactions (HIPCAR, 2012).

The regulatory framework for cybersecurity can also influence the choice which cloud service customers make between different types of cloud configurations. For example, the cyber-control measures put in place by the Government of China have contributed to greater reliance on nationally based cloud services because of higher latency experienced when using servers located outside the country. According to one study, the Chinese firewall – the Golden Shield Project, which has been used since November 2003 – has led to an increase in the loading time by 450 ms or more for an object hosted on a server outside of China.[7]

(iii)   Weaknesses in the wider business environment

The third set of external barriers concerns the wider business environment and the extent to which a 'digital culture' has developed. This is partly a matter of business performance, including performance in trade in goods and services, and partly of the availability of underlying skills and resources within society.

The shortage of IT skills is a significant concern especially in low-income countries, where IT education (at school and university levels) is underdeveloped and where those with IT skills have opportunities to earn more and build more attractive careers if they take their skills elsewhere. The migration of skills outside the country is a particularly serious problem for smaller countries, such as island states in the Caribbean and the Pacific. Even with a shift to the cloud, expertise is still required at the cloud service customer level in both use of the technology and its legal and regulatory requirements. IT skills are even more important where countries and businesses are seeking to establish new business opportunities through the cloud, whether managing data centres, acting as cloud aggregators or establishing new cloud services targeted at export or domestic markets. The lack of training infrastructure, and of skilled personnel benefiting from it, can be a significant barrier to cloud adoption and successful leveraging of cloud computing in developing countries.

The drivers and barriers to cloud adoption described above are summarized diagrammatically in figure III.2. While the drivers illustrated in the figure are broadly similar for businesses and other potential users in all countries, the barriers differ significantly depending on a country's level of development and business and communications environments.

3. Assessing drivers and barriers to cloud adoption in developing countries

Potential cloud service customers, be they in business or Government, should weigh potential gains (such as lower operational and transaction costs) against additional costs which they may incur by using the cloud (notably for communications and migration). It is possible to overestimate the internal savings that may result from migration to the cloud as well as underestimate the costs of the migration itself. Like other new technologies, cloud computing can prove significantly more successful if accompanied

Figure III.2. Drivers and barriers to cloud adoption

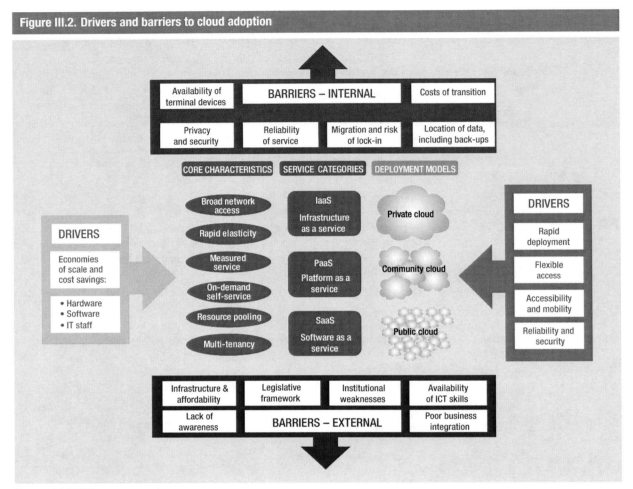

Source: UNCTAD.

by organizational change that enables a business or organization to make proper use of it, a point emphasized above. Making the necessary changes may take time and require new investment.

Factors of particular significance in developing countries that may lead to different decisions from those that would be made by decision-makers in a more developed economy include the following:

- The lesser prevalence of ICT use in Government and business in developing countries;
- Cloud costs: the cost of fees paid to cloud service providers and for communications access and usage, ISP charges and the hardware and software costs incurred when accessing the cloud are likely to be significantly higher in developing-country environments, and so form a higher proportion of the total costs of cloud provisioning;
- The presence or absence of Internet exchange points (IXPs) and local data centres that can

reduce costs and address challenges caused by international connectivity;
- The risks and potential costs associated with unreliable communications networks and high latency. Cloud-based systems may experience more downtime in developing countries and are likely to suffer slower connectivity;
- Inadequacies in the legal and regulatory framework to address concerns related to data protection and privacy;
- The costs of automating processes that can be done efficiently by human staff. Labour costs are likely to be significantly lower in developing countries, making it more cost-effective to use personnel rather than to automate some functions;
- The availability of content and applications that are specifically addressed to the requirements of developing country or local enterprises and organizations;

- The ability to source equipment and software in a timely manner for service provision, whether using conventional computing or the cloud. Established sources of conventional supply may be preferable if potential gains from cloud provisioning are relatively small;
- The extent to which potential users are likely to take up cloud services that may be offered to them. This is likely to be lower in developing countries because communications networks are less widespread and less affordable.

The outcome of calculations of the expected net benefit will vary between countries according to their level of cloud readiness. It will also vary between organizations, according to the contexts, data and services involved. And it will evolve over time as the level of cloud readiness in national communications environments improves.

It should be recognized, too, that if firms and Governments adopt cloud provisioning they may not always do so systematically. While some large firms and some Governments are developing overarching cloud strategies, in others, decision-making is devolved to individual divisions or departments. Some of these may adopt cloud services while others eschew them, and different departments may contract with different providers. SMEs, conscious of the risk to their businesses of getting things wrong, may move more cautiously towards the cloud, adding cloud applications one by one, rather than adopting a comprehensive approach. In some cases, cloud services may already be used extensively, without any management decision in favour of such use having been taken. Staff in government and the private sector often prefer to make use of cloud services (such as webmail) for work purposes rather than using in-house email and other facilities if they are deemed inconvenient or less reliable.

An organization-wide strategic approach aimed at integrating changes in management and operational systems with a coordinated move towards the cloud is more likely than ad hoc approaches to leverage cloud benefits successfully. An organization-wide approach can enable more efficient procurement of cloud services, whether from a single cloud provider or through an aggregator, avoiding potential problems of incompatibility between cloud services and enabling systematic integration of legacy and cloud services throughout the business. As indicated by the high incidence of integration problems (Dynamic Markets Ltd., 2013), companies at all levels and Governments would benefit from more coherent consideration of cloud options by senior management.

It is by no means certain that cloud adoption and the cloud economy will evolve in similar ways in developing countries as in developed countries. As suggested above, for example, some potential cloud service customers value a local presence of the cloud provider. Different situations in terms of the affordability and QoS of broadband networks may tilt the balance in favour of more national or regional rather than global cloud provision. Meanwhile, as in developed countries, some cloud service customers will prefer to forgo some potential cost savings and opt for private rather than public cloud facilities, in the belief that these can provide better security, greater control of data, lower risk of becoming dependent on a cloud provider and more certainty about communications costs.

B. CLOUD ADOPTION IN SELECTED COUNTRIES: EXPERIENCES AND OPPORTUNITIES

The cloud economy ecosystem described in chapter I and the discussion of drivers and barriers outlined above provide a framework for considering levels of adoption and potential opportunities for the cloud economy. The evidence base concerning cloud adoption in developing countries is very limited. Substantial differences are nevertheless evident in the extent to which the cloud economy has emerged in countries with diverse characteristics. Much of the variation that can be identified can be attributed to differences in the national business and communications environments (chapter II).

This section draws on available evidence of cloud development in selected countries to explore opportunities on both the supply and the demand sides of the cloud economy ecosystem. The discussion leverages the experience of countries with a high level of readiness as well as those with nascent cloud economies.

1. Supply-side cloud opportunities in developing countries

The most significant activities and potential opportunities for enterprises on the supply side of the cloud economy in developing countries are concerned with the following: (a) data centre and related cloud provision; (b) the development and provision of local cloud services for groups of customers, including local businesses and individual citizens; (c) cloud aggregation, system integration, brokerage and related services. In addition to these explicitly cloud-based areas of activity, opportunities exist for national communications businesses (telecommunications operators and ISPs) which can gain from increased data traffic using their networks.

(a) Provision of data-centre services

Major cloud service providers own and manage the computing infrastructure (the interconnected data centres and related facilities that store data) and enable services on behalf of cloud service customers. As stressed earlier (chapter I), the cloud business model is highly dependent on economies of scale and the ability to manage networks of data centres or server farms with huge computational and storage capacity. Very high levels of capital investment are needed to challenge their predominance and few potential competitors may have the resources to do so. However, the dominance of the incumbent providers may be somewhat challenged by growing concerns among cloud customers about data privacy and security.[8]

Only a few larger and more technologically advanced emerging economies such as the BRICS countries (Brazil, the Russian Federation, India, China and South Africa), Malaysia, Singapore and Thailand meet the scale and connectivity requirements for global data centre operations.[9] However, there is potential for a wider range of developing countries and developing country businesses to establish data centre operations which could attract customers from a regional level. This potential is likely to be greatest in countries with large and dynamic ICT sectors, with strongly established IT businesses and with an established role as regional business or communications hubs.

Despite the advantages of leading global cloud service providers, there are various other factors that may offer scope for local or regional data centres to expand in developing countries, such as the following:

- **Demand for private cloud solutions.** The fact that large corporations as well as Governments have hitherto preferred private over public clouds suggests that they have preferred to eschew significant economies of scale to ensure a greater sense of security and control over their data and services;

- **Non-cost factors which may require local presence (such as national data protection laws).** Some Governments and businesses are required (by law or corporate policy) to locate their data within national jurisdictions, or prefer to do so for security or geopolitical reasons. Such policies may increase demand for local cloud service provision;

- **High degree of alternative added value.** More effective customer service or familiarity which may be enhanced by a local or regional presence are examples;

- **High costs of or unreliable international broadband connectivity, making it more advantageous to rely on local data centres.** While these hamper and reduce potential benefits from cloud adoption in general, inadequate infrastructure may also undermine the cost advantage of global cloud provision in developing countries.

Reducing the physical distance between cloud computing resources and end users would reduce the costs of broadband communication and reduce latency. As noted in a recent report on cloud computing in Africa (ITU-D, 2012):

> Despite the development of international data transmission links between Africa and the rest of the world, the costs associated with the bandwidth necessary for transferring "African data" to and from cloud computing resources located outside Africa… are so high that it is more advantageous to construct data storage centres in Africa than to pay for accessing centres located tens of thousands of kilometres away from the continent.

An increasing number of Governments are establishing their own data centres to manage government data and services. These can form the basis for what are in effect private clouds (box III.2). In other cases, new data centres are being established by the communications providers. In Nigeria, for example, the state-owned provider of connectivity, ICT services and applications, Galaxy Backbone, is in the process of implementing a national cloud infrastructure that will deliver IaaS, PaaS and SaaS (Research ICT Africa, 2013). Meanwhile, the Nigerian telecommunications operator Globacom has set up a large Internet Data Centre in Lagos to provide co-location, disaster recovery and dedicated hosting services to its clients all over the country.[10] In Kenya, Safaricom began to host its MPESA mobile money service at a local data centre in 2011. This was in

---

Box III.2.   Government data centres in developing countries

Different approaches have been used by Governments to set up national data centres, sometimes involving the public–private partnership (PPP) sector. A few examples are provided below.

- The Government of Kenya has developed data centre capacity for its own use as well as for public access in order to reduce costs for businesses and organizations that need to host data in-country. Such intervention is not uncontroversial, since government-owned data centres may compete with commercial businesses operated in the private sector (Research ICT Africa, 2013).

- The Government of Ghana is constructing three data centres that will host data from all government ministries, departments and agencies (Research ICT Africa, 2013).

- In India's roadmap to develop the "GI Cloud" (see also chapter V), the Government opens the possibility of inviting private cloud service providers to set up dedicated government clouds or to manage them according to the policy, standards and guidelines adopted for the government cloud (India, Department of Electronics and Information Technology, 2013).

- Ecuador has included the implementation of a national data centre in its Digital Ecuador Strategy. The centre is to be established and operated under a PPP arrangement led by the Ministry of Telecommunications and Information Society.[a]

Source: UNCTAD.

[a] See eLac2015 newsletter, number 19, July 2012, available at http://www.cepal.org/socinfo/noticias/paginas/3/44983/newsletter19ENG.pdf (accessed 7 October 2013).

---

response to downtimes caused by problems related to international broadband connectivity. However, it has been difficult to convince other local businesses to adopt cloud services in Kenya due to concerns over issues associated with connectivity and power availability.[11]

An alternative opportunity for local cloud service providers and data centres is to develop partnerships with global providers with the objective of offering customers more control over their data while still leveraging economies of scale. A hybrid cloud arrangement utilizing local data centres may allow sensitive government or corporate data to be retained in-country while less sensitive data can be distributed across a global public cloud. There are both cost and strategic advantages for global cloud providers in locating data centres in different world regions, whether operating these within their own estates or making use of data centres established by locally based partners.

There has been significant investment by TNCs in data centres in developing countries since the final years of the last decade. IBM, for example, has opened a number of cloud centres in China and India since 2008, providing services to local businesses, universities and software developers. Other international firms that have established cloud operations in India include the software provider, Parallels, the business applications provider Salesforce and the virtualization specialist VMware (Kshetri, 2010). At the same time,

local companies in developing countries have also been developing their own cloud facilities, including significant international players such as the Indian telecommunications company, Airtel, and the South African firms MTN and Dimension Data.

One factor to keep in mind for countries aiming to encourage the creation of new large-scale data centres is the need for low cost, sustainable power. Data centres have enormous electricity demands, much of it for cooling servers. Estimates of their total power consumption are hard to clarify, though it has been asserted that they consume between 1.1 and 1.5 per cent of total electricity consumption worldwide, equivalent to the output of thirty nuclear power stations.[12] Countries with fragile power supplies or regular shortages of power simply cannot accommodate large data centres without placing significant additional burdens on existing electricity users.

(b) Cloud service provision

The second, and perhaps most significant, area of supply-side potential within the cloud economy lies in the development and marketing of new cloud services. Because of the versatility of cloud provisioning, the range of potential services is wide, as is the range of potential target clients (chapter I). Countries with established communities of IT professionals and entrepreneurs will be best placed to develop more innovative, sophisticated cloud applications and services.

For low-income countries at a nascent stage of cloud readiness, IaaS is likely to be the first category of cloud services to be demanded. Businesses and Governments in developing countries are recognizing this opportunity. In Ghana, for example, a number of companies already provide various types of cloud services (table III.1). By contrast with the global pattern observed in chapter II, most of the cloud services in Ghana are in the areas of IaaS and PaaS, which together accounted for 69 per cent of the market, exceeding SaaS deployments, with IT training and consulting services making up the rest (Yeboah-Boateng and Cudjoe-Seshie, 2013). The majority of the companies listed in the table act as local representatives of global cloud providers. In Nigeria, similarly, most cloud adoption appears so far

to be focusing on IaaS (Research ICT Africa, 2013). The emphasis on storage and infrastructure services by virtually all cloud providers in that country can be seen as a natural evolution following on from the significant investments made in recent years by various TNCs, banks and other large enterprises in their own network infrastructure, particularly data centres and hosting. As of early 2013, however, there was very limited PaaS and SaaS activity in the country.

As the market for IaaS matures, the scope for PaaS and SaaS tends to expand. Some of the services which are being made available in developing countries replicate the success of global applications (such as social networks) at a national or regional level, offering a more targeted experience. Other cloud services have been developed in response to more specific, localized requirements (box III.3).

Table III.1. Selected cloud service providers in Ghana, 2013

Cloud service provider	Cloud delivery model(s)	Target market segment	Comment
Locally owned providers			
CIS Ghana	PaaS, IaaS	SMEs, ASPs	
DreamOval	SaaS	SMEs, individuals	
Gesatech Solutions	IaaS	SMEs	Linked to Kaspersky Security software
Ghana Dot Com	IaaS	SMEs, individuals	
Maafo-Visions	IaaS	SMEs, individuals	Targets regional markets
National Information Technology Agency	BPaaS, PaaS, IaaS	Government	Government agency
NetSolutions Ghana	PaaS, IaaS	SMEs	
Radius Consulting	PaaS, IaaS	SMEs	Targeting West African markets. Part of several vendor accreditation schemes (Cisco, Dell, Microsoft, Symantec Gold, and the like)
Rancard Mobility	PaaS	Mobile operators, content providers, mobile marketers, developers	Established in 2001, grew regional in 2010 (office in Nigeria)
Red Mango	SaaS, IaaS	SMEs	Has a network of global partners including Cisco, HP, Microsoft
Sylversys Consulting	SaaS, PaaS, IaaS	SMEs	Offices in Ghana and Mali and targets West African markets
Foreign affiliates			
ACT ICT	SaaS	Government, SMEs	Founded by ACT ICT (Israel) in partnership with Lifeforms (Ghana)
Huawei	IaaS	Enterprises, Government	Huawei (China)
IIHT Ghana	SaaS, PaaS	SMEs, individuals	Owned by Indian Institute of Hardware Technology, India's leading IT services training company
Internet Solutions	IaaS	SMEs, individuals	Pan-African division of Dimension Data (South Africa), which is owned by NTT Group (Japan). Partner of Cisco, Microsoft, Symantec
MTN	SaaS, PaaS, IaaS	SMEs	Affiliate of MTN Group (South Africa)

Source: UNCTAD, adapted from Research ICT Africa (2013).

Box III.3.   Examples of cloud service provision in developing countries

The following list includes examples of the provision of cloud services that either provide a local version of globally successful applications or that are targeted to specific local needs:

- Sonico.com is a social networking website headquartered in Argentina, with over 48 million users, the majority in Latin America. To compete with global giants such as Facebook and LinkedIn it needed to keep costs down. Sonico uses Amazon Web Services applications for file storage and sharing of more than 1 billion images uploaded by its members. The company says that this has led to a 70 per cent cost saving over its previous file management architecture.[a]

- A host of domestic cloud service providers has emerged in China, offering services for the local market which are significantly protected from global competitors by language and regulatory constraints. Examples include e-commerce platforms (such as Alibaba and Taobao) and indigenous web platforms for micro blogging and social networking (such as Sina Weibo and Renren) and local search engines (such as Baidu) (UNCTAD, 2012a).

- Viet Nam Technology and Telecommunication offers server storage capacity and system capability for its clients, mainly SMEs. It has the intention to launch applications that are designed specifically for construction and for real-estate companies.[b]

- India-based AdventNet's Zoho division operates a suite of web-based applications. As of September 2009, Zoho had over 2 million users, the bulk of which were from North America and Europe and some 20 per cent from India and China. Zoho's applications are used by hospitals and banks in India to develop new products and services and by some insurance companies to develop innovative services such as a personalized insurance for diabetics (Kshetri, 2010).

- Cloud services can be focused on individual or neighbouring countries rather than international markets. Ping.sg is a blog aggregator and blogging community in Singapore, whose site brings together more than 100,000 blogs. As its business grew, it chose to migrate its data and services to the cloud. It has derived cost savings and other benefits from the ability gradually to increase computing capacity rather than having to procure new equipment as the business expands.[c]

- A growing range of cloud services are targeted at enterprises. The South Africa-based media and telecommunications company MTN launched a suite of cloud services for SMEs in Ghana and Nigeria in December 2012, following pilot projects in six countries. It offers packages to support small business accounting, human resource and customer-relations management as well as webmail and videoconferencing, storage and backup. It also offers an SaaS application that provides microfinance institutions with a platform on which to run their banking operations. According to MTN, this package has been adopted by SMEs in the manufacturing, hospitality, microfinance and advertising industries (Research ICT Africa, 2013). Pamoja Cloud Services, which is owned by the South African-led submarine cable company SEACOM, is also targeting growing demand for IT-as-a-Service from SMEs in Africa (Research ICT Africa, 2013).

Source: UNCTAD.

[a] See http://aws.amazon.com/solutions/case-studies/sonico/ (accessed 8 October 2013).

[b] See "VNTT rides on cloud to deliver new services", search SMB Asia, 31 August 2009, available at http://www.searchsmbasia.com/en/content/vntt-rides-cloud-deliver-new-services?page¼0%2C0 (accessed 8 October 2013).

[c] See http://aws.amazon.com/solutions/case-studies/ping-sg/ (accessed 8 October 2013).

In countries where national broadband coverage is inadequate, but where mobile connectivity is widespread, there may be opportunities to leverage a combination of cloud and mobile services. The mothers-2-mothers (m2m) organization, a South African NGO, combines the cloud with database technology and mobile services to reduce the incidence of HIV/AIDS transmission from mothers to children.[13] The m2m NGO digitizes patient records and shares them with counsellors across its networks of more than 700 sites in Africa. The records contain information on treatment plans, and advanced reporting tools that allow quick response. Women in African villages authenticate children's medication with text messages via short message service (SMS).[14] As of 2011, m2m served more than 1.5 million women in nine sub-Saharan African countries. In a similar way, the core customer interface of MPESA in Kenya relies on SMS, but its underlying data and applications management reside in the cloud.

Although PaaS applications of cloud services are less widespread than IaaS and SaaS deployments, they can offer supply-side opportunities for small scale IT businesses in developing countries, which may be expected to grow in coming years. The *Information Economy Report 2012* emphasized in that respect the important role that local IT sectors, including local software developers, have in building a culture of digital innovation in developing countries. Innovation centres like the iHub in Nairobi and Campus Tecnológico in Guatemala (UNCTAD, 2012a) have brought together vibrant groups of developers and entrepreneurs producing software, developing applications and supporting the adoption of ICTs by enterprises.

Most developing countries now have at least a small number of individuals with the skills to develop software applications, but their business development is often hampered by limited access to development tools, by the cost of necessary hardware, and by small domestic markets for their services. A critical advantage of cloud computing for innovative firms, particularly such entrepreneurial start-ups, is that they can access the ICT capabilities they need to innovate without significant capital expenditure.

The cloud can support open source software development, which is preferred by many application developers. The software company, Canonical, for example, has built cloud capabilities into its Ubuntu Server platform,[15] and offers a developer store platform on top of its application store, Ubuntu Software Center.[16] The Ubuntu App Developer allows developers anywhere in the world to create Linux applications for the Ubuntu platform and make them available either for a fee or free of cost. These applications can be directly downloaded to the Ubuntu Linux Desktop and Server platforms (UNCTAD, 2012a). There are other platforms that allow such entrepreneurs to develop new ideas, such as mobile applications, at low cost, using the latest available tools, and then offer them to global rather than national markets, where they may generate enough revenue to become sustainable and finance the next phase of enterprise development. Global or national PaaS providers could partner with these enterprises, sharing the risk, cost and profit associated with the development of new products. OrangeScape is one of several examples of Indian companies that offer a PaaS application. This enterprise claims to be "the world's only cross-cloud PaaS platform".[17]

(c) Cloud aggregation, integration and related services

A third area of opportunity for the supply of cloud services in developing countries is in the provision of aggregation, consultancy and brokerage services that facilitate the relationship between cloud providers and their government or corporate clients. Cloud aggregators work on behalf of government or corporate customers to assemble packages of services from different cloud providers that suit their clients' overall requirements, rather like system integrators in more traditional IT environments. Aggregators assume the role of identifying the most suitable cloud services, integrating these with one

---

Box III.4. Selected cloud aggregators in developing countries

- Aggregation is one of the services offered by the IT company Clogeny, based in Pune, India. It works with businesses and organizations on a range of issues across the spectrum of cloud management, offering services in areas such as cloud assessment and planning, application development and cloud testing to end-to-end cloud support. It acts as an intermediary between clients and major cloud computing providers.[a]

- A number of indigenous and foreign-owned cloud aggregators and system integrators are active in the Nigerian market (Research ICT Africa, 2013). Nigerian companies providing aggregation services include Computer Warehouse, Resourcery, City Business Computers and Computer Information System Nigeria. The companies generally offer aggregation alongside other IT services, helping their clients to integrate cloud provisioning more effectively within their overall IT strategy.

- Smaller businesses are less likely to need the services of an aggregator, but may benefit from consultancy and procurement services offered by a specialist broker with the expertise and connections to identify and negotiate the most appropriate cloud deals. Descasio, for example, describes itself as "the leading Google Apps and cloud computing solutions provider in Nigeria and the sub-region", and as offering "the bridge between cloud-based solutions and legacy on-premise solutions".[b]

Source: UNCTAD.

[a] See http://www.clogeny.com/.

[b] See http://www.descasio.com/ (accessed 8 October 2013).

another, managing relationships with cloud providers, and thereby offer clients a simpler interface for their IT and cloud activities. Box III.4 provides some examples of such businesses in developing countries.

The aggregator/broker market is a promising area for developing-country IT firms to explore. While larger, transnational firms may prefer to obtain aggregation services at a multinational level, national businesses are more likely to see value in working with local partners. They can leverage their experience of their national business and communications environments, including the particularities of national legislation in areas such as data protection, the preferences of national client groups, and the availability of national or regional cloud providers.

The discussion above illustrates opportunities on the supply side of the cloud for potential developing-country businesses. A number of factors will influence the extent to which these are likely to emerge in the next few years. Some developing countries are clearly better placed to take advantage of supply-side opportunities than others – particularly larger countries with more developed economies, large domestic IT businesses and more sophisticated communications networks. Countries in which connectivity is reliable and cheap will be at a considerable advantage over others. So will countries that already have the skills to develop IT services for domestic and export purposes. Political and other factors also play a part. When looking for potential providers, cloud service customers in both government and the private sector are likely to give significant weight to the quality of security protection afforded by cloud providers and to the risk that data will be accessed by third parties.

2. Cloud use by different stakeholders in developing countries

This section reviews the available evidence concerning cloud adoption in developing countries within four groups of potential cloud service customers – citizens and others using mass market cloud services; Governments and government agencies; TNCs and large national businesses; and SMEs.[18]

(a) Mass market use of free cloud services

There has been extensive adoption by individuals in developing countries of free-to-use cloud services such as webmail and online social networks. This is true in almost all countries, though particularly so in those with higher levels of Internet use and cloud readiness. The most popular cloud-based applications are generally those provided at a global level. Facebook, for example, by the end of 2012 had some 835 million registered users worldwide, more than 10 per cent of the global population.[19] It is estimated that more than 40 per cent of Internet users on any given day access the Facebook site.[20] The video file-sharing site YouTube, owned by Google, is estimated to reach around 35 per cent of global Internet users.[21] Both appear among the top four websites in all the 17 African countries for which statistics are available.[22] In the few national markets where these global services are not available, such as China, local equivalent cloud services are equally predominant (see box III.3). Social media platforms are increasingly accessed on mobile phones rather than computers, and through apps rather than through the conventional Internet.[23]

There is widespread anecdotal evidence that cloud-based webmail services are extensively used by Government and business professionals when they consider the in-house email systems to be less efficient or reliable (which is the case in many developing countries). Data-storage and file-sharing services that are available on the public cloud are also experiencing increased use in both developed and developing countries. Many users of these services may be unaware that they are cloud-enabled, but their widespread use illustrates the growing pervasiveness of the cloud in core aspects of personal and professional use of computing and the Internet.

Publicly-available mass market cloud services are of value not just to individuals but throughout the supply chain. As has already been noted, they are free because data mining enables their providers to target advertising much more precisely on likely customers than conventional media, and so to attract advertising revenue. They are also potentially useful, however, for small business users. Social media platforms allow SMEs to build customer relationships by sending occasional text messages or emails, or by building their profiles through Facebook (and similar) pages rather than conventional websites. Social media, in this sense, add a new dimension to the "word of mouth" on which many small businesses have always depended to extend their market reach. Following their customers' interests online can even offer SMEs an opportunity to target their own services more precisely on consumer trends. Cloud-based information services also offer opportunities for marketing. Public cloud services can therefore add value to SMEs, particularly those that deal directly with individual consumers, though care needs to be taken to protect the privacy and security of both SMEs themselves and of their customers.

(b) Government use of the cloud

In many developing countries, Governments are the largest purchasers of IT, spending substantial amounts annually on hardware, software and ancillary goods and services, including in-house IT management. Much of this procurement – for example, of software licences – exceeds requirements as the majority of authorized users rarely need more than basic applications. The availability of in-house IT management s kills is also often a challenge in Governments of developing countries.

Government agencies are increasingly considering cloud solutions to manage large data sets of the kind on which modern administration and service delivery depend, in some cases building their own estates of data centres. Coordination among government departments to maximize the value of cloud solutions requires proper managerial structures as well as national strategies. In the Republic of Korea, the decision to build a government cloud has generated significant benefits in terms of cost reductions, improved security and greater client satisfaction (box III.5). Several developing and transition economies are moving towards greater government use of the cloud. A few examples are given in the following paragraphs.

- Thailand's Electronic Government Agency launched its government cloud in 2012, bringing together 200 different IT systems from more than 100 government agencies. A PPP approach was adopted, with local software companies developing SaaS products that enable legacy government systems to be redeployed in the cloud and reduce duplication between different agencies.[24] The Electronic Government Agency has signed a memorandum of understanding with the Cloud Security Alliance – a not-for-profit organization which promotes the use of best practices for providing security assurance within cloud computing – and plans to make Cloud Security Alliance certification frameworks mandatory for cloud service providers.[25]

- The Government of Moldova launched its Moldova Cloud, developed in partnership with the private

---

Box III.5. Government cloud use in the Republic of Korea

The Government of the Republic of Korea has been a leading exponent of network connectivity and data centre management. It enjoys very high broadband connectivity, has among the highest average download and upload speeds in the world, and enjoys low levels of latency (annex table 5). An important part of the Government's overall strategy to boost the cloud economy has been the holistic development of its own cloud use.[a]

When Korean agencies were responsible for building and operating their own e-government systems, a number of problems frequently arose – includingoverlapping infrastructure investment, lack of relevant expertise, inadequate provisioning of facilities, weak security systems and inferior computing environments. The National Computing and Information Agency (NCIA) was established in 2005 under the Ministry of Security and Public Administration to serve as a government integrated data centre and build the foundation for more reliable and sustainable e-government.

In order to provide government cloud services, it was decided that the co-location of ICT resources was needed, followed by hardware integration through hardware pooling and the organization of software platforms (Kang et al., 2011). As a first step, a standardized and automated government integrated data centre management system – the National Total Operation Platform System – was developed. To reduce the risk of serious government-wide impacts caused by natural disasters or terror attacks, a disaster recovery system was built, including two inter-copied centres in Daejeon and Gwangju to ensure business continuity. K-net (Korea net), an intranet separated from commercial networks, was also established to provide safe, secure and scalable communication services to central and local government agencies and public organizations.

Government-wide integration of hardware resources began in 2008, involving the conversion of multiple servers into one unified hardware platform by applying virtualization technologies. Since 2011, the Government of the Republic of Korea has started the process of embedding service platforms in integrated hardware to enable cloud computing. The cloud computing platform, G-Cloud, was deployed in 2011. In the same year, a comprehensive

Box III.5.   Government cloud use in the Republic of Korea *(continued)*

defense system, the Electronic Advanced National Security Infrastructure, which implemented physical and cyber security and access control, was also put in place.

NCIA today has the ICT resources and operational management needed for government agencies to conduct their business electronically. It also provides a reliable e-government platform, which offers the general public some 1,200 e-government services at all times of the day and night. By 2015, half of all the ICT resources of central agencies and a smaller percentage of those of local agencies and their affiliates will have been moved into cloud environments.

NCIA provides various forms of PaaS and a validated standard environment:

- **The G-cloud platform service** provides government agencies with a server, storage and a network in a virtualized environment on demand along with the eGovFrame software environment;[b]

- **The G-mobile platform service** offers common systems and test environments for the development of mobile government services, including basic systems (link, security, authentication, mobile device management, push) needed for developing mobile or web applications;

- **The Smart office platform service** provides an environment for flexible working by mobile workers; it also designs and provides a cloud PC infrastructure architecture.

Finally, NCIA provides a business continuity guarantee service, which offers ICT-based government services without interruptions even in the event of a disaster.

More efficient management of national ICT resources has generated significant cost savings, estimated at about $300 million per year. Government agencies have been able to reduce their budgets for the purchase and operation of ICT resources by 30 per cent through better procurement, shared resources and integrated development of common functions and services. The total investment involved was recouped seven years after the establishment of NCIA. Other returns on investment continue to be generated in the areas of security, operation, resource integration and maintenance. In addition, on the power usage effectiveness (PUE) scale, energy efficiency improved from 2.0 in 2006 to 1.71 as of June 2013, that is, the second highest level.[c]

One of the reasons for entrusting NCIA with the task of operating cloud services in-house, rather than outsourcing these to the private sector, was to ensure that data owned by the Government would be protected. NCIA has strengthened its cyber response system to detect and block external attacks automatically.[d] In addition, using dual-power supply equipment and generators, the e-government system equipment downtime has been dramatically reduced; the monthly average downtime per item of equipment fell from 67 minutes in 2004 to only 3.04 seconds in June 2013.

Public satisfaction with e-government services has increased. Government agencies are now able to provide such services anytime and anywhere. By ensuring the quality of services through the application of service level agreements between each agency and NCIA, the level of satisfaction among government agencies has also increased. Each agency is now able to improve its business competencies and productivity by using NCIA's various ICT resources as well as managerial and technical support.

Source: Ministry of Security and Public Administration, Republic of Korea.

[a] In 2009, the "Government-wide Cloud Computing Promotion Master Plan" was announced which was followed in 2011 by the "Strategy for Promoting the Expansion and Competitiveness of Cloud Computing".

[b] eGovFrame (e-Government Standard Framework) is a standardized set of software tools for developing and running e-government applications. It was developed by the Government of the Republic of Korea.

[c] The PUE indicates the annual power consumption of a data centre. The closer the number gets to 1, the more power efficient it is. The average PUE for data centres around the world is 1.8.

[d] Over 99 per cent of invasion attempts are cut off automatically. Known "distributed denial of service" attacks can be blocked in real time, whereas unknown new attacks can be blocked within ten minutes by applying the rule-sets (about 18,500 as of June 2013).

sector, in February 2013 as part of the country's e-Transformation Agenda. The cloud makes standardized IaaS, SaaS and PaaS services available to government agencies to reduce costs, improve information management and share data. It also consolidates capacity in government data centres to improve resource allocation and lower maintenance costs. The Government now applies a cloud first policy, requiring every agency to consider using the Moldova Cloud before procuring hardware or upgrading legacy IT systems.

- Galaxy Backbone, a state-owned company which provides infrastructure for government entities in Nigeria, is in the process of developing a national cloud infrastructure which will offer its public sector clients backup and disaster recovery, IP

telephony and unified communications, and IT project management, in addition to other IaaS, SaaS and PaaS services (Research ICT Africa, 2013). One of Nigeria's state governments – in Rivers State – has launched its own private cloud (known as RivCloud) to provide public agencies with storage and application hosting, likely to include an application for tax filing (Research ICT Africa, 2013).

- The Government of India is taking steps to develop a government cloud, which will serve both the national and state government levels (box III.6).

These national government cloud initiatives are new, and it remains to be seen how they will work out in practice. As well as large-scale coordinated cloud

---

Box III.6. Towards a government cloud in India

The Government of India has taken a proactive stance in fostering government cloud use. The Department of Electronics and IT (DeitY) unveiled its national "GI Cloud" initiative in 2013.[a] The GI Cloud is a private cloud computing environment that will be used by government departments and agencies at the national as well as state levels. It is intended to support the implementation of the National e-Governance Plan of India. Ultimately, the GI Cloud will provide services to government departments, citizens and businesses over both the Internet and mobile phones.

To provide strategic direction and guidance to DeitY on matters pertaining to the functioning of the GI Cloud, an "Empowered Committee" has been proposed under the chairmanship of the Secretary of DeitY, with representation from Central/State line ministries and other government entities. In addition, a task force has been set up to give direction to the creation of a detailed cloud strategy, including cloud architecture, cloud implementation and a roadmap for future activity. This task force comprises representatives not only from national and state governments but also from the private sector (National Association of Software and Service Companies, Gartner, Tata Consultancy Services, Cisco, Microsoft and HP).

The DeitY in April 2013 released a roadmap to GI Cloud. This assesses the ICT infrastructure currently in place and sets out an implementation plan.[b] The roadmap underlines that cloud computing environments will be established at the national and state levels using new and existing data centres. There are already large national data centres (NDCs) run by the National Informatics Centre in Delhi, Hyderabad and Pune. Another NDC is being set up at Bhubaneswar. The largest NDC, in Delhi, is at an advanced stage of virtualization. State data centres in 21 states have been made operational and in four states are in an advanced stage of implementation. As of 2013, in about 10 of these centres, infrastructure utilization had reached more than 50 per cent.

The roadmap also identifies potential challenges, such as those related to security and interoperability, shortage of technical competencies and the need for changes in government procurement norms. In terms of security-related aspects, DeitY will prescribe standards around interoperability, integration, data security, portability, operational aspects and contract management for the cloud. A dedicated unit will be responsible for defining guidelines on security and for prescribing appropriate steps to mitigate risks.

Ultimately, the GI Cloud will provide IaaS and PaaS as well as SaaS. It is anticipated that the national cloud will be able to provide computing, storage and network infrastructure, backup and recovery, and application development as a service, supported by the state clouds. Different business models will be considered, such as pay-per-use, subscription or offering services free of charge. The national cloud will be owned and run by a central government agency.

Source: India, Department of Electronics and Information Technology (2013).

[a] See http://deity.gov.in/sites/upload_files/dit/files/GI-Cloud%20Strategic%20Direction%20Report%281%29.pdf (accessed 9 October 2013).

[b] See http://deity.gov.in/sites/upload_files/dit/files/GI-Cloud%20Adoption%20and%20Implementation%20Roadmap %281%29.pdf (accessed 9 October 2013).

deployments, individual government agencies also have experience of using cloud applications to deliver specific public services, for example in the education and health areas.[26] In education, there is potential to extend the range of content available to students at all levels – both through access to published material and greater accessibility for teaching resources. Health records managed through the cloud may be much more accessible at point of need, and more easily shared between health professionals, enabling better coordination of patient care. Cloud applications can also be used to deliver other government services, including transactions such as bill payments and individual certification (driving licences, pension entitlements, land records, and the like). Data protection and privacy considerations, however, are obviously important in these contexts.

There are differences in the ways government departments and enterprises make use of cloud provisioning.

First, Governments are likely to have many more data sets available. Aggregating these data sets is likely to add value for both administration and service delivery (though it may also have privacy implications). For these benefits to be achieved, Governments need to ensure that different Government departments have the necessary resources to share data effectively and that the cloud services which they commission are interoperable. A government-wide approach to cloud procurement can help to maximize administrative benefits from cloud provisioning, while joint procurement should also reduce costs. The experience of the Republic of Korea is illustrative in this context (UNCTAD, 2012a).

Secondly, Governments may have particular security concerns, and may be more constrained by legal restrictions on where national data can be held, inhibiting the use of data centres that are distributed around the world. Given the volume of government data, and the potential scale of cloud provisioning, these constraints offer opportunities for local data centres and cloud providers. Partnerships between local data centres and global cloud providers, locating sensitive and non-sensitive data in separate locations, could enable Governments to maximize cost benefits while fulfilling requirements for security and control. Successful local data centres and cloud providers in one country may subsequently be able to provide a service for neighbouring countries, particularly within regional economic communities.

A shift to the cloud may generate some additional opportunities for Governments. Some Governments use cloud applications to enhance e-government initiatives which are explicitly targeted to businesses, including transaction interfaces concerned with trade facilitation, licensing and taxes. The introduction of single-window processes in trade facilitation is an example, which, like open data, can be implemented through the cloud or through managed proprietary systems (Adam et al., 2011). Cloud provisioning can make it easier for different government agencies to make official data available, and to do so flexibly, enabling businesses, citizens and NGOs to target and make innovative use of information about their own localities. The cloud is also well suited to support open data and other transparency initiatives aimed at making public information more widely accessible.

(c) Large business customers

At the global level, almost all major TNCs are now using cloud computing to some degree. For example, it has been estimated that in 2012, 80 per cent of Fortune 1000 enterprises were paying for some cloud services.[27] The cloud strategies of large international businesses with operations in developing countries are determined at a global rather than national level. Like Governments, such companies often rely on private cloud arrangements with global providers that can meet their needs in every country and maximize the value of economies of scale. Sometimes, businesses deploy their own resources in this way. However, where global corporations (such as banks and large retail businesses) reach extensively into domestic markets, they may make use of local cloud providers and cloud services to extend beyond their own marketing and customer relations operations.

Large national businesses are also adopting cloud and cloud services where these offer competitive advantage in managing their businesses. This is clearly the case in developed countries. In the United States, the share of businesses adopting cloud services doubled between 2010 and 2011, from 22 per cent to 45 per cent of large companies, from 17 per cent to 36 per cent of medium-sized businesses and from 7 per cent to 13 per cent of small ones (Gentzoglanis, 2012). It is also increasingly the case in developing countries. In Kenya, for example, all large companies in the Nairobi Stock Exchange are in the cloud in one way or the other (Kituku, 2012). To varying degrees they have moved messaging, collaboration, human resources, payroll, CRM/sales management, accounting, finance, project management and application development to the cloud.

Anxieties about reliability, security and control influence decisions by major corporations as well, as confirmed in a study of companies listed on the Nairobi Stock Exchange (Kituku, 2012). Similar concerns also featured prominently during a 2013 meeting of chief information officers (CIOs) in South Africa. They stressed the importance of looking at the relative merits of different solutions, including the competing benefits of traditional and cloud-based approaches to business management, and of integrated and non-integrated approaches to cloud deployment.[28] Many businesses have experienced difficulties in integrating cloud applications with their existing software and business practices (Dynamic Markets Ltd., 2013): "68 per cent of cloud adopters have attempted integration, but 86 per cent of these encountered negatives along the way – in fact, 55 per cent have tried and failed".Many businesses in the same survey had abandoned at least one cloud application in frustration.[29] This further underlines the importance of making thorough and realistic assessments of likely outcomes of cloud adoption rather than relying on assumptions that gains will be made.

(d) Small and medium-sized enterprises

The SME category of enterprises is highly diverse. Depending on the nature of their size, industry, nature of activities and geographical location, they may be more less intensive users of ICTs.[30] Consequently, the adoption of cloud services by SMEs is unevenly distributed. Those with very few employees have significantly lower adoption rates. For example, a survey of SMEs commissioned in 2012, covering 13 countries (including Brazil, China, Turkey and the Russian Federation) confirmed that cloud use is greater in medium-sized than in small firms (Microsoft, 2012). However, almost all respondents expected their use of the cloud to grow in the next few years. This would suggest that cloud provisioning will displace legacy systems in the majority of the SMEs surveyed as and when the latter come to need upgrading.

Many SMEs may find webmail services preferable to proprietary alternatives, particularly when they are able to cloak these in their own commercial identities. Some, as discussed earlier in this chapter, can gain considerably from the use of other cloud-based social media services in marketing and customer

relations. In some cases, specialist cloud services will be particularly valuable – for example, for some professional freelancers or for SMEs in sectors such as tourism that relate to large groups of remote potential customers.

On the other hand, as mentioned above, the challenges of integrating cloud and legacy software and the loss of control over data and applications can make migration undesirable for some SMEs. Some small businesses report having moved away from the cloud altogether in light of such experience. Some start-ups, for example, have benefitted from the cloud initially but then found that they were better off investing in their own equipment as their businesses mature and stabilized; others may experience a different or opposite trajectory.[31]

Among the SMEs that have adopted cloud services, the number of applications that have been taken up is low. On average, the 3,000 respondents that took part in the survey cited earlier were using four paid services (in addition to free services such as webmail) (Microsoft, 2012). They expected this to increase to an average of six applications over a two to three year period. Based on the results from that survey, the cloud experience for SMEs to date, even in developed countries, seems to relate mostly to standard, consumer-oriented cloud services which are available cost-free or at low cost, rather than to specialized services oriented explicitly at businesses. The most commonly used services included:

- Webmail (40 per cent of current users);
- Voice communications (23 per cent);
- Instant messaging (23 per cent);
- Data storage and back up (22 per cent);
- File-sharing (21 per cent).

In the same study, informants reported using a range of sources to obtain information about cloud options, the most commonly cited being the websites of cloud providers and other software companies, industry analysts and blogs, IT consultants with whom they were familiar and business associates. Thus, even where they have access to a wide range of potential sources of advice, SMEs may not be assessing options systematically and may benefit from the kind of services offered by cloud brokers and aggregators.

For many small firms, mass-market free-to-use services can provide effective resources for marketing and customer relations management. Medium-sized firms, however, and those in more complex markets,

Box III.7.   Benefiting from the cloud's elasticity – the case of Zenga Media

Zenga Media is an Indian company that provides real-time access to video and television content for mobile phones. Zenga saw the demand for its services rise from 50,000 to 7 million users over a period of about six years. It now delivers more than 50 million items of video content to its users every month. Cloud computing enabled this growth to take place smoothly, without recurrent capital expenditure peaks to upgrade server capacity. It also allowed it to manage large surges in demand at particular times, such as during the Indian Premier League cricket season. Transition to cloud-based delivery has taken place gradually, but almost all content is now delivered using cloud resources. The company has at the same time reduced the number of IT professionals managing its services from 35 to 4 while benefiting from increased turnover.

Source: See http://www-07.ibm.com/in/city/pdf/cloudburst_for_smes.pdf (accessed 10 October 2013).

could gain advantage from using more sophisticated cloud services where possible, as illustrated by the case of Zenga Media (box III.7). At the other end of the scale, independent professionals can also benefit from cloud services. Global online marketplaces allow independent entrepreneurs to enter product and service markets, including North–South and South–South markets, which were previously unavailable to them because there were no suitable procurement channels for low-value service exports.

These services give small developing-country enterprises with suitable skills the opportunity to market services beyond their local communities. The economic value which individuals derive from them comes not from cost savings but from improved access to markets. Where this access is international, it contributes to national export performance as well as revenue generation for individuals. However, much more analysis is needed to assess the significance of these job-search services in developing countries.

Developing-country SMEs need to consider the pros and cons of using cloud-based applications for their specific businesses and business models. This consideration includes benefits and potential disadvantages for their customers, the costs and benefits for the SME itself, the risks that may be incurred by relying on services that run in the cloud, and the risks of not using the cloud when competitors do so. The calculation of these costs and benefits will depend partly on the circumstances of the firm itself, and partly on the wider business and communications environment in which it operates. Much will depend on how easily the gains attributable to the cloud can be secured in practice. Migrating data and services to the cloud may make sense for a company offering a particular range of consumer services in one location, but not for a company offering identical services elsewhere, if the infrastructure is less adequate or

reliable. The value of cloud migration will also change over time as national communications environments evolve.

C. CONCLUSIONS

Cloud computing is only in its early stages in developing countries, but its reach is rapidly growing and is likely to continue to do so. There are several potential advantages for businesses and other organizations in adopting cloud services related to cost reduction, lower capital expenditures and improvements in the quality of administration and services to end users. But risks also need to be accounted for, related to data security and privacy, integration challenges and reliability of services. It is difficult to assess the overall impact on the national economy of different countries, for example, in terms of employment, productivity and growth, which depends on the extent and nature of cloud uptake, and on the degree to which domestic enterprises will be able to expand and develop on the supply side of the cloud economy.

There is already significant cloud usage within countries by citizens making individual use of available public cloud services, including in their work places. Foreign affiliates of TNCs make extensive use of the cloud as part of their parent companies' global networks. With some wariness, Governments in developing countries are also moving towards the cloud. Some Governments are developing systematic cloud strategies, as part of broader ICT strategies or sometimes in parallel (chapter V). There is increasingly significant planned adoption of the cloud in domestic enterprises, though this appears to be less extensive than anticipated by cloud advocates. Important barriers need to be overcome within companies. Nevertheless, the trend is towards more adoption, across a growing range of services. Where government departments and larger corporations are concerned, there is so far a general preference for private over public cloud approaches.

The potential for cloud adoption is inhibited by underlying infrastructure and legislative/regulatory barriers, which raise the costs and reduce the benefits of adoption. Security concerns are also holding back movement towards the cloud. Government initiatives to promote improvements in the availability, reliability and affordability of infrastructure, and to revise legal and regulatory frameworks for e-commerce and data protection would be necessary to overcome such barriers (see chapter IV).

Businesses, Governments and other organizations should carefully examine the potential for cloud services to improve their management and service delivery. They should migrate data and services to the cloud only when this can offer significant benefits and few attendant risks. Both public and private cloud solutions should be considered in this context, taking into account implications for data security and privacy.

When doing so, internal systems need be adapted to reap maximum gains from the change. Cloud providers can tailor their offerings more clearly for developing-country markets, recognizing the infrastructure constraints within those markets and the security and other concerns of potential customers.

Although the cloud provisioning market is dominated by a relatively small number of very large providers, there are opportunities for developing-country firms to participate on the supply side of the cloud economy. These include data-centre provision and management, both independently and in conjunction with global cloud providers; cloud aggregation and integration services; and the development and provision of cloud services to different groups, including local businesses and individuals. It is important that, when they are designing national ICT strategies, or dedicated cloud strategies, Governments take the supply side as well as the demand side of the cloud fully into account (see chapter V).

NOTES

1   The survey aimed to gain a better understanding of the state of the technical infrastructure of NGOs, nonprofits and charities and their future plans for adopting cloud technologies. Answers were received from more than 10,500 respondents in 88 countries (Tech Soup Global, 2012).

2   For example, in a survey of 3,000 SMEs, where four out of ten informants felt that cloud services remained unproven and therefore risky, security and control were the prime concerns (Microsoft, 2012). About 40 per cent of the SMEs responding were in a developing or transition economy. More than two thirds of the SMEs were anxious to know where their data would be located, and more than half expressed that concerns over data privacy would deter them from moving some functions to the cloud.

3   See CIO East Africa "103 Government of Kenya websites hacked overnight", available at http://www.cio.co.ke/news/main-stories/103-Government-of-Kenya-websites-hacked-overnight (accessed 4 October 2013).

4   The survey collected responses from 1,355 companies with revenues of £50 million (about $80 million) or more. The companies were based in 17 countries, including Brazil, China, India, the Russian Federation, Singapore, South Africa, Turkey and the United Arab Emirates. At least 50 responses were collected from each country.

5   See, for example, "Why more SMEs are embracing cloud computing", Times of India, 2 July 2013; Research ICT Africa (2013) and Tech Soup Global (2012).

6   For example, the UNCITRAL Model Law on Electronic Signature from 2001 has so far been adopted by 26 developing economies. See http://www.uncitral.org/uncitral/en/uncitral_texts/electronic_commerce/2001Model_status.html (accessed 7 October 2012).

7   For a typical website hosted in Asian cities such as Hong Kong (China), Singapore or Tokyo, the firewall allegedly added 10 to 15 seconds to load in China. For a website hosted in the United States, it would take 20 to 40 seconds to load in China. See "How to do online business with China", TechWeek Europe, 22 February 2013, available at http://www.techweekeurope.co.uk/comment/how-to-do-online-business-with-china-108291 (accessed 7 October 2013).

8   The Information Technology and Innovation Foundation estimates that United States cloud service providers might lose between 10 per cent and 20 per cent of the non-United States market for cloud provision as a result of recent revelations concerning government surveillance of data communications, (see Castro, 2013).

9   See also Source8 et al. (2013).

10   See "Glo to build Nigeria's biggest data centre", BiztechAfrica, 27 June 2013, available at http://www.biztechafrica.com/article/glo-build-nigerias-biggest-data-centre/6327/ (accessed 7 October 2013).

11   See "Safaricom offers locally hosted cloud service: Plans to run its Mpesa pan-African mobile money offering on new platform", Computerworld Kenya, 1 November 2011, available at http://www.pcadvisor.co.uk/news/mobile-phone/3314899/safaricom-offers-locally-hosted-cloud service/ (accessed 7 October 2013).

12   See "Power, pollution and the Internet", The New York Times, 22 September 2012, available at http://www.nytimes.com/2012/09/23/technology/data-centers-waste-vast-amounts-of-energy-belying-industry-image.html?pagewanted=all&_r=2& (accessed 8 October 2013). See also http://www.analyticspress.com/datacenters.html (accessed 8 October 2013).

13   See "African NGO taps IT to help prevent HIV transmission", Computer World, 28 January 2011, available at http://news.idg.no/cw/art.cfm?id=E669CBCD-1A64-67EA-E47FFECA76A12C2A (accessed 8 October 2013).

14   See Leo Apotheker (2011), "Opinion: Connectivity is no longer a tool but a global way of life", San Jose Mercury News. 3 December. Available at http://www.mercurynews.com/opinion/ci_17596575?nclick_check%C2%BC1 (accessed 8 October 2013).

15   Canonical was founded by a South African entrepreneur, Mark Shuttleworth. It is registered in the United Kingdom. See also Ubuntu Linux Cloud, http://www.ubuntu.com/download/cloud (accessed 8 October 2013).

16   See Ubuntu Software Center, https://wiki.ubuntu.com/SoftwareCenter (accessed 8 October 2013).

17 See http://www.orangescape.com/paas/platform-as-a-service/ (accessed 8 October 2013).

18 NGOs are similarly moving to cloud services, notably standardized public cloud services. The 2012 survey of
    ICT decision-makers in more than 10,000 NGOs cited earlier in this chapter found that the most frequently
    used applications were webmail, social networking and web 2.0 applications, file storage and file sharing, web
    conferencing and office productivity (Tech Soup Global, 2012).

19 See http://www.internetworldstats.com/facebook.htm (accessed 8 October 2013).

20 See http://www.alexa.com/siteinfo/facebook.com (accessed 8 October 2013).

21 As estimated by the web information provider Alexa, see http://www.alexa.com/topsites/countries (accessed
    8 October 2013).

22 See www.alexa.com (accessed 8 October 2013).

23 For example, Facebook's revenue from mobile advertising increased from virtually nothing a year ago to 41 per cent of
    its total advertising revenue of $1.6 billion in the second quarter of 2013. See, for example, http://bits.blogs.nytimes.
    com/2013/07/25/daily-report-facebooks-mobile-ad-revenue-cheers-investors/ (accessed 8 October 2013).

24 See "Govt pushing its agencies into the cloud", The Nation, 28 May 2013, available at http://www.nationmultimedia.
    com/technology/Govt-pushing-its-agencies-into-the-cloud-30206986.html (accessed 9 October 2013).

25 See "Cloud Security Alliance and Electronic Government Agency (EGA) of Thailand partner to drive cloud
    computing adoption in the Association of Southeast Asian Nations." Cloud Security Alliance press release.
    Available at https://cloudsecurityalliance.org/csa-news/csa-electronic-government-agency-ega-of-thailand-
    partner/ (accessed 9 October 2013).

26 See, for example, Cowhey and Kleeman (2012) and http://www.grameenfoundation.org/sites/grameenfoundation.
    org/files/MOTECH_Suite_Overview_Nov2012.pdf (accessed 10 October 2013).

27 See "Cloud computing – An enterprise perspective", presentation by Raghavan Subramanian, Infosys Technologies,
    available at http://research.microsoft.com/en-us/people/sriram/raghu-cloudcomputing.pdf (accessed 9 October 2013).

28 See http://www.brainstormmag.co.za/index.php?option=com_content&view=article&id=4756%3Acio-roundtable-
    castles-in-the-clouds&Itemid=124 (accessed 9 October 2013).

29 For an assessment of cloud experience, see Trip Advisor, available at http://highscalability.com/blog/2012/10/2/
    an-epic-tripadvisor-update-why-not-run-on-the-cloud-the-gran.html (accessed 9 October 2013).

30 The different impacts of ICTs on these different types of SME, and the different policy approaches appropriate to
    them, were explored in the Information Economy Report 2010 (UNCTAD, 2010).

31 See "Why some startups say the cloud is a waste of money", Wired, 15 August 2013, available at http://www.wired.
    com/wiredenterprise/2013/08/memsql-and-amazon/ (accessed 9 October 2013).

32 See http://www.freelancer.com/?utm_expid=294858-31.GWNoRHpfQwCRcsmjo9a25Q.0 (accessed 10 October
    2013) and https://www.odesk.com/ (accessed 10 October 2013).

GOVERNANCE, LAW AND REGULATION OF CLOUD SERVICES IN DEVELOPING COUNTRIES

4

The rapid emergence of cloud computing has inevitably raised concerns about the legal and regulatory implications of such developments. From the regulatory characterization of cloud services to the privacy implications of processing personal data remotely, policymakers, legislators, regulators, service providers and users all have an interest in the governance of cloud services. Governments will want to protect national interests, including the protection of their citizens; service providers require a stable framework to facilitate innovation and investment; users require assurance and trust to encourage the take-up of such services. This chapter examines some legal developments relating to the cloud, identifies emerging regulatory responses, and considers certain issues of particular concern for developing countries.

A. INTERNATIONAL LEGAL AND REGULATORY TRENDS

As discussed in preceding chapters, cloud computing can be seen both as a return to an earlier model of computing, as well as an innovation in the exploitation of ICTs, through the exploitation of shared and location-independent processing infrastructure. This duality of perspective is also reflected in the governance debates surrounding cloud computing. Concerns about data sovereignty and privacy[1] first appeared during the 1970s, as the emergence of more sophisticated telecommunication systems made it feasible for large TNCs to move bulky data sets between countries to take advantage of more advanced technological capabilities available in certain locations, primarily the United States, as well as economies of scale. Such transborder data flows (TDFs) were viewed by some with concern (Seidman, 1986). For some Governments, the transfer of critical commercial data to another country was seen as generating an unwelcome dependency and vulnerability for the State, with implications for national security, analogous to recent concerns about the provision of energy. In response, countries, including Brazil and Canada, introduced legislation requiring that certain data remain within the national territory. National security was not the only concern; the economic impact in terms of a perceived loss of domestic economic activity from TDFs also lay behind some such policy responses. A parallel and related concern arose from the fact that TDFs could enable companies to circumvent emerging national privacy laws, especially in Europe, which were designed to protect the privacy of citizens in an age of computing (Walden and Savage, 1990).

The economic and data-sovereignty concerns of the 1970s generally dissipated in the face of the liberalization of trade in services, manifest in the General Agreement on Trade in Services (GATS) in 1994, under the auspices of the World Trade Organization (WTO). The TDFs that underpin the cross-border provision of services were seen as offering greater benefits to nations than any concurrent enhanced vulnerability. Developing countries, in particular, have reaped comparative economic advantages in certain sectors, with the emergence of services such as the offshoring of

business processes. However, data-sovereignty concerns have re-emerged as a governance issue within cloud computing for a number of reasons (*CIO*, 2012). First, there are concerns that data placed with global cloud service providers may be accessible by law-enforcement agencies of their home country. Second, as Governments increasingly look to improve their efficiency and effectiveness through e-government initiatives, there are concerns that data fundamental to the functioning of Governments may move offshore into the cloud (see, for example, United Kingdom, Cabinet Office, 2011). Third, the threat of cybercrime, and even cyberwarfare, and the associated vulnerability of critical national infrastructure and data, is another manifestation of the national security concern (Kshetri, 2010).

In response to the privacy concerns of the 1970s, legal instruments, particularly European data-protection laws, expressly addressed the possibility of restricting TDFs. Some harmonization measures in the field were driven primarily by the desire to reduce the possibility that privacy rules would operate as a barrier to international trade, the leading example being the 1980 OECD Guidelines (OECD, 1980). Others, such as the 1981 Council of Europe Convention, included default rules stating that TDFs should only take place between jurisdictions with "equivalent" levels of privacy protection (Council of Europe, 1981).[2] Indeed, under the GATS, there is specific provision permitting member States to provide for a general exception from the liberalized and non-discrimination provisions for the purpose of protecting privacy and confidentiality.[3] Over the intervening years, while the nature of TDFs has evolved way beyond that imagined some 40 years ago, concerns about the potential erosion or circumvention of national privacy protections remain at the forefront of the policy response to cloud computing. There is no harmonized international privacy framework regulating data transfers across borders (see box IV.1), but developing countries could benefit from implementing strong domestic privacy regimes.

The governance framework for cloud computing can be divided broadly into two parts. On the one hand, there are laws and regulations adopted by Governments, public administrations and independent regulatory authorities – collectively referred to as "public law" for the purpose of this chapter – that are either directly targeted at the provision or use of cloud services, or impact such provision and usage by virtue of being

Box IV.1.   Protecting personal data in the cloud – different options and challenges

While the importance of protecting personal data in a cloud environment is broadly accepted, jurisdictions diverge significantly over the most appropriate regulatory mechanisms to achieve this, reflecting differing cultural and social attitudes towards the concept of privacy and its protection. As of mid-2013, there were some 99 countries with data-privacy laws of varying types (Greenleaf, 2013). European Union law imposes a general prohibition on transfers to jurisdictions without "adequate" protection, to ensure that individual rights are not subverted by moving data outside the jurisdiction, and requires the oversight of an "independent supervisory authority". Examples of such national authorities are the Office of the Information Commissioner in the United Kingdom and La Commission nationale de l'Informatique et des Libertés in France.

By contrast, the Asia-Pacific Economic Cooperation Privacy Framework (2005), to which the United States is party, subjects data transfers to an "accountability" principle,[a] but no general prohibition on transfers to countries with no data protection laws. There is no requirement for an independent enforcement authority.

These very real differences in approach present developing countries with potentially difficult choices when adopting domestic data-protection measures. Such adoption is often driven more by international trade concerns than by domestic policy concerns. Yet data protection regimes – as with all legislation – also represent a bureaucratic and compliance cost to developing-country Governments and domestic businesses. The current absence of an international consensus on what constitutes an "adequate" data-protection regime, in terms of core content principles, as well as procedural and enforcement mechanisms, can itself represent a barrier to cloud computing (Kuner, 2013).

Source: UNCTAD.

[a] According to article 26 of the Asia-Pacific Economic Cooperation Privacy Framework "A personal information controller should be accountable for complying with measures that give effect to the Principles stated above. When personal information is to be transferred to another person or organization, whether domestically or internationally, the personal information controller should obtain the consent of the individual or exercise due diligence and take reasonable steps to ensure that the recipient person or organization will protect the information consistently with these Principles."

applicable across a range of similar activities or behaviour (such as data-protection laws). To date, the public law response to cloud computing has primarily been of the latter kind, that is, applying existing rules in a cloud-based environment. A second governance framework comprises the contractual agreements entered into between the various providers of the cloud ecosystem and the end users of the services. While such "private law" arrangements are given legal recognition and enforceability by the public-law framework of a State, including the incorporation of national mandatory requirements, the provisions contained within such agreements more directly impact on the operation of the cloud economy, for providers and users.

These public and private law aspects to the governance of cloud should be viewed as complementary layers of protection, rather than as substitutes. Public law approaches are more comprehensive at meeting public policy objectives (for example, cloud promotion) and addressing public policy concerns (for example, consumer protection), although they can be time-consuming to adopt and require adequate resources to ensure effective implementation and enforcement.

B. PUBLIC LAW AND CLOUD SERVICES

1. Cloud as a regulated activity

A fundamental distinction exists between activities subject to the general law and those that are subject to specific legal and regulatory obligations by virtue of the type of activities being undertaken (such as banking and finance, and health services and telecommunications). Therefore, one question raised by cloud computing is whether it falls within existing regulatory spheres and, if not, whether it should be made subject to some form of cloud-specific regime.

The cloud-economy ecosystem includes the provision of transmission services to enable data to be transferred to and from remote data centres (chapter I). The provision of such transmission services is generally subject to sectoral regulation as a form of telecommunications. Progressive global liberalization of the telecommunications sector since the 1980s has resulted in a broadly harmonized but complex regulatory environment, which can be represented by the WTO "Telecommunications services: Reference paper" for telecommunications.[4] National regulatory authorities exercise varying degrees of control and oversight over market participants, imposing specific obligations on the provision of services.

Companies that provide PaaS and SaaS are generally viewed as falling outside the regulatory concept of a telecommunication service. However, certain SaaS applications that provide call-handling functionality for enterprises could be regarded as a regulated telecommunication service, depending on a country's particular regulatory regime.[5] While such cloud services are dependent on telecommunication networks and services for communicating with their customers, they are not per se generally characterized as being a telecommunication facility, network or service. Certain IaaS, however, may provide processing, storage and connectivity services that may be viewed as a telecommunication service depending on the primacy of the connectivity component (ITU, 2012a). In 2012, the Korean Communications Commission published a proposed "Bill for the development of cloud computing and protection of users", which would have classified cloud computing as a telecommunications service. The proposal met with strong opposition from cloud providers and was being reconsidered at the time of preparing this report.[6]

In some jurisdictions, primarily in developing countries, the regulatory net is cast wider than the provision of telecommunication services to include the provision of data processing services.[7] In such cases, cloud services – be they SaaS, PaaS or IaaS – are likely to fall squarely within the regulatory sphere. Such regimes enable Governments to impose conditions on the supply of services and might help address concerns including data sovereignty and privacy. In Indonesia, for example, recent regulations require those providing "electronic systems" for the provision of public services to locate the applicable data and disaster-recovery centres for public services in Indonesian territory "for the purpose of law enforcement, protection and enforcement of national sovereignty to the data of its citizens".[8]

In other countries, while cloud services are not subject to comprehensive sectoral regulatory regimes, they may fall within regulatory concepts designed to shield certain service providers from liability for the content that they make available on behalf of others. In South Africa, for example, the provision of "information system services", which would extend to most cloud services, is subject to special provisions limiting the liability of service providers in respect of unlawful content made available by others.[9]

Uncertainties over the regulatory characterization of cloud computing may deter its acceptance until legislators or regulators clarify the situation. Issues of administrative competence are obviously linked to such uncertainty. If viewed as a telecommunications service, then the telecommunications regulator can exercise jurisdiction. If a cloud service is seen as a data-processing service, then competence may lie with the national ICT regulator, if there is one, or alternatively the media regulator if it is viewed as a content-like service. Such sectoral regulators may also have to operate in conjunction and cooperation with any horizontal national regulators, such as data-protection or consumer-protection authorities, in respect of certain issues.

To date, few jurisdictions have attempted to draft regulations expressly designed to regulate the provision of cloud services. This probably reflects both the broad range of services that fall within the concept of cloud, as well as the flexibility of scope within existing regulatory concepts. As far as is known, Mexico is the only country which has adopted cloud-specific provisions in relation to data protection (box IV.2). Some of these rules are merely restatements of generally applicable obligations, while others are more "cloud appropriate", designed to address concerns that have arisen in a cloud context, specifically regarding transparency about the layered nature of the cloud supply chain (see also section IV.C), regarding the treatment of user data following service termination, and regarding law enforcement access (Bradshaw et al., 2011). The Mexican approach intends to encourage the domestic take-up of cloud solutions.

2. Regulating in a multi-jurisdictional environment

If regulatory characterization is one key concern for policymakers, another is the perceived loss of oversight and control over applications and data resulting from the remote nature of cloud service provision. Location independence is a key characteristic of cloud computing, which exploits the "death of distance" made possible where adequate communication networks are in place (Cairncross, 1997).[10] This results in a multiplicity of jurisdictions potentially competing to govern the various parts of a cloud service. The

---

Box IV.2.   Legislating for cloud: the case of Mexico

Policies on ICT and the regulatory framework constitute a basis for developing cloud computing services in Mexico. In relation to privacy and data protection, a federal law on the "Protection of Personal Data Held by Private Parties" was adopted in 2010. Regulations made under this law were adopted in December 2011 and include specific provision for cloud computing.

Article 52 imposes certain obligations on cloud service providers offering "services, applications, and infrastructure" to data controllers "by general contractual conditions or clauses". The provider must ensure that it (the provider):

(a)   Complies with at least the following:

    (i)   Policies to protect personal data similar to the applicable principles and duties set out in the Law and its regulations;

    (ii)   Makes transparent any subcontracting that involves information about the service which is provided;

    (iii)   Abstains from including conditions, when providing the service, that authorize or permit the provider to assume the ownership of the information related to the service provided;

    (iv)   Maintains confidentiality with respect to the personal data associated with the service provided.

(b)   Ensures that the contract contains mechanisms at least for:

    (i)   Disclosing changes in its privacy policies or conditions of the service it provides;

    (ii)   Permitting the data controller to limit the type of processing of personal data associated with the service provided;

    (iii)   Establishing and maintaining adequate security measures to protect the personal data associated with the service provided;

    (iv)   Ensuring the suppression of personal data once the service has been provided to the data controller and ensuring that the latter may recover the data;

    (v)   Impeding access to personal data by those who do not have proper access or in the event of a request duly made by a competent authority, to inform the data controller.

The user of the cloud services, as "data controller", is obliged not to use services that "do not ensure the proper protection of personal data".

Source: Mexico, Federal Institute for Access to Public Information, see http://inicio.ifai.org.mx/_catalogs/masterpage/ifai.aspx (accessed 22 October 2013).

---

movement of data into and out of a cloud service will often result in the data becoming subject to the rules of both the cloud user's jurisdiction and those of the providers of the cloud and inter-cloud services. The transfer of data out of the user's jurisdiction is often opaque to the user, raising issues of control and, for the relevant national regulator, effective oversight and audit. For some regulated sectors, such as financial services, cloud-related transfers and storage outside the jurisdiction of the regulated entity may itself breach national rules by failing to provide national authorities with "effective access" to the data.[11]

Due to concerns about sovereignty, national regulators may be unwilling to surrender jurisdiction to a foreign authority unless adequate mutual recognition arrangements are in place. For some types of processing, such as those relating to national security, no foreign involvement may be acceptable

and a national solution will be required. Effective mutual recognition requires greater transparency, more dialogue and closer cooperation between national regulators to resolve conflicts of law and regulation in a cloud environment, and to facilitate the free flow of data. Significant examples of cooperative networks of national regulators and law enforcement agencies already exist in the areas of consumer protection, cybercrime and data protection,[12] while legislative proposals have been put forward to facilitate international cooperation and interoperability with respect to cloud.[13] The European Commission, in its cloud strategy, noted that "being born global", cloud computing called for "a reinforced international dialogue on safe and seamless cross-border use", including the need for "legal adjustments to promote efficient and effective cloud roll-out" (European Commission, 2012).

Another dimension of the multi-jurisdictional nature of cloud is concern about the potential implications of the regulatory regime of the country of origin of the cloud provider. This has been highlighted, for example, in the context of data placed with global cloud service providers and the possibility for law-enforcement agencies to access such data even if stored outside of the jurisdiction of their home country. As noted in a recent report for the European Parliament (Bigo et al., 2012):

> Cloud providers are transnational companies subject to conflicts of international public law. Which law they choose to obey will be governed by the penalties applicable and exigencies of the situation, and in practice the predominant allegiances of the company management.

The launch of Microsoft's Office 365 in June 2011, for example, was accompanied by expressions of concern that Microsoft would not guarantee that data of European customers could not be accessed by agencies acting under United States jurisdiction.[14] Similar concerns were behind statements by the Government of the Netherlands, suggesting that cloud providers from the United States in government bids and contracts could be excluded.[15] In Australia, the Office of the Victorian Privacy Commissioner in 2011 warned government agencies about the use of cloud computing, suggesting that it could be "impossible" to protect personal information held about Australians when located offshore or even outside Victoria.[16]

In 2013, media reports brought the issues of law enforcement access to cloud-based services to the forefront of the policy debate on cloud, indicating that the United States National Security Agency was obtaining large volumes of data from leading cloud service providers, such as Apple, Facebook, Google, Microsoft, Yahoo and Skype.[17] The service providers have denied suggestions that their services permit some form of "back-door" access to national agencies, but have accepted that they regularly disclose customer data in response to requests from law-enforcement agencies in a number of countries.[18] It has been stressed that such disclosures, whether carried out under legal mandate or voluntarily, might expose the cloud service provider to liability under the laws of the customer's jurisdiction (Bigo et al., 2012; Walden, 2011).

Related concerns may widen the scope for new competitors to enter and expand in the market.[19] Some European providers have called for certification schemes that would indicate where data is protected from such access.[20] At the same time, almost all countries have legislation that gives their authorities the right for reasons of national security to request data on cloud services stored in their jurisdiction.[21] The issue is ensuring that these powers are used only when necessary.

To the extent that cloud computing services are located outside the domestic jurisdiction, policy and legal issues arise as to whether large-scale data transfers are appropriate or permissible and whether regulatory control measures can be imposed or maintained once the data have left the jurisdiction. Harmonized statutory regimes would significantly mitigate such concerns, but at present, contractual agreements between providers and customers are the main mechanism available to address them, at least to some extent.

C. PRIVATE LAW AND CLOUD SERVICES

As noted earlier, the cloud ecosystem is to a high degree built on private law agreements between service providers and between service providers and cloud service customers. Such contracts offer service providers and customers a self-regulatory mechanism for generating a framework of legal certainty and security in cloud computing. Cloud contractual arrangements come in varying shapes and sizes, but will generally comprise four distinct components, whether in a single agreement or a set of linked documents (generically referred to as the "cloud contract"):

- **Terms of service**, detailing the key features of the relationship, both cloud-specific and general boilerplate provisions (for example, choice of law);
- **Service-level agreement**, detailing the service features being provided, the standards that they should meet (for example, service uptime) and any compensation mechanism when the standards are not met;
- **Acceptable-use policies**, detailing permitted or impermissible conduct by users (for example, copyright infringement);
- **Privacy policy**, detailing the approach taken to the storage and processing of user data, particularly consumer information.

The terms of a cloud contract can be distinguished into standard terms and cloud-specific provisions. The standard terms will include such matters as provider liabilities, dispute resolution and applicable law. Both are of equal importance in terms of defining the provider–user relationship. The cloud-specific provisions generally focus on two key aspects: first, the treatment of the data submitted by the cloud user into the cloud service; second, the specifications of the service being offered to the cloud user.

With respect to the treatment of data held in the cloud, "cloud appropriate" terms would include provisions ensuring that the users' rights of ownership over the data are not compromised, that the data are secure against inadvertent or unauthorized disclosure, and that they will reside on infrastructure located in a specified jurisdiction or region. On the service side, users will want cloud-appropriate service levels that address concerns about dependency on the cloud service (see for example, European Network and Information Security Agency, 2012).[22] Conversely, providers will generally argue that the utility and commodity nature of a "public" cloud service must limit their responsibilities concerning issues such as the integrity and backup of user data (Hon et al., 2012).

From a public policy perspective, self-regulation through contractual agreements can raise concerns when market practice facilitates a situation where contracts do not result in a fair balance of liabilities and responsibilities between cloud providers and customers, especially when the latter are SMEs and individuals. In addition, contractual terms can have implications for third parties that not a part of the agreement, particularly regarding privacy and data protection issues. In these circumstances, regulatory intervention in the freedom to contract may be considered necessary to rebalance the relationship with a view to protecting third parties or the wider public interest. Such intervention may occur through the imposition of obligations that cloud providers are required to address in any cloud contractual process or agreement (see box IV.2), through certain terms and conditions being statutorily implied in any agreement, or the development of model cloud industry terms and conditions or service-level agreements.[23] For example, the European Commission recently stated that model terms may be needed "to create transparent and fair cloud services contracts" following calls from respondents to a survey.[24] For most developing countries, however, the challenge of intervening in cloud contracts is obviously much greater, with domestic consumer laws often being either inadequate or unenforceable.

A cloud service customer will only contract directly with the cloud service provider and, usually, a communication service provider, and this customer may be unclear in their understanding of the entire chain of suppliers providing elements of the cloud service, such as IaaS. This may represent a risk, since the customer may not be aware of the layers of contracts that underpin the provision of the service and, significantly, whether commitments entered into by the contracting service provider are adequately reflected at each stage of the supply chain. One proposed regulatory response is to impose transparency obligations on the cloud service provider (ITU, 2012b).

In the consumer market, cloud service providers will generally dictate the terms on which the service is offered. Such standard terms and conditions are often biased in favour of the provider, even though they may vary considerably according to the markets from which the cloud provider originates: providing hardware, software, outsourcing, communications services or retail products. At the enterprise level, however, service providers are increasingly being forced to negotiate agreements that have provisions more favourable to the customer in order to win the business (Hon et al., 2012). It has also been stressed that certain market entrants, such as cloud integrators and aggregators,[25] seem to be willing to offer more user-orientated terms (Hon et al., 2012). The issues on which most negotiation takes place with respect to the terms of service are: provider liability, service-level agreements, data protection and security, and intellectual property rights. In terms of the mechanism of the agreement itself, the right of service providers to unilaterally amend service features and termination rights are key areas of dispute. While enterprise cloud contracts will remain distinct from the consumer segment, some of the concessions achieved in enterprise negotiations may later trickle down into the provider's standard terms of business, especially if regulators become more involved (Hon et al., 2012).

Another obvious influence on the contractual environment for cloud services is the procurement practices of government administrations, as they are usually among the largest customers in the emerging cloud market. As public authorities embrace cloud services for the provision of e-government-related services, they are – similarly to large enterprise users – in a potentially strong position to negotiate more favourable terms and conditions with cloud service providers, including measures to protect the privacy interests of data subjects/citizens. In addition, they can utilize their "procurement weight", expressed in national public procurement rules, to promote other policy objectives, including "open technologies and secure platforms" (European Commission, 2012: 3.2) that benefit the wider user community. In the United States, for example, the Chief Information Officer within the Office of Management and Budget has issued best practice guidance for the acquisition of cloud services (United States, Federal CIO Council and Chief Acquisition Officers Council, 2012). This guidance addresses the selection of the service provider, the service-level agreement, end-user agreements, e-discovery and record-keeping issues. Inevitably, a key concern for the public sector is that of security in the cloud.

While contractual arrangements are not a substitute for public law measures, especially when protecting third party interests, they comprise an important layer of cloud governance that should be acknowledged and can be influenced to help address certain policy concerns. However, the ability to negotiate and enforce contractual obligations can vary considerably, especially in a developing country context.

D. IMPLICATIONS FOR DEVELOPING COUNTRIES

Despite calls for new cloud laws from certain sectors in both developed and developing countries,[26] what exactly would such regulatory and governance measures address for developing countries? This chapter has identified three overlapping areas: (a) the provision of cloud services; (b) the conditions under which such services are provided to end users; (c) the treatment of data placed in the cloud service. These areas are generic and relevant for all jurisdictions – whether in developed or developing countries – but achieving effective resolution through law and regulation is generally more difficult in developing countries.

1. Provision of cloud services

Should the provision of cloud-related services be a distinct regulated activity? Governing the right to establish and/or supply a cloud service in the domestic jurisdiction, through some form of prior licensing or authorization requirement, is about enabling regulatory

control over market entry. In developed countries, there are few, if any, examples of such cloud-specific regulations. Some components of the cloud ecosystem, particularly the communication network component, already fall within existing regulatory regimes, but those regimes are typically designed to facilitate market entry and competition, rather than to constrain market participants.

For developing countries, while the dominance of foreign companies offering cross-border services may be a concern, it is both practically and legally difficult to address this market reality through regulatory intervention. From a practical perspective, preventing access to foreign cloud services would likely require a radical intervention in the global connectivity of the State, especially in respect of the Internet. From a legal perspective, a majority of developing countries are members of the WTO and signatories to the GATS, committing themselves, at least in some sectors, to liberalized trade in services, including through cross-border supply.[27] As such, regulatory intervention is permissible only under limited exceptions, including the protection of the privacy and confidentiality of data.

An alternative policy response is to encourage the establishment of domestic cloud services, either by offering foreign service providers a favourable environment to invest in the building of local infrastructure (such as data centres) or encourage domestic enterprises to enter the supply side of the cloud economy. However, the former approach would not necessarily overcome the problem of the application of foreign laws, as outlined above, especially if the local entity remains under the control of the foreign parent. Such measures may involve regulatory components, such as imposing "localization" requirements, but would be designed to facilitate the provision of cloud services rather than to constrain them. As noted in chapter III, several Governments of developing countries are also taking steps to build government clouds to serve the needs of the Government itself and sometimes also other cloud service customers.

2. Conditions of supply

Irrespective of whether the establishment and provision of cloud services is regulated, Governments may choose to intervene to impose certain conditions on the supply of cloud services to address specified public policy concerns, such as data security and privacy. Such conditions may be applicable only to certain types of cloud services (for example, SaaS), certain types of end users (for example, consumers or public administrations) or be imposed upon all cloud services. The conditions may directly impose behavioral obligations on cloud service providers, such as requirements to retain some types of data within certain geographical locations or for certain periods of time, or they may indirectly govern the contractual arrangements between the provider and end user, such as rendering certain "unfair" terms unenforceable. Such public law intervention in the conditions of supply may also have an impact on a user's cost–benefit analysis for cloud adoption, if it results in a higher cost service, which should be factored into any initiative.

Among developed countries, there has been little adoption of cloud-specific obligations to date (Business Software Alliance and Galexia, 2012). Instead, relevant regulatory authorities have tended to issue opinions as to how existing obligations, whether for particular sectors (for example, financial services) or of a general nature (for example, data protection) should be applied within a cloud context (United Kingdom, Cabinet Office, 2011).[28]

In Mexico, the Government has gone one step further, imposing an express obligation on all regulatory authorities to draft guidelines in relation to the cloud.[29] For most other developing countries, relevant laws and regulations – where they exist – are more likely to be considered an obstacle to cloud adoption rather than a facilitator, as was the case with the emergence of e-commerce during the first decade of the century. Indeed, many e-commerce and cyberlaw reform initiatives are directly relevant to cloud computing, and the emergence of cloud computing can act as a further spur towards the comprehensive implementation of these reforms.[30]

The ability to enforce any regulatory obligations upon a cloud service provider will depend, in reality, on whether the provider is either in some way established within the jurisdiction (such as having a local office, against which any enforcement action can be pursued), or if the provider is prepared to voluntarily submit itself to local rules, or at least comply with them, even though these may be unenforceable. A key example of the latter case are foreign service providers responding to domestic law enforcement requests in relation to content considered illegal, which is held and made available via the provider's remote servers.

Companies such as Google and Microsoft have made public their handling of such requests in respect of specific jurisdictions, whilst noting that they are often not legally required to cooperate.[31]

Another strategy for regulators in developing countries is to make reference, in laws or regulations, to international technical and business standards that specify certain good practices that are either generally applicable to,[32] or specifically designed for cloud computing.[33] Requiring compliance with such standards, particularly when they are implemented through an external and independent audit and certification procedure, carried out by an accredited certification body,[34] can offer end users, third parties and regulators some assurance with respect to the provision of trustworthy and quality cloud services.

3. Treatment of data

In addition to regulating the conditions under which cloud services are supplied to cloud service customers, there are also public policy concerns that extend beyond the relationship between provider and customer. Data placed in the cloud can engage third-party interests that may require regulatory intervention, whether concerning personal privacy, commercial secrecy or national security. Within data protection laws, for example, imposing security-breach notification obligations on cloud service providers provides transparency about vulnerabilities and enables mitigating measures to be taken in a timely manner.

Governments will have particular data security concerns where the end users are public administrations, involving data about citizens or data considered relevant to national security, as is the case with Indonesia. In February 2013, for example, the European Commission published a proposal for a Directive on information security that would require member States to designate a competent authority to provide regulatory oversight, establish a national computer emergency response team (CERT) to handle security incidents and risks, and require certain "market operators" that enable the provision of online services, including cloud service providers, to notify the competent authority of security breaches and undergo security audits when required.[35] These proposals are equally valid recommendations for consideration in developing countries, where the vulnerabilities and risks associated with cloud computing are shared.

A growing number of developing countries are also establishing CERTs and are at different stages of development in their operations, procedures and related activities. Many of these countries are also faced with challenges, particularly in the areas of capacity building, funding, the legislative framework and other soft and hard resources. Africa has the smallest number of CERTs.[36]

E. CONCLUDING REMARKS AND POLICY RECOMMENDATIONS

Cloud computing is another manifestation of a rapidly evolving ICT environment that confronts both developed and developing countries. How to respond appropriately to cloud computing from a legal and regulatory perspective is not obvious and can involve different approaches, ranging from a do-nothing attitude to the adoption of cloud-specific laws. The nature of the response will often depend on whether the implications of cloud computing are viewed overall to be positive, and therefore to be facilitated, or negative, and therefore to be constrained. Given the immature state of the cloud market, especially in developing countries, considerable caution and care should be taken by both policymakers and regulators in terms of rushing to legislate for cloud.

While there is no imperative to develop specific laws or regulations on cloud computing, some of the areas requiring law reform are relatively clear: privacy, data protection, information security and cybercrime measures.[37] As noted earlier, these are issues of equal importance to e-commerce and other aspects of the networked economy. This, in itself, indicates that approaching cloud computing issues in isolation would not be advisable. For Governments of developing countries, it is essential that appropriate laws and regulations are adopted in these areas and enforced.

Governments and public administrations, as potential users of the cloud, can offer leadership to the national market in terms of addressing areas of concern for users. Regulators can also assist, by issuing guidance on the applicability to cloud solutions of the regimes for which they are responsible. This could include, for

example, explicit recognition that certified compliance with international technical and business standards, especially concerning information security, will be accepted as prima facie evidence of good market practice. For many developing countries, such initiatives will require the provision of external assistance to users, policymakers and regulators, on the technical, managerial and legal issues raised by cloud computing.

Several additional steps can be taken by policymakers in developing countries when considering the appropriate policy response to cloud computing:
- Consider the need to draft and ensure a coherent and appropriate national cloud strategy, of which legal and regulatory issues are one component. The drafting process should be inclusive and transparent to stakeholders (see chapter V);
- Review existing legal frameworks and enact comprehensive laws relating to, as a minimum, privacy and data protection, information security and cybercrime. Aligning such laws with leading international legal instruments in these areas is highly recommended to achieve a harmonized set of laws and regulations. Such instruments include the United Nations Committee on International Trade Law texts on e-commerce,[38] in particular the United Nations Convention on the Use of Electronic Communications in International Contracts,[39] the Council of Europe Convention for the Protection of Individuals with regard to Automatic Processing of Personal Data,[40] and the Council of Europe Convention on Cybercrime;[41]
- Build capacity to ensure enactment and enforcement of laws and regulations, including establishing CERTs, training regulatory agencies and the judiciary, and making use of support from international organizations such as UNCTAD (box IV.3);
- Consider the use of public procurement rules as a vehicle for promoting particular cloud-related policy objectives, such as enhanced privacy protection;
- Promote awareness-building in government institutions and public administrations on the potential that cloud computing technologies offer;
- Monitor regulatory developments in the field of cloud computing. For such an evolving area it is important to stay abreast of regulatory developments, in particular in cross-border cooperation between regulatory and law-enforcement authorities.

Box IV.3.   UNCTAD support to e-commerce legislation harmonization

UNCTAD's E-commerce and Law Reform Programme assists member States in preparing legal and regulatory frameworks to facilitate e-commerce and e-government. It has become the leading capacity-building programme within the United Nations system in support of the harmonization of legal frameworks governing the use of electronic services in developing countries. In addition to training workshops and briefing sessions for policy and law makers, including parliamentarians, UNCTAD reviews existing legislation and helps prepare domestic laws and regional legal frameworks to facilitate this process. Key legal issues addressed include electronic transactions, electronic signatures and authentication, data protection and privacy, consumer protection, computer crime, intellectual property, competition, taxation and information security at large.

To date, UNCTAD has assisted more than 35 countries, notably in the Association of Southeast Asian Nations (UNCTAD, 2013), Central America (UNCTAD, 2009a), Latin America (UNCTAD, 2009b), the East African Community (UNCTAD, 2012b) and the Economic Community of West African States. This has successfully contributed to raising the profile of cyberlaw issues at the national and regional level and has resulted in the adoption of law reforms. For example, in August 2013, the second phase of the East African Community Framework for Harmonized Cyberlaws was approved for implementation by the tenth meeting of the Sectoral Council on Transport, Communications, and Meteorology. This and the first phase of the Framework were developed with UNCTAD assistance. Partner States are currently advancing in their implementation of domestic laws in the relevant areas.

Source: UNCTAD.

NOTES

1   See, for example, chapter 6, "Protecting privacy rights in an online world" in UNCTAD (2004).

2   What constitutes "equivalent" protection is not further defined, but is considered to require a higher standard of harmonization than the term "adequate" adopted under European Union data protection law (see box IV.1).

3   See GATS, article XIV(c)(ii).

4   Available at http://www.wto.org/english/tratop_e/serv_e/telecom_e/tel23_e.htm (accessed 22 October 2013).

5   For example, CaaS solutions are available from companies such as Level 3, Cisco and Skype.

6   See BSA case study on the Republic of Korea, available at http://cloudscorecard.bsa.org/2013/assets/PDFs/case_studies/2013Scorecardcs_Korea.pdf (accessed 22 October 2013). See also ETNews "Cloud Computing Act came to a deadlock due to opposition by global cloud service providers", 16 November 2012, available at http://english.etnews.com/computing/2677775_1301.html (accessed 22 October 2013).

7   See, for example, Indonesia, Law No. 11 on Electronic Information and Transactions 2008, which at article 1(6) regulates the provision of "electronic systems". A more recent regulation, No. 82 of 2012 on the Operation of Electronic Systems and Transactions, furthermore requires, inter alia, that data centres and disaster-recovery centres for public services have to be located in Indonesia, and that Indonesian citizens are employed in certain cases. Moreover, under the GATS, "data processing services" is a category of business service distinct from "communication services", such as telecommunications. For further information, see WTO, "Services sectoral classification list", MTN.GNS/W/120, 10 July 1991. See also WTO, "Communication from the United States", S/C/W/339, 20 September 2011: "notwithstanding convergence, the category of computer and related services remains the fundamental locus for cloud computing under the GATS", available at http://www.wto.org/english/thewto_e/minist_e/min11_e/brief_ecom_e.htm (accessed 22 October 2013).

8   Regulation No. 82 of 2012, at article 17(2).

9   South African Electronic Communications and Transactions Act 2002, chapter XI.

10 However, it is worth noting that the "tyranny of distance" is not overcome for all services; for example, content delivery networks, or applications (for example, real-time financial trading systems), where minimizing latency is critical.

11 See European Commission Directive 2006/73/EC implementing Directive 204/39/EC "as regards operational requirements and operating conditions for investment firms and defined terms for the purposes of that Directive" (OJ L 241/26, 2.9.2006), at article 14(2)(i).

12 For example, the International Consumer Protection and Enforcement Network (icpen.org) and the Global Privacy Enforcement Network (www.privacyenforcement.net).

13 See, for example, United States Senator Amy Klobuchar's Cloud Computing Act of 2012 (S. 3569), available at http://beta.congress.gov/bill/112th/senate-bill/3569/text (accessed 22 October 2013).

14 See, for example, "Patriot Act and privacy laws take a bite out of US cloud business", Arstechnica, 8 December 2011, available at http://arstechnica.com/tech-policy/2011/12/patriot-act-and-privacy-laws-take-a-bite-out-of-us-cloud-business/ (accessed 22 October 2013) and "BAe Systems: Office365 doesn't fly", Computer Weekly, 5 December 2011, available at http://www.computerweekly.com/blogs/it-fud-blog/2011/12/bae-systems-office365.html (accessed 22 October 2013).

15 See the statement (in Dutch) by Dutch Minister for Security and Justice, Ivo Opstelten, available at https://zoek.officielebekendmakingen.nl/ah-tk-20102011-3516.html (accessed 22 October 2013).

16 See "Offshore cloud privacy may be 'impossible', says commissioner", Delimiter, 4 May 2011, available at http://delimiter.com.au/2011/05/04/offshore-cloud-privacy-may-be-impossible-says-commissioner/ (accessed 22 October 2013), and Office of the Victoria Privacy Commissioner (2011).

17 See "NSA Prism program taps in to user data of Apple, Google and others", The Guardian, 7 June 2013, available at http://www.theguardian.com/world/2013/jun/06/us-tech-giants-nsa-data (accessed 22 October 2013), and the statement by the President of the United States on 7 June 2013, available at http://www.whitehouse.gov/the-press-office/2013/06/07/statement-president (accessed 22 October 2013).

18 See, for example, "PRISM scandal: tech giants flatly deny allowing NSA direct access to servers", The Guardian, 7 June 2013, available at http://www.theguardian.com/world/2013/jun/07/prism-tech-giants-shock-nsa-data-mining (accessed 22 October 2013).

19 It has been estimated that United States cloud service providers might lose between 10 per cent and 20 per cent of the non-United States market for cloud provision as a result of recent revelations concerning government surveillance of data communications (Castro, 2013). See also http://www.cio.com/article/734919/European_and_US_cloud_providers_go_head_to_head_after_NSA_revelations (accessed 22 October 2013).

20 See "Deutsche Telekom wants 'German Cloud' to shield data from US", Business Week, 14 September 2011.

21 See, for example, "Patriot Act not a cloud computing threat: IDC", ContinuityCentral, 24 October 2012, available at http://www.continuitycentral.com/news06514.html (accessed 22 October 2013); "GCHQ taps fibre-optic cables for secret access to world's communications", The Guardian, 21 June 2013, available at http://www.guardian.co.uk/uk/2013/jun/21/gchq-cables-secret-world-communications-nsa (accessed 22 October 2013); "En France, la DGSE au cœur d'un programme de surveillance d'Internet", Le Monde, 11 June 2013, available at http://www.lemonde.fr/international/article/2013/06/11/en-france-la-dgse-est-au-c-ur-d-un-vaste-programme-de-surveillance-d-internet_3427837_3210.html (accessed 22 October 2013).

22 For example, European Network and Information Security Agency (2012).

23 For example, Cloud Industry Forum, "Code of practice for cloud service providers", available at http://www.cloudindustryforum.org/code-of-practice/code-of-practice (accessed 22 October 2013).

24 See European Commission (2012: 3.4) and IDC (2012).

25 That is, entities that do not themselves own much of the cloud "stack", but offer users integrated ICT solutions that will increasingly comprise cloud components.

26 "New cloud laws needed for business data", TechWeek Europe, 16 August 2012, available at http://www.techweekeurope.co.uk/comment/cloud-laws-update-eu-89567 (accessed 23 October 2013).See also ITU-D (2012).

27 For example, Indonesia's Schedule of Specific Commitments under the GATS: GATS/SC/43, 15 April 1994.

28 For example, United Kingdom, Information Commissioner's Office, "Guidance on the use of cloud computing", September 2012, available at http://www.ico.org.uk/news/latest_news/2012/~/media/documents/library/Data_Protection/Practical_application/cloud_computing_guidance_for_organisations.ashx (accessed 25 October 2013).

29 Regulations to the Federal Law on the Protection of Personal Data Held by Private Parties (2011), at article 52, (see further box IV.2).

30 For example, the East African Community Cyberlaws Framework, see UNCTAD (2012b).

31 See http://www.google.com/transparencyreport/ (accessed 23 October 2013) and http://www.microsoft.com/about/corporatecitizenship/en-us/reporting/transparency/ (accessed 23 October 2013).

32 For example, ISO/IEC 27001 for information security management systems.

33 For example, recommendation ITU-T Y.3510, "Cloud computing infrastructure requirements", which has recently reached first-stage approval. ISO/IEC WD 27018 is a proposed "Code of practice for data protection controls for public cloud computing services" being developed under the ISO 27001 family. See also the work of the Cloud Security Alliance, which is developing mechanisms such as the CloudTrust protocol (for further details see https://cloudsecurityalliance.org/research/ctp/, accessed 23 October 2013).

34 See the International Accreditation Forum, available at http://www.iaf.nu/ (accessed 23 October 2013).

35 European Commission, proposal for a Directive "Concerning measures to ensure a high common level of network and information security across the Union", COM(2013) 48 final, 7 February 2013.

36 With the support of the ITU, the region has recently established four new such teams and another four are underway; see http://www.itu.int/en/ITU-D/Cybersecurity/Pages/Projects.aspx (accessed 23 October 2013).

37 Other identified areas include protecting intellectual property, ensuring data portability and liberalizing trade rules. See, for example, Business Software Alliance and Galexia (2012).

38 See http://www.uncitral.org/uncitral/uncitral_texts/electronic_commerce.html (accessed 23 October 2013).

39 Ibid.

40 See http://conventions.coe.int/Treaty/Commun/QueVoulezVous.asp?NT=108&CL=ENG (accessed 23 October 2013).

41 In signatories to the Budapest Convention on Cybercrime, domestic law-enforcement agencies can ask foreign ISPs for disclosure of data, but only on a voluntary basis. See http://conventions.coe.int/Treaty/Commun/QueVoulezVous.asp?NT=185&CL=ENG (accessed 23 October 2013).

POLICY RECOMMENDATIONS

5

The emergence of the cloud economy has implications for countries at all levels of development. Whereas a general shift to the cloud can stimulate major gains in efficiency, productivity and economic growth, these are not automatic. Where they are realized, they will be unevenly distributed, geographically, within societies and over time. There are also potential pitfalls, some of the most important of which are related to data security and privacy. It is important, therefore, for both individual Governments and the international community as a whole to consider policy responses that can help bring about development outcomes from the cloud economy which are as favourable as possible.

This final chapter builds on the analysis in earlier chapters of the report and makes recommendations to Governments and their development partners. Given the early stage of development of the cloud economy in developing countries, and an evidence base which is still thin, the policy advice remains at a fairly general level. This chapter is intended to provide a basis for policymakers in developing countries and their partners as they seek to enable the development of a cloud economy and translate its potential into development gains. It identifies specific areas and aspects that should be considered when designing a strategic response.

A. RECOGNIZING THE DIVERSITY OF CLOUD ADOPTION STRATEGIES

Cloud computing has the potential to offer users in developing countries access to unprecedented resources of computing power and storage. This is a welcome development which is likely to expand further in the future. At present, however, cloud adoption in developing countries is low and most countries face significant barriers to participating effectively in the cloud economy.

This report has sought to demystify the cloud phenomenon and to analyse its implications. While the metaphor of the "cloud" suggests something rather new, cloud computing can also be seen as the latest stage in the long-term evolution of computing and communications services, enabled by greatly expanded computing power, storage capacity and reliable broadband communications networks. As a consequence, however, the lack of adequate ICT infrastructure and power supply in many developing countries holds back their ability to make productive use of the cloud. Cloud policy needs to be formulated and implemented in this wider context of ICT markets and usage.

While the adoption of cloud services in developing countries is motivated by more or less the same basic drivers that attract users in developed countries, there are significant barriers that are more acute in developing economies. Depending on the country, these include insufficient broadband connectivity, high costs for broadband access and use, unreliable power supply, long distances to data centres (with higher latency as a result), a lack of skills to make effective use of ICTs and inadequate legal protection of data. The level of cloud adoption is greatly affected by such contextual factors. As a result, notwithstanding the significant potential benefits that can be derived from cloud computing, cloud-based solutions are not always preferable to alternative approaches. Moreover, different cloud configurations will be more or less appropriate in different contexts.

The first question for Governments, enterprises (large and small) and other organizations is whether to migrate services to the cloud or not. Their response will be influenced by their assessment of potential advantages and risks/disadvantages (table V.1)

Potential adopters will be influenced by the nature of their operations as well as by the national context. Some businesses and organizations are better positioned to reap the benefits of a shift to the cloud or can gain greater advantage than others because of the nature of their activities or business model. This is the case, for example, for those that have high fixed costs in maintaining in-house IT departments, recurrently need IT software and hardware, face large or unpredictable variations in demand for IT resources or can gain substantial added value from more efficient exploitation of data and market opportunities. The outcome of an individual business or organization's assessment will also depend on the economic and communications environment in which it operates.

As a potential cloud service customer, a business or organization needs to think through a number of issues if it decides to migrate significant services to the cloud. The business or organization must explore the range of cloud solutions available to find that which best meets its needs. While it is beyond the scope of this report to make technical recommendations on what solutions to adopt, businesses and organizations may consider the following:

Table V.1. Potential advantages and risks/ disadvantages of cloud adoption	
Potential advantages	**Potential risks/disadvantages**
Reduced costs for rented IT hardware and software compared to costs for in-house equipment (cost advantages can be reaped through the economies of scope and scale of cloud solutions and from the shift from capital to operational expenditure)	Increased costs of communications (to telecommunication operators/ISPs)
Reduced cost of in-house IT management	Increased costs for data or service migration and integration
Enhanced elasticity of storage/ processing capacity as required by fluctuation in demand	Reduced control over data and applications
Greater flexibility and mobility of access to data and services	Data security and privacy concerns
Immediate and cost-free upgrading of software	Unreliable services, e.g. due to inadequate ICT or power infrastructure
Enhanced reliability/security of data and services	Risk of vendor lock-in (limited interoperability and data portability) with providers in uncompetitive cloud markets

Source: UNCTAD.

- Whether to opt for a public, private, community or hybrid cloud solution
- Whether to opt for a national, regional or global cloud solution
- What activities and data to migrate (taking data protection and privacy concerns into account)
- What changes are required within the organization and what business processes need to be re-engineered in order to benefit fully from migration
- How the need for IT, procurement and organizational skills may be affected
- Possible legal implications of choosing different types of cloud provisioning.

The efficiency-enhancing potential of cloud computing is a strong incentive for organizations in the private and public sectors to move increasingly to the cloud. However, there are important trade-offs to be made, for example, between cost savings on the one hand and considerations related to data protection and privacy on the other. Different cloud customers will assess the opportunities and risks associated with the cloud differently, therefore opting for different solutions. As noted in chapter III, there are visible differences between cloud adoption strategies even among large enterprises in the United States and in continental Europe, respectively, reflecting different preferences and risk assessments. Similarly, the options for cloud adoption available to enterprises in low-income countries look very different from those in developed countries. The future shape of the cloud economy at the global level, as well as its regional and national configurations, will also be influenced by government policies.

B. RECOMMENDATIONS TO GOVERNMENTS

There is good reason for Governments to take a proactive role in the development of the cloud economy ecosystem. Although there is, as yet, no statistical analysis of the relationship between the cloud economy and economic growth, it seems likely that by generating cost savings, leveraging new opportunities and participating in learning processes, enterprises that are early adopters of cloud computing can gain a competitive advantage.

There is no case for government policy and regulation to generally discourage migration towards the cloud. Policies and regulatory approaches should seek to create an enabling framework that supports firms

and organizations that wish to migrate data and services to the cloud in doing so easily and safely and that enables the introduction of new cloud services at the national level where there is the necessary infrastructure to support them. At the same time, cloud-based solutions are not always preferable to alternative approaches, and there are multiple ways of using cloud technology. Governments should focus on those which seem most likely to deliver wider economic benefits to their countries.

The remainder of this section offers a number of policy recommendations that can be used as a foundation for Governments in developing countries and for development partners that wish to translate the potential of the cloud into tangible development gains. These recommendations relate to both the demand and the supply sides of the cloud economy ecosystem.

1. Designing strategic policy approaches to the cloud

Government policies towards the cloud need to be rooted in a thorough understanding of existing ICT and cloud use within countries. This requires research and analysis. Policies should recognize the diversity of business models and services within the cloud, the diversity of customers of cloud services and the complexity of the cloud economy ecosystem described in this report (chapter I). These various understandings need to be brought together to tailor policy approaches to the particular circumstances of individual countries and economies, consistent with each country's overall strategic framework for national economic development and for the use of ICTs in development.

(a) Assess the cloud readiness of the country

There is no one-size-fits-all strategy that Governments can apply to benefit from the cloud. Governments should therefore start by carefully assessing the current situation in their countries, to identify how best to make countries "ready" to leverage the opportunities offered by the cloud and to address concerns associated with increased cloud adoption. This report has pointed to a number of tools that can be used in this context (chapter II). Moreover, it may be useful to establish a national task group with representatives of different stakeholder communities (including relevant government ministries/agencies, private sector businesses on supply and demand sides of the cloud economy, civil society and other stakeholders). The assessment undertaken by this task group should help to identify bottlenecks and weaknesses that need to be addressed if the cloud is to be effectively exploited and clarify what kind of cloud solutions are most propitious.[1]

Reliable evidence about a country's cloud readiness and economy should be collected as a critical starting point in assessing policy objectives. In most developing countries, there is as yet little reliable quantitative information about the extent of cloud adoption or about business attitudes towards the cloud. Empirical evidence, including data from studies of both perceptions and practice on the demand side of the cloud, can help policymakers better understand the needs of different categories of cloud service customers. A baseline of knowledge derived from such sources will give both government departments and local enterprises a better platform on which to take decisions about what is feasible within specific contexts.

(b) Develop a national cloud strategy

Based on the assessment described above, a national cloud strategy could be drafted. This could either be a stand-alone policy document or an integral part of the national ICT strategy. In either case it is crucial that the cloud strategy be consistent with the ICT strategy and that appropriate synergies be drawn. It should also be linked to a national broadband strategy where one has been adopted.

A separate national cloud strategy may be most appropriate in developing countries which are planning extensive government use of cloud computing, which have markets of sufficient size to support local cloud provision and/or which already have highly developed sectors engaged in the outsourcing of IT services and business processes. Elsewhere, it may be better to integrate the cloud dimension into broader ICT for development strategies, as in the case of Kenya (box V.1). Many of the measures required for a positive enabling environment for cloud computing – such as improvements in infrastructure and in legal and

---

Box V.1.   Promoting the cloud economy in Kenya

The implementation of cloud services in Kenya mirrors global trends in terms of service and deployment models, but its success is dependent on local conditions. Presently, most of the cloud services offered are data backup, archiving and disaster recovery, i.e. mainly IaaS. While Kenyan SMEs are at an incipient stage of cloud adoption, all large companies listed on the Nairobi Stock Exchange have started migrating some services to the cloud, including messaging, payroll, accounting, human resources and customer relationship management. For large companies, the main concerns with regard to cloud adoption are related to data security, privacy and service reliability. Cloud adoption by SMEs is hampered by the lack of awareness and trust, high cost of broadband services and limited access to electricity.

The Government of Kenya recognizes the potential benefit of cloud computing for the economy at large and has designed a strategy to address relevant constraints. The basis for the Government's activities in this area is the national ICT policy that was launched in 2006 and which mainstreamed ICT into governance and social and economic applications.

The cloud economy is promoted through several actions. A key policy priority is to enable a large-scale, nation-wide expansion of broadband infrastructure. The Government has invested in international submarine optical fibre projects and in a national fibre optic network. Furthermore, the Communications Commission of Kenya has promoted a competitive environment to facilitate network expansion while reducing costs and improving the quality of services. In addition, the elimination of certain taxes on ICT goods and services has led to lower prices for computers, software and cellular phones, which has helped to raise ICT use in the country.

As noted in chapter III, the Government has also established national data centres aimed at meeting the needs of the Government itself and to serve as a neutral provider of SaaS to citizens and private sector customers. To raise awareness among citizens and consumers, some e-government services have been migrated to the cloud, and the Government has become one of the most significant cloud adopters in Kenya. The next step is the adoption of data protection legislation, which is to be presented shortly to Parliament.

Source: Research ICT Africa (2013).

regulatory frameworks, and enhancements to the ICT skill base – are also relevant to the broader ICT for development agenda.

A review by the Economic and Social Commission for Asia and the Pacific of its 58 member economies in Asia and the Pacific in 2013 concluded that 14 had already adopted a specific cloud computing strategy or featured cloud computing prominently in their overall ICT for development strategies.[2] This group includes both OECD countries and LDCs. Moreover, the Broadband Commission has stated that as of mid-2013 there were 134 national broadband plans in place, though these were of varying type and quality, and there was still a need to assess to what extent they address cloud computing as such (Broadband Commission for Digital Development, 2013).[3]

Whether concerned with ICTs in general, broadband or the cloud economy in particular, such strategies should be informed by inputs from a wide variety of government departments, not just those concerned with communications. Ministries for trade and economic development are important in this context, as are those concerned with education and research. Ministries of finance need to be involved, because of the implications for taxation, job creation and economic growth, while ministries of justice need to be engaged to develop an adequate legal and regulatory system. Strategies should also be informed by close interaction with other stakeholders, for example, through the task group proposed above.

As mentioned before (chapter III), however, migration to the cloud can also have less desirable impacts. Examples may include job displacement within cloud service customer businesses and reduced demand for the services offered by local SMEs in the IT sector when users opt for global cloud providers. These potential negative aspects of the cloud economy need to be considered in a strategy alongside potential benefits.

In terms of scope, a cloud strategy should include policy measures to address at least the following main areas: infrastructure, legal and regulatory issues, the supply side of the cloud economy ecosystem, human resources, government cloud use and financial implications. It should address the role of development partners, set realistic targets and allocate responsibility for implementation and follow-up with a view to leveraging macroeconomic gains – such as improved productivity, job creation, innovation and economic

growth – from the cloud economy. These areas are discussed below.

2. Addressing the infrastructure challenge

Fulfilling the potential of the cloud depends on action to address a range of infrastructure challenges set out below.

(a) Improve the provision of reliable broadband infrastructure

Without reliable broadband networks, the cloud economy can have only a limited impact in a country. Governments in developing countries are increasingly facilitating the deployment of broadband networks, often through public–private partnerships and/or with finance derived from government revenues or loans from international financial institutions. International bandwidth has improved in most countries, especially through improved access to submarine cables, and more attention is now being devoted to national broadband networks and to regional interconnection (e.g., for landlocked countries in Africa). Making access to data and services in the cloud a seamless experience requires attention to backbone and backhaul infrastructure, and also to local access networks, both wireline (where available) and wireless (for the majority of developing country users in the short to medium term).

At the same time, cloud services do not all have the same communications needs. Some require high traffic volumes but are not time-sensitive, while others – such as more sophisticated services that may be used for customer relations management or in the financial sector – need reliable, high-quality infrastructure capable of implementing complex applications in real time. Wireless broadband access, which is the predominant form available in many developing countries, does not offer the same capabilities at present as fixed alternatives. Global and local public and private clouds are likely to have different infrastructure needs. Where international communications are unreliable or very expensive, this will favour the use of local data centres over international ones (ITU-D, 2012). However, in many developing countries, local data centres and cloud providers are absent. As one entrepreneur described the situation in Kenya:[4]

For now we have to make do with international hosts... Their products are miles ahead in terms of offerings and they are at the bleeding edge of innovation, set on making those offerings even better. Their prices are pretty reasonable... There's just one problem. They are continents away! They do not have data centres anywhere near here. When I host my service with them, any new data has to travel across oceans to get to my user. The undersea fibre-optic cables suffer cuts every so often and those of us who rely on their data capacity are routinely left waiting for days till things return to normal. This is no life for web-based innovation – which whether or not we like it is something we will need to make everything else thrive. The sooner we acknowledge this as an industry, the better off we will all be. We need to invest in support structures for the ecosystem we keep talking about.

(b) Pay attention to quality

Cloud applications put higher demands on the quality of service of broadband networks than many other forms of ICT use. In addition to download speeds, the user experience is greatly affected by upload speeds and latency. Low levels of latency are particularly important where a service has to be provided in real time. Network redundancy is also crucial to ensure that access to data and services is not disabled by natural disaster, accident, equipment failure or criminal activity. As noted in chapter II, many developing countries currently suffer from inadequate quality of service in their networks, with high latency and poor upload speeds representing critical bottlenecks.

In order to be able to make informed decisions, Governments should improve the measurement of quality of service of broadband networks. Such measurement is in the interests of all stakeholders. Regulators mandated to act in the interest of consumers need information in order to set standards, define policies and resolve disputes based on evidence. Regulated businesses need information on their performance, not least in comparison

with other operators, in order to maximize revenue. Consumers need data to make informed decisions when selecting service providers and broadband plans, as well as for lodging complaints (Epitiro, 2011). In this context, several approaches can be considered to ensure the most accurate data (box V.2).

(c) Make connectivity more affordable

Connectivity needs to be competitively priced to avoid having the cost advantages from holding data and using applications in multi-tenancy data centres be cancelled out by high communication costs. While the costs of broadband communications in developed countries are now relatively low, this is not the case in many developing countries (chapter II). In order to address the affordability challenge, attention needs to be given to the roles of network operators, Internet exchange points and related regulation.[5]

(d) Implement effective communications regulations

The infrastructure improvements referred to above are fundamental requirements for the effective use of all ICTs in developing country contexts, not only cloud computing. They also need to be accompanied by competent, effective and independent regulation of the telecommunications markets that underpin them. This includes liberalization of markets and regulatory intervention to promote competition. Competitive and interoperable ICT markets, facilitated by independent regulators, should deliver services that are higher quality, more reliable and affordable. As broadband usage grows in developing country markets dependent on wireless networks, policymakers and regulators also need to make radio spectrum available to communications operators to ensure that cloud services can be reliably accessed through the wireless networks which are currently the norm for local access in developing country markets.

Box V.2.   Approaches to measuring the quality of broadband services

There are advantages and disadvantages to the measurement of quality of service being conducted by different stakeholders (Wattegama and Kapugama, 2009).

- **Independent consumer measurements** typically lack uniformity in the methodology adopted, making comparability and representativeness a challenge. A number of factors (e.g. operating systems, browsers and virus-infected machines) can reduce the accuracy of the results. Nonetheless, consumer-based initiatives are valuable for holding networks operators accountable.

- **Network operators** usually produce diagnostics for internal quality monitoring purposes. However, they often consider those network segments with the best connectivity rather than the average performance of the network.[a] Diagnostic results may therefore differ from what consumers actually experience.

Box V.2.   Approaches to measuring the quality of broadband services *(continued)*

- A number of **national regulatory authorities** measure broadband performance. In addition to securing the necessary resources, the challenges for them include the adoption of a sound methodology and ways of presenting data transparently, in a manner that can be easily understood by the general public.

Several approaches are currently used to measure broadband quality. "SamKnows" (http://www.samknows. com) is a hardware-based approach that has been adopted, for example, by the United Kingdom, the European Commission, the United States and Singapore. In this case, a box directly linked to the consumer's network utilizes network idle time to run a series of tests. Although it is less intrusive on the network and offers high levels of accuracy, this method may be too expensive for widespread adoption. Some regulatory authorities carry out software-based tests, while others set guidelines and request operators to report results periodically, with possible financial penalties for non-compliance. Examples of software include Ookla, Speed Test, AT Tester and in-house solutions.

Irrespective of the approach taken, certain principles should be considered.

- **Scope of measurement**. The approach should be able to test multiple metrics. Download speeds, upload speeds and latency are particularly relevant for cloud services.

- **Time dependent variance**. Tests should be run over a period of time, on multiple days (both weekdays and weekends) and at multiple time slots each day.

- **File size**. When testing download and upload speeds, the file should ideally consume the whole bandwidth to increase the accuracy of measurement.

- **User willingness to engage in tests**. Desktop applications that run speed tests offer high levels of accuracy. However, users may see downloading a test application as a potential security threat and the uptake of such applications may be reduced.

- **Network features**. Quality of service experience is among other things a function of the physical medium used in the access network (e.g., copper, fibre) and the distance from the exchange/base transceiver station. In the case of wireless networks, the number of users of a base transceiver station also varies. Therefore, a country's broadband performance derived from results received in only one location can be misleading as an indicator of quality at the country level. For transparency reasons, it may be better to report results for a city or locality rather than the whole country.

In South Asia, a testing methodology designed by LIRNEasia and the Indian Institute of Technology (Madras) has been applied to measure broadband quality of service. The software measures quality along various dimensions (download and upload speeds, RTT, jitter, packet loss and availability) at six time slots a day, on multiple days per week including weekends (Galpaya and Zuhyle, 2011). It can carry out the tests in different domains – within the ISP network, nationally (within the country but through a server located on the network of a different ISP) and internationally. This distinction can help detect problematic segments of the network.

At a meeting in 2012, the ITU Expert Group on Telecommunication/ICT Indicators[b] agreed on two indicators on fixed broadband quality of service (service activation time and complaints per 100 fixed (wired)-broadband subscriptions) and one on mobile broadband QoS (complaints per 100 mobile broadband subscriptions). These three indicators will be included in the statistical data collection of the ITU. The indicator on data transmission speed achieved should be collected at the national level (upload and download speed), for both fixed and mobile broadband. Other indicators, such as on jitter, throughput, packet loss and latency, should be collected at the national level using a representative sample and a verified methodology, as that developed by LIRNEasia.

Source: UNCTAD.

[a] The access network is only a part of the entire end-to-end connection. While easy to measure, good QoS in the access network does not necessarily imply good QoS experience for the end user.

[b] The ITU Expert Group on Telecommunication/ICT Indicators is open to all ITU members and experts in the field of ICT statistics and data collection (see http://www.itu.int/en/ITU-D/Statistics/Pages/definitions/ default.aspx; accessed 14 October 2013).

(e) Promote the establishment of Internet exchange points

IXPs should also be established to reduce the cost of Internet access and bring down latency. There are different kinds of IXPs (chapter II). Rather than prescribing the model to apply, public policy may focus on supporting an environment of fair competition and establishing a licensing structure that can enable IXPs to succeed (Ryan and Gerson, 2012). A key challenge is to ensure effective cooperation with the ISPs in each market. As was noted in chapter II, there is a particular need for more IXPs in Africa. The African Union has obtained financial support to help remedy this situation (box V.3).

(f) Ensure access to reliable power

The power infrastructure is another critical bottleneck to cloud adoption in many countries. Regular power outages which disrupt communications between cloud customers and providers – as well as between different cloud service providers – are a serious problem. Power outages are common in developing countries, and smaller countries are often dependent on their neighbours for a substantial part of their power supply. For countries aspiring to host international data centres, which consume considerable amounts of electricity, access to a reliable power supply is even more essential (see below).

3. Strengthening the legal framework

A national cloud strategy needs to address a number of legal and regulatory issues related to cloud adoption, ensuring that the interests of cloud service users are properly protected. Concerns over data protection and security are among the most frequently mentioned. Most developing countries still lack much of the legislation required to address such concerns. While there is not necessarily a need to develop laws or regulations which are specific to cloud computing, legal reforms are clearly required in areas including privacy, data protection, information security and cybercrime. It is essential that Governments of developing countries adopt and enforce appropriate laws and regulations in these areas. Putting such legislation in place will give local businesses, including local entrepreneurs, new opportunities to innovate in services and applications, seeking to address export as well as domestic markets. While public law is essential to secure the basic rights of end users, private law contractual agreements between cloud service providers and cloud service customers also directly impact on the operation of the cloud economy. Governments may wish to consider the following recommendations in this context.

(a) Assess the adequacy of current legislation

An important starting point is to review current legislation to see if it adequately addresses relevant areas for cloud adoption and to begin to consider ways of further improving the legal framework. This is one area in which international organizations, including UNCTAD, can offer assistance.

(b) Clarify situation concerning the location of data

Many Governments and other cloud service customers have serious concerns about data security. These are most pronounced when data are kept on servers located in other jurisdictions. In particular, there are concerns that holding national data overseas may make them more accessible to third parties (including the Governments of other countries). At the same time, it is important that regulations do not restrict the ability to take advantage of cost savings where there are not, in practice, real security threats. Assessing this balance is challenging, and there are no simple solutions. As part of their response, Governments

---

Box V.3.   The African Internet Exchange System Project

The African Union Commission signed an agreement in 2012 with the Luxembourg Development Cooperation to support the implementation of the African Internet Exchange System project funded by the European Union–Africa Infrastructure Trust Fund and the Government of Luxembourg. This project seeks to secure the establishment of IXPs in Member States of the African Union. The project also seeks to make real-time and historical traffic data accessible via web-based visualization system and to develop a certificate curriculum on Internet exchange technologies. A first steering committee meeting was held in May 2012. Capacity-building and technical assistance to support establishment of regional Internet exchange points was to begin in 2013.

Source: African Union. Available at http://pages.au.int/axis/about (accessed 14 October 2013).

may consider the value of data centres situated locally, including the potential of these centres to interact with private-sector cloud providers in hybrid (public/private, local/global) clouds. Such ideas are being explored in both developed and developing countries. In Europe, for example, there have been calls from the highest political level for the development of a secure European cloud,[6] and the Government of France has launched a sovereign cloud project to offer an alternative source of cloud provision to French and other European enterprises.[7]

(c) Facilitate electronic transactions and payments

The business model based on "pay as you go" that is often applied to monetize many cloud services requires a legal and regulatory framework which accommodates electronic transactions and payments. The ability to make secure micropayments is an essential part of many services offered over the cloud, including those that could provide new business opportunities for SMEs in developing countries.

(d) Address the cybersecurity challenge

Growing use of the cloud is driving the demand for adequate security solutions. The concentration of data in a few locations represents an attractive target for cybercriminals. In addition, the interaction of different laws and regulatory schemes in various jurisdictions increases the complexity of data security in the cloud. All relevant stakeholders need to take action to limit the vulnerabilities of their systems. Governments need to design cybercrime and data protection laws and regulations that take cloud vulnerabilities adequately into consideration (chapter IV). Cloud providers need to implement robust security enforcement tools. End users also have a responsibility to be prudent when making use of cloud services (and the Internet more generally).[8] Countries should also continue moving towards the establishment of CERTs to handle security incidents and risks and to ensure that the responsible authorities are notified of security breaches.

(e) Take international legal frameworks into account

Aligning relevant national laws with international legal instruments and models is highly recommended to achieve an internationally harmonized set of laws and regulations (chapter IV). Governments should monitor regulatory developments in the field of cloud computing to be able to adjust as appropriate to changes in markets and technologies. In view of the limited resources available to many Governments of developing countries, there is a potential role here for regional economic communities to advise Governments, possibly with financial support from international development partners.

4. Map opportunities on the supply side

A national cloud strategy should not only consider the implications for potential cloud customers in the public and private sectors. Three areas of supply-side opportunity in particular were highlighted in chapter III: the development of national data centres and related cloud provision, the potential for cloud aggregation and the scope for new cloud services to be developed for both domestic and export markets.

(a) Explore the market for national data centres and cloud provision

The market for cloud provision, at a global level, is currently dominated by a small number of very large corporations which are predominantly headquartered in the United States (chapter II). Moreover, it has been estimated that as much as 85 per cent of data centres offering co-location services are in developed economies (chapter II). For many Governments and businesses in developing countries, this raises questions about the security and control of their data and of critical applications. It also raises questions concerning the dependence of developing countries on developed countries to manage data resources that are critical to their social and economic development, something which can be considered a new dimension of the digital divide.

Global cloud providers, notably in the United States, have the advantages of being first movers and having achieved economies of scale. Whereas these same advantages can represent formidable entry barriers for new competitors, there are opportunities for local IT companies in the cloud economy in developing countries, either independently or in collaboration with international cloud service providers. Some of these arise from a desire of cloud customers to exercise greater control over their data and applications. As noted above, the high cost of international communications may also favour local data centre provision.

Several developing countries are actively promoting the development of national data centres, either by companies in the ICT sector or by the Government itself (chapter III). Data centres which offer commercial storage and application may be oriented purely towards domestic markets and/or towards export markets. National data centre markets are most likely to arise in developing countries with large domestic markets such as Brazil, China, India, Nigeria and South Africa. Governments that wish to foster the development of data centre markets oriented towards exports need to pay particular attention to the adequacy of power and communications infrastructure, cybersecurity arrangements and the cost of international bandwidth.

(b) Consider the inclusion of cloud-related activities in foreign direct investment promotion strategies

In countries that offer the right conditions for cloud services, it may be appropriate to include cloud-related activities as a new focus in national strategies for the attraction of foreign direct investment. Several developed countries are actively promoting themselves as strategic locations for the establishment of international data centres. Some developing countries may offer attractive conditions in this area. Foreign cloud providers may also be interested in supporting the development of domestic capacity to store and process data.

(c) Explore the market for the aggregation and brokerage of cloud services

Cloud service customers often need to rely on several different cloud providers to meet their varying needs. A market has emerged for cloud aggregators packaging services from different providers on behalf of customers and brokers providing advice and guidance on the best cloud options for different businesses. This activity offers opportunities for IT companies in developing countries with local expertise. Policymakers can engage in dialogue with the local industry on the main areas of opportunity as well as current bottlenecks.

(d) Support the development of cloud applications for local needs

A growing number of IT companies are developing and deploying cloud services targeted at national or regional communities or at niche groups within them. In low-income countries at a nascent stage of cloud readiness, IaaS is likely to be the first category of cloud services to be demanded. As the infrastructure

situation improves in low-income countries and in countries with an expanding SME market with more purchasing power, the market for SaaS will become more important and eventually dominant as it is today in developed countries. Cloud services cover a wide range of activities, from the distribution of retail goods to providing access to major content libraries. Opportunities for local offerings may be particularly relevant in countries where international connectivity is expensive and latency is high.

5. The human resource challenge

Many of the underlying factors that influence propensity to benefit from the cloud economy apply not just to cloud services but to the ICT sector as a whole. This is clearly the case for the national skill base, particularly for the ICT sector itself.

The relationship between education/human resource development, enterprise and the ICT sector was discussed in the *Information Economy Report 2010* (UNCTAD, 2010). Many developing countries have struggled to incorporate IT skills development within their school and education systems, not least because of the shortage of IT-skilled teachers. Meanwhile, without adequate skills on both the supply and user side of the cloud economy, it is difficult to achieve proper integration of new cloud applications. It is therefore important for Governments, together with the private sector and academia, to consider how skill shortages within the ICT sector and elsewhere may affect their capacity to take advantage of cloud computing, and what priority interventions they should make in order to address these shortfalls.

A national strategy could map skill requirements. Likely areas to consider include:
- IT and software skills, for managing the migration and integration
- Management and organizational skills, for addressing the need for reorganization and re-engineering of business processes
- Legal and procurement skills, to ensure that contracts with providers or cloud services respond well to the needs of the user.

Government and the private sector should work together to address these human resource challenges, from the revision of curricula at different stages in the education system, to in-work training and the development of specialized professional skills. Among the many challenges involved, developing countries face significant loss of skilled IT personnel through migration to more lucrative job markets in developed countries. A continual flow of IT-skilled recruits into employment is therefore required. The most successful countries in leveraging the potential of the cloud in the longer term may be those that are able to build up a significant group of skilled IT entrepreneurs with the capability of developing innovative cloud-based businesses.

6. Government use of the cloud

One way in which government action can affect the development of the cloud economy is through its own cloud use for administration and for the provision of public services. Governments are among the most important – in smaller developing countries often the largest – purchasers of IT equipment and services. Computer equipment and software licences represent significant expenditure for Governments, and the possible cost savings are important drivers for government cloud adoption. Government policies vis-à-vis cloud adoption are hence important.

(a) Consider the role of the Government in the establishment of national data centres

Governments in developing countries should consider investing directly in data centre capacity, taking into account the experience of other countries.

(b) Improve e-government services through government cloud use

There are many instances in which individual government services are being provided through, or supported by, the cloud. In education, cloud services can make available larger libraries of content. They can also support the delivery of mass-market services that rely on personal data, such as health, tax and benefit/welfare systems. Similarly, processes such as business registration, customs administration and the payment of taxes and licence fees can be facilitated through online provision or through the cloud. Some Governments have adopted a "cloud first" approach (e.g., the Republic of Moldova and the United States), requiring government agencies to consider cloud provisioning before more conventional alternatives.

Although some cloud-related initiatives form part of comprehensive government strategies, in many countries, decisions to introduce particular cloud services are being taken on an ad hoc basis by individual government departments. One consequence is that cloud provisioning can become unsystematic, risking limited interoperability between systems that deal with the same citizens and losing some of the economies of scope and scale that might otherwise have been realized.

(c) Use public procurement as a tool to support local IT sector development

There is a strong case for more coordination in government procurement of cloud services (as indeed there is for other IT services).[9] In this context, Governments can seek to ensure that their procurement practices are conducive to greater involvement of domestic suppliers, especially SMEs. This involves attention to transparency, openness and clarity of specifications. There are also various ways in which the structuring of the procurement process can be adapted to fit the skills and capabilities of software SMEs. At the same time, local IT firms will only be able to compete effectively if they have the necessary skills and capabilities. Thus, it is important to connect the public procurement strategy with efforts aimed at strengthening the capabilities of the local IT industry (UNCTAD and Germany, Federal Ministry for Economic Cooperation and Development, 2013; UNCTAD, 2012a).

7. Implementation and follow-up of the strategy

Given the cross-cutting and multipurpose nature of ICTs and cloud computing, with consequences for both public service delivery and business competitiveness, it is important to integrate any cloud strategy into the overall national development plan. Moreover, a detailed approach should be crafted for strategy execution, monitoring and evaluation.[10] To allow for effective follow-up, realistic and measurable goals in each area should be set for use when assessing performance. The choice of indicators should reflect discussions with relevant stakeholders to ensure that targets are shared across society.

8. Raising awareness

Once a strategy has been formulated in collaboration with relevant stakeholders, it is important to raise awareness concerning its content. There is still much confusion and uncertainty about the meaning and implications of the cloud economy. This extends to government officials and business leaders and affects important issues in determining the potential for cloud computing.

Efforts to demystify the cloud, in order to build awareness of its potential and limitations for businesses and national economies, should be made by Governments and business associations alike. Regulators can assist by issuing guidance on the applicability to cloud solutions of the regimes for which they are responsible. Governments may need to build capacity in various departments to ensure enactment and enforcement of laws and regulations and to promote awareness in government institutions and public administrations of their implications. Awareness-raising activities should seek to help potential users (including SMEs) better understand the potential gains from using cloud-based solutions as well as the potential costs and risks associated with such migration. There may, for example, be a need to educate users on available approaches to protect data that are transmitted to and stored in the cloud (e.g., through encryption techniques), contracting with cloud providers and government policies vis-à-vis the cloud.

C. RECOMMENDATIONS TO DEVELOPMENT PARTNERS

The differential between developed and developing countries in access to and use of ICTs – the digital divide – has been a significant concern of Governments and international development agencies since "The missing link" (ITU, 1985), known as the Maitland Report, was published by the ITU almost 30 years ago. Since that time, the nature of the digital divide has changed. The gap in access to basic telephone services, which was once very substantial, is now greatly diminished and expected almost to disappear in the next few years. In its place has come a gap in access to the Internet and particularly in access to broadband services, i.e. to services which have the capacity to deliver a full Internet experience and enable access to the full range of data communications opportunities which can now be made available. A digital divide in broadband capacity and quality leads in turn to a divide between countries in the extent to which they and businesses located in them are able to take advantage of ICT innovations.

Many developing countries face considerable challenges in seeking to benefit fully from the evolving cloud economy. Addressing these challenges will require both expertise in various fields and substantial financial resources. In order to reduce the risk that the move towards the cloud economy at the global level results in a further widening of the digital divide,

development partners should ensure that cloud-related development challenges are included on their agendas, particularly where low-income countries and those with limited IT-management capacity are concerned. Development partners may explore the need for bilateral support in specific areas in different countries. In addition, there are several horizontal issues for which support from bilateral and multilateral donors will be needed.

At a country level, assistance may be relevant in some or all of the following areas:

- **Empirical analysis and research** is needed to map the current state of the cloud economy, assess potential implications of greater cloud adoption and make policy recommendations. As the evidence base expands, it will be possible to make better assessments of the implications of the cloud economy for economic growth, employment, productivity and trade. Special attention may also be given to the link between cloud computing and climate change, taking into account the intensive use of energy by huge data centres.

- **Financing of broadband infrastructure**, including public–private partnerships. Different infrastructure layers need to be addressed separately from a policy and financing perspective, rather than using a one-size-fits-all approach (Broadband Commission for Digital Development, 2012). Adequate attention should also be given to power infrastructure, whose deficiencies undermine the capabilities of communications networks.

- **Support for the establishment of appropriate legal and regulatory frameworks**. Many developing countries still lack appropriate legislation and ancillary institutions for electronic commerce, data protection and cybersecurity. Development partners can support Governments of developing country in transposing existing legislative models into national legal and regulatory frameworks.

- **Capacity-building activities**. Development partners can provide support through technical training in the deployment, procurement and integration of cloud services as well as by advising on law reforms and undertaking policy reviews.[11]

International agencies could facilitate this assistance through some of their existing activities. For example, the ITU, UNCTAD and United Nations regional commissions could facilitate an exchange of experiences with regard to the policy challenges that developing countries face in deriving benefits from the cloud economy and avoiding pitfalls. This could be based on evidence-gathering from Governments, cloud providers and cloud customers in developing countries, with the aim of building a nuanced analytical framework to help policymakers in government and business address the challenges and seize the opportunities of the cloud economy as it develops.

Another area of significance for developing countries concerns international standards for cloud services, which are essential to facilitate interoperability and to help customers understand what they are purchasing. The number of interfaces presently used by cloud service providers can make it difficult for customers to move from one system to another. The various standard-setting activities that are currently undertaken in this area (Sakai, 2011) are overwhelmingly in and by developed countries, whose interests in cloud services may differ from those of developing countries. Standardization forums should consider how to engage developing countries and their users in standard-setting activities so as to ensure that their specific needs and requirements are addressed.

This report has summarized the experience to date with the cloud economy in developing countries and raised a number of issues which need to be addressed by Governments and businesses. The cloud economy is, however, a recent phenomenon, and the evidence base available for analyses of the kind in this report is still limited. It is important to build a stronger evidence base for decision-makers that relies more on empirical evidence and independent analysis than on marketing and other advocacy literature. More research is needed in a number of areas, including:

- **The extent of cloud adoption in developing countries**. In addition to national reviews required for national policymaking purposes, developing countries would benefit from a systematic and comprehensive overview of the extent and manner in which cloud services are being adopted in the developing world as a whole and perceptions of the cloud by developing country businesses. National case studies in countries with diverse experience would also be valuable.

- **The macroeconomic implications of cloud computing**. Currently, the evidence base does not allow for empirical assessments of the cloud's impact on various macroeconomic variables.

It is important to deepen the analysis to better understand the implications for countries at different levels of development and for the global economy as a whole.

- **Implications for data security and privacy**. Research into perceptions of cloud security and data protection in determining attitudes towards the cloud would be valuable in understanding how related concerns affect cloud adoption. Research might include assessment of the potential for moving towards a common global approach to data protection, rather than the diverse approaches currently found in different jurisdictions (see chapter IV).

- **Competition in the cloud provider market**. Research into the extent to which cloud markets are currently competitive and the potential impact on competitiveness, and viability, of new cloud businesses based in developing countries would be valuable.

- **The impact of the cloud on taxation**. Many cloud services, including mass market services, depend on cross-border connectivity and transactions. Some displace markets for physical goods or services traded in more conventional ways in either domestic or export markets. The impact of this changing business model on taxation could be significant. Research into the cloud's impact on tax revenue and into appropriate means of avoiding double taxation when cloud services are supplied across borders would be valuable.

- **The impact of the cloud on trade in services, particularly IT-enabled services**. Research into the impact of the cloud on trade in services would be valuable to Governments concerned about maximizing export potential and would indicate where domestic sectors may be vulnerable to service competition from developed countries. Research into the impact of the cloud on IT-enabled services, such as BPO, and into its impact on intraregional trade would be particularly valuable.

- **The scope for South–South collaboration**. The ICT sector has seen significant South–South collaboration, including public–private partnerships in infrastructure investment and the growth in South-based TNCs providing communications services. Research would be valuable into the experience and particularly the potential of South–South collaboration in the cloud, especially at the regional level.

As with other ICT areas, the pace of change in cloud technology and markets is rapid. The experiences described in this report relate to present circumstances. The nature of cloud services and of the cloud economy will continue to develop quickly and may be very different in five years' time. Governments, businesses and development partners need to bear these changes in mind and re-evaluate their policies and strategies concerning the cloud regularly in order to ensure that they continue to maximize potential benefits and minimize potential risks to their citizens, businesses and customers.

NOTES

1   In India, for example, the Government has established an Empowered Committee with representatives from different government departments, and a special task force with private sector participation, to develop a strategy towards the development of a government cloud (box III.6).

2   Australia, Bangladesh, Bhutan, China, India, Japan, Kazakhstan, Malaysia, New Zealand, the Philippines, the Republic of Korea, Singapore, Sri Lanka and Thailand (Economic and Social Commission for Asia and the Pacific, 2013).

3   The Broadband Commission was established in May 2010 to boost the importance of broadband on the international policy agenda. It is co-chaired by President Paul Kagame of Rwanda and Mr. Carlos Slim Hélu, Honorary Lifetime Chair of Grupo Carso. Mr. Hamadoun Touré, Secretary-General of ITU, and Ms. Irina Bokova, Director-General of the United Nations Educational, Scientific and Cultural Organization (UNESCO), serve as joint Vice-Chairs. See http://www.broadbandcommission.org.

4   Hapa Kenya (2013). Why Kenyan telcos need to start thinking like web companies. Available at http://www.hapakenya.com/why-kenyan-telcos-need-to-start-thinking-like-web-companies/ (accessed 10 October 2013).

5   See, for example, http://broadbandtoolkit.org/en/home and http://www.broadbandcommission.org/work/documents.aspx.

6   Charlemagne (2013). Reaching for the clouds. The Economist. 20 July.

7   See, for example, Reuters (2013), Analysis: European cloud computing firms see silver lining in PRISM scandal, 17 June. Available at http://www.reuters.com/article/2013/06/17/us-cloud-europe-spying-analysis-idUSBRE95G0FK20130617 (accessed 11 October 2013).

8   For links to more information on the adoption of regionally and internationally harmonized, appropriate legislation against the misuse of ICTs for criminal or other purposes, see, for example, http://www.itu.int/en/ITU-D/Cybersecurity/Pages/Legal-Measures.aspx.

9   The Info-Communications Development Authority of Singapore facilitates public sector procurement of public cloud services through several "bulk tenders" (Singapore, Info-Communications Development Authority, 2013). In India, the roadmap to the GI Cloud highlights the importance of procurement and recognizes the importance of adjusting current practices (India, Department of Electronics and Information Technology, 2013; p. 36).

10 A useful tool for governments to consider in this context are the IT sector manual and toolbox developed by the Federal Ministry for Economic Cooperation and Development of Germany (Germany, Federal Ministry for Economic Cooperation and Development, 2011).

11 An assessment of cloud computing in Africa identified training needs in several areas, including understanding cloud computing, technical considerations, data centres, broadband connectivity and QoS (ITU-D, 2012).

REFERENCES

Aberdeen Group (2008). Application performance management: The lifecycle approach brings IT and business together. Aberdeen Group. June. Available at http://www.riverbed.com/docs/WhitePaper-Riverbed-ApplicationPerformanceManagement_LifeCycle.pdf (accessed 11 October 2013).

Adam L, Souter D, Jagun A and Tusubira FF (2011). Transformation-ready: The strategic application of information and communication technologies in Africa. ict Development Associates Ltd.. Report prepared for the African Development Bank, the World Bank and the African Union. Available at http://siteresources.worldbank.org/EXTINFORMATIONANDCOMMUNICATIONANDTECHNOLOGIES/Resources/282822-1346223280837/RegionalTradeandIntegration_Fullreport.pdf (accessed 9 October 2013).

Armbrust M, Fox A, Griffith R, Joseph AD, Katz RH, Konwinski A, Lee G, Patterson DA, Rabkin A, Stoica I and Zaharia M (2009). Above the clouds: A Berkeley view of cloud computing. No. UCB/EECS-2009-28. Electrical Engineering and Computer Sciences University of California at Berkeley. Berkeley. Available at http://www.softwareresearch.net/fileadmin/src/docs/teaching/SS09/VS/Above_the_Clouds.pdf (accessed 1 October 2013).

Asia Cloud Computing Association (2012). Cloud Readiness Index 2012. Available at http://www.asiacloud.org/index.php/2012-07-17-08-34-39/2012-11-12-10-08-55/index-2012 (accessed 11 October 2013).

Berry R and Reisman M (2012). Policy challenges of cross-border cloud computing. *Journal of International Commerce and Economics*. May.

Bradshaw S, Millard C and Walden I (2011). Contracts for clouds: A comparative analysis of terms and conditions for cloud computing services. *International Journal of Law and Information Technology*. 19(3): 187–223.

Bigo D, Boulet G, Bowden C, Carrera S, Jeandesboz J and Scherrer A (2012). Fighting cyber crime and protecting privacy in the cloud. Directorate General for Internal Policies. Policy Department C: Citizens' Rights and Constitutional Affairs. Study commissioned by the European Parliament's Committee on Civil Liberties, Justice and Home Affairs. Available at http://www.europarl.europa.eu/studies (accessed 25 October 2013).

Broadband Commission for Digital Development (2011). *Broadband: A Platform for Progress*. ITU and UNESCO. Geneva and Paris. Available at http://www.broadbandcommission.org/Reports/Report_2.pdf (accessed 11 October 2013).

Broadband Commission for Digital Development (2012). *The State of Broadband 2012: Achieving Digital Inclusion for All*. ITU and UNESCO. Geneva and Paris.

Broadband Commission for Digital Development (2013). *Planning for Progress: Why National Broadband Plans Matter*. ITU and UNESCO. Geneva and Paris.

Business Software Alliance and Galexia (2012). *BSA Global Cloud Computing Scorecard: A Blueprint for Economic Opportunity*. Washington D.C.. Available at http://cloudscorecard.bsa.org/2012/assets/PDFs/BSA_GlobalCloudScorecard.pdf (accessed 16 October 2013).

Cairncross F (1997). *The Death of Distance: How the Communications Revolution Will Change Our Lives*. Harvard Business Review Press. Boston.

Capgemini (2012). Trends in cloud computing: Secure journey to the cloud – a matter of control. Available at http://www.capgemini.com/resources/trends-in-cloud-computing-secure-journey-to-the-cloud--a-matter-of-control (accessed 2 October 2013).

Castro D (2013). How much will PRISM cost the U.S. cloud computing industry? The Information Technology and Innovation Foundation. Washington D.C..

CIO (2012). Strategy guide: Data sovereignty and security. Available at http://www.cio.com.au/whitepaper/371067/strategy-guide-data-sovereignty-and-security/download/?type=other&arg=0&location=tag_detail_page (accessed 21 October 2013).

Cisco Analysis (2012). Cisco Global Cloud Index: Forecast and Methodology, 2011–2016. Cisco. Available at http://www.cisco.com/en/US/solutions/collateral/ns341/ns525/ns537/ns705/ns1175/Cloud_Index_White_Paper.pdf (accessed 2 August 2013).

Council of Europe (1981). Convention for the Protection of Individuals with regard to Automatic Processing of Personal Data. http://www.conventions.coe.int/Treaty/en/Treaties/Html/108.htm (accessed 21 October 2013).

Cowhey P and Kleeman M (2012). Unlocking the benefits of cloud computing for emerging economies – a policy overview. Univesity of California, San Diego.

Crémer J, Gassot Y, Lanvin B and Pupillo LM, eds. (2012). Introduction. Communications & Strategies. 85 (1st Quarter): 13–21.

Dynamic Markets Ltd. (2013). *Cloud for business managers: the good, the bad and the ugly*. Commissioned by Oracle. Dynamic Markets Ltd.. Abergavenny, United Kingdom. Available at https://emeapressoffice.oracle.com/imagelibrary/downloadmedia.ashx?MediaDetailsID=2905&SizeId=-1 (accessed 10 October 2013).

Economic and Social Commission for Asia and the Pacific (2013). A review of cloud adoption by Asia–Pacific Governments. United Nations. Unpublished.

Epitiro (2011). Regulatory challenges for measuring national broadband performance. Epitiro. Cardiff, United Kingdom. Available at http://www.epitiro.com/assets/files/20-102-1008.001%20Challengers%20for%20Regulators.pdf (accessed 7 November 2013).

Ernst and Young (2010). Cloud adoption in India. Available at http://twelvedot.com/blog/wp-content/uploads/2011/07/Cloud_computing_adoption_in_India.pdf (accessed 2 October 2013).

European Commission (2012). Unleashing the potential of cloud computing in Europe. No. COM(2012) 529. European Commission. Luxembourg. Available at http://eur-lex.europa.eu/smartapi/cgi/sga_doc?smartapi!celexplus!prod!DocNumber&lg=EN&type_doc=COMfinal&an_doc=2012&nu_doc=529 (accessed 22 October 2013).

European Network and Information Security Agency (2012). *Procure Secure: A guide to Monitoring of Security Service Levels in Cloud Contracts*. ENISA. Heraklion, Greece. Available at http://www.enisa.europa.eu/activities/Resilience-and-CIIP/cloud-computing/procure-secure-a-guide-to-monitoring-of-security-service-levels-in-cloud-contracts (accessed 22 October 2013).

European Telecommunications Network Operators' Association (2011). ETNO reflection document replying to the public consultation on cloud computing. ETNO. Brussels. Available at http://www.etno.be/home/positions-papers/2011/32 (accessed 7 November 2013).

Galpaya H and Zuhyle S (2011). South Asian broadband service quality: Diagnosing the bottlenecks. Social Science Research Network, No. 1979244. Rochester, United States. April.

Gentzoglanis A (2012). Evolving cloud ecosystems: Risk, competition and regulation. *Communications & Strategies*. 1(85): 87–108.

Germany, Federal Ministry for Economic Cooperation and Development (2011). *IT Sector Promotion in Developing and Emerging Countries: Manual*. Deutsche Gesellschaft für Internationale Zusammenarbeit (GIZ) GmbH. Bonn and Eschborn.

Gonsalves TA and Bharadwaj A (2009). Comparison of AT-tester with other popular testers for quality of service experience (QoSE) of an Internet connection. TeNet Group, Department of Computer Science and Engineering, Indian Institute of Technology Madras.

Greenleaf G (2013). Global tables of data privacy laws and bills (third edition). University of New South Wales Law Research Paper No. 2013-39. Available at http://ssrn.com/abstract=2280875 (accessed 21 October 2013).

Hamilton P (2011). Measuring backbone transmission networks. Document C/10-E. Paper presented at the ninth World Telecommunication/ICT Indicators Meeting, Mauritius, 7 December. Available at http://www.itu.int/ITU-D/ict/wtim11/documents/cont/010-E.pdf 8 (accessed 16 October 2013).

Hilbert M and López P (2011). The world's technological capacity to store, communicate and compute information. *Science*. 332: 60–65.

HIPCAR (2012). Electronic transactions: Assessment report. ITU. Geneva.

Hon WK, Millard C and Walden I (2012). Negotiating cloud contracts: Looking at clouds from both sides now. *Stanford Technology Law Review*. 16(1): 79–128.

IDATE Foundation (2012). *Digiworld Yearbook 2012: The Challenges of the Digital World*. Idate. Montpellier, France.

IDC (2012). Quantitative estimates of the demand for cloud computing in Europe and the likely barriers to up-take. No. 2011/0045. D4 final report. Available at http://ec.europa.eu/information_society/activities/cloudcomputing/docs/quantitative_estimates.pdf (accessed 22 October 2013).

India, Department of Electronics and Information Technology, Ministry of Communications and Information Technology (2013). GI cloud (Meghraj) adoption and implementation roadmap. New Delhi.

Information Warfare Monitor and Shadowserver Foundation (2010). Shadows in the cloud: Investigating cyber espionage 2.0. Available at http://www.scribd.com/doc/29435784/SHADOWS-IN-THE-CLOUD-Investigating-Cyber-Espionage-2-0 (accessed 5 November 2013).

Intel (2011). Over 6 decades of continued transistor shrinkage, innovation. Available at http://download.intel.com/newsroom/kits/22nm/pdfs/Intel_Transistor_Backgrounder.pdf (accessed 5 November 2013).

ITU (1985). The missing link: Report of the Independent Commission for World Wide Telecommunications Development. *Telecommunication Journal*. 52(2):67–71.

ITU (2012a). Focus Group on Cloud Computing technical report part 1: Introduction to the cloud ecosystem: definitions, taxonomies, use cases and high-level requirements. ITU. Geneva.

ITU (2012b). GSR12 Best Practice Guidelines on regulatory approaches to foster access to digital opportunities through cloud services. ITU. Geneva. Available at https://www.itu.int/ITU-D/treg/Events/Seminars/GSR/GSR12/consultation/GSR12_BestPractices_v3_E.pdf (accessed 24 October 2013).

ITU-D (2012). Cloud computing in Africa: Situation and perspectives. ITU Regulatory and Market Environment Division. Geneva. April. Available at http://www.itu.int/ITU-D/treg/publications/Cloud_Computing_Afrique-e.pdf (accessed 23 October 2013).

Kang HY, Lee HH, An HS and Yang HD (2011). Cloud computing: Its implication on industries and strategic direction. No. 11-08. Korea Information Society Development Institute (DISDI). Gwacheon.

Kituku KM (2012). Adoption of cloud computing in Kenya by firms listed in the Nairobi Stock Exchange. MBA thesis. School of Business, University of Nairobi. Available at http://erepository.uonbi.ac.ke:8080/xmlui/handle/123456789/13578 (accessed 9 October 2013).

KPMG (2012). Exploring the cloud: A global study of government's adoption of cloud. Available at http://www.kpmg.com/BS/en/IssuesAndInsights/ArticlesPublications/Documents/exploring-cloud.pdf (accessed 4 October 2013).

Kshetri N (2010). Cloud computing in developing economies. *IEEE Computer*. 43(10): 47–55.

Kuner C (2013). *Transborder Data Flow Regulation and Data Privacy Law*. ISBN 9780199674619. Oxford University Press.

Kushida KE, Murray J and Zysman J (2012). The gathering storm: Analysing the cloud computing ecosystem and implications for public policy. *Communications & Strategies*. 1(85)(first quarter): 63–85.

LIRNEasia (2011). Broadband quality of services experience (QOSE) indicators. No. Q3 2011. LIRNEasia. Colombo. Available at http://lirneasia.net/wp-content/uploads/2010/10/Broadband-QoSE-report-OCT-2011_V5.pdf (accessed 16 October 2013).

Manyika J, Chui M, Bughin J, Dobbs R, Bisson P and Marrs S (2013). Disruptive technologies: Advances that will transform life, business and the global economy. McKinsey Global Institute. Available at http://www.mckinsey.com/insights/business_technology/disruptive_technologies (accessed 5 November 2013).

Microsoft (2010). The economics of the cloud. Available at http://www.microsoft.com/en-us/news/presskits/cloud/docs/the-economics-of-the-cloud.pdf (accessed 1 October 2013).

Microsoft (2012). Drivers & inhibitors to cloud adoption for small and midsize businesses. Available at http://www.microsoft.com/en-us/news/presskits/telecom/docs/SMBCloud.pdf (accessed 2 October 2013).

National Institute of Standards and Technology (2011). The NIST definition of cloud computing. Available at http://csrc.nist.gov/publications/nistpubs/800-145/SP800-145.pdf (accessed 1 October 2013).

OECD (1980). *OECD Guidelines on the Protection of Privacy and Transborder Flows of Personal Data*. OECD Publishing. Paris. Available at http://www.oecd.org/internet/ieconomy/oecdguidelinesontheprotection-ofprivacyandtransborderflowsofpersonaldata.htm (accessed 21 October 2013).

Pierre Audoin Consultants (2013). PAC webinar: Cloud services – six key opportunities for software and IT services providers. 21 March.

Poletti F, Wheeler NV, Petrovich MN, Baddela N, Numkam Fokoua E, Hayes JR, Gray DR, Li Z, Slavic R, Richardson DJ (2013). Towards high-capacity fibre-optic communications at the speed of light in vacuum. *Nature Photonics*. 7(4): 279–284.

Pyramid Research (2012). Enterprise cloud readiness index excerpt. Available at http://www.pyramidresearch.com/enterprise-cloud-readiness-index-excerpt.htm?sc=PRN121012_PPCRI (accessed 16 October 2013).

Ramos D (2012). *How Latin American Telcos Are Tackling the SME Cloud Opportunity*. Pyramid Research, Inc.

Renda A (2012). Competition, neutrality and diversity in the cloud. *Communications & Strategies*. 85 (1st quarter): 23–44.

Research ICT Africa (2013). Cloud computing country reports prepared for the UNCTAD *Information Economy Report 2013*. Unpublished.

Ryan PS and Gerson J (2012). A primer on Internet exchange points for policymakers and non-engineers. Social Science Research Network, No. 2128103. 12 August.

Sakai H (2011). Standardization activities for cloud computing. *NTT Technical Review*. 9(6): 1–6.

Seidman DR (1986). Transborder data flow: Regulation of international information flow and the Brazilian example. *Journal of Law and Technology*. 31 (Spring).

Singapore, Info-Communications Development Authority (2013). Cloud computing in Singapore: Empowering the next generation businesses. Singapore.

Source8, hurleypalmerflatt and Cushman & Wakefield (2013). Data Centre Risk Index: Informing global investment decisions. Available at http://www.business-sweden.se/PageFiles/9118/DCRI%202013.pdf (accessed 7 October 2013).

Stork C, Calandro E and Gamage R (2013). Future of broad band in Africa. 13 May. Available at: http://www.researchictafrica.net/presentations/Presentations/2013_Stork_Calandro_Gamage_-_The_Future_of_Broadband_in_Africa.pdf (accessed 16 October 2013).

Tech Soup Global (2012). 2012 global cloud computing survey results. Available at http://www.techsoupglobal.org/2012-global-cloud-computing-survey (accessed 4 October 2013).

TeleGeography (2013). Global Bandwidth Research Service: Executive summary. Available at http://www.telegeography.com/page_attachments/products/website/research-services/global-bandwidth-research-service/0003/8368/gb13-exec-sum.pdf (accessed 16 October 2013).

Tweneboah-Koduah S (2013). Unleashing the potential of cloud computing: what is it and what does it mean for public organizations in Ghana. Paper presented at the GhanaTechnology University Centre for Information and Media of University of Aalborg conference. Accra. 16–17 May.

UNCTAD (2004). *E-Commerce and Development Report 2004*. United Nations publication. UNCTAD/SDTE/ECB/20. New York and Geneva.

UNCTAD (2009a). *Estudio sobre las Perspectivas de la Armonización de la Ciberlegislación en Centroamérica y el Caribe*. United Nations publication. UNCTAD/DTL/STICT/2009/3. New York and Geneva.

UNCTAD (2009b). *Study on Prospects for Harmonizing Cyberlegislation in Latin America*. United Nations publication. UNCTAD/DTL/STICT/2009/1. New York and Geneva.

UNCTAD (2010). *Information Economy Report 2010: ICTs, Enterprises and Poverty Alleviation*. United Nations Publication. UNCTAD/IER/2010. Sales No. E.10.II.D.17. New York and Geneva.

UNCTAD (2011a). *ICT Policy Review Egypt 2011*. United Nations publication. UNCTAD/DTL/STICT/2011/6. New York and Geneva.

UNCTAD (2011b). *Information Economy Report 2011: ICTs as an enabler to private sector development*. United Nations publication. UNCTAD/IER/2011. Sales No. E.11.II.D.6. New York and Geneva.

UNCTAD (2012a). *Information Economy Report 2012: The Software Industry and Developing Countries*. United Nations publication. Sales No. E.12.IID.14. UNCTAD/IER/2012. New York and Geneva.

UNCTAD (2012b). *Harmonizing Cyberlaws and Regulations: The Experience of the East African Community*. United Nations publication. UNCTAD/DTL/STICT/2012/4. New York and Geneva.

UNCTAD (2013). *Review of E-commerce Legislation Harmonization in the Association of Southeast Asian Nations*. United Nations publication. UNCTAD/DTL/STICT/2013/1. New York and Geneva.

UNCTAD and Germany, Federal Ministry for Economic Cooperation and Development (2013). *Promoting local IT sector development through public procurement*. United Nations publication. UNCTAD/DTL/STICT/2012/5. New York and Geneva. Available at http://unctad.org/en/PublicationsLibrary/dtlstict2012d5_en.pdf (accessed 21 October 2013).

United Kingdom, Cabinet Office (2011). Government ICT offshoring (international sourcing) guidance. Available at https://www.gov.uk/government/publications/government-ict-offshoring-international-sourcing-guidance (accessed 21 October 2013).

United States, Federal CIO Council and Chief Acquisition Officers Council (2012). *Creating Effective Cloud Computing Contracts for the Federal Government: Best Practices for Acquiring IT as a Service*. February. Available at https://cio.gov/wp-content/uploads/downloads/2012/09/cloudbestpractices.pdf (accessed 22 October 2013).

Walden I (2011). Accessing data in the cloud: The long arm of the law enforcement agent. Queen Mary School of Law Legal Studies Research Paper No. 74/2011. Queen Mary College, University of London. London. November.

Walden I and Savage N (1990). Transborder data flows. In: Walden I, ed., *Information Technology and the Law*. Macmillan. London: 121.

Wattegama C and Kapugama N (2009). Prospects of volunteer computing model in performance data gathering for broadband policy formulation: A case study from South Asia. Available at http://lirneasia.net/wp-content/uploads/2009/10/Broadband-Quality-of-Service-Experience_LIRNEasia.pdf (accessed 14 October 2013).

Yeboah-Boateng E and Cudjoe-Seshie S (2013). Cloud computing: The emerging of application service providers (ASP) in developing economies. *International Journal of Emerging Technology and Advanced Engineering*. 3(5): 703–712.

STATISTICAL ANNEX

Annex table 1.   Enterprise Cloud Services Readiness Index, 2012

Americas		Europe		Asia-Pacific		Africa and Middle East	
2. United States	5.54	3. Germany	5.33	1. Japan	5.74	9. United Arab Emirates	4.4
5. Canada	5.03	6. France	4.87	4. Republic of Korea	5.17	16. Saudi Arabia	3.71
13. Argentina	4.11	7. United Kingdom	4.64	8. Taiwan Province of China	4.56	19. Turkey	3.63
18. Mexico	3.64	11. Spain	4.14	10. China	4.24	21. Israel	3.47
20. Brazil	3.61	12. Italy	4.13	14. Hong Kong, China	3.94	30. South Africa	2.71
24. Colombia	3.31	17. Romania	3.7	15. Philippines	3.88	34. Morocco	2.37
27. Puerto Rico	2.85	19. Turkey	3.63	22. Malaysia	3.47	36. Egypt	2.07
28. Venezuela (Bolivarian Republic of)	2.75	23. Russian Federation	3.45	26. India	3.01	42. Nigeria	1.65
29. Costa Rica	2.74	25. Poland	3.02	33. Viet Nam	2.43		
31. Chile	2.61	39. Czech Republic	1.91	35. Singapore	2.31		
32. Panama	2.47			38. Thailand	1.95		
37. El Salvador	2.02			40. Indonesia	1.87		
41. Guatemala	1.75						
43. Peru	1.59						
44. Ecuador	1.46						
45. Uruguay	1.38						
46. Bolivia (Plurinational State of)	0.94						
47. Honduras	0.76						
48. Paraguay	0.67						
49. Nicaragua	0.44						

Source: Pyramid Research.

Rank	Economy	Overall score	Data privacy	Security	Cybercrime	Intellectual property	Support for industry-led standards and international harmonization of rules	Promoting free trade	ICT readiness and broadband deployment
	Annex table 2. 2013 BSA Global Cloud Computing Scorecard								
1	Japan	83.3	8.8	8.4	10	17.2	8.8	9.2	20.9
2	Australia	79.2	7.9	6	9.4	17.6	10	7	21.3
3	Germany	79	6.6	6.4	10	16.8	9.8	9.2	20.2
4	United States	78.6	6.5	7.6	8.8	16.6	9.4	8	21.7
5	France	78.4	6.5	7.6	10	16.4	9.6	8.8	19.5
6	Italy	76.6	6.2	7.6	9.6	17.4	9.8	8.8	17.2
7	United Kingdom	76.6	6.9	8	6.8	17.4	9.2	6.8	21.5
8	Republic of Korea	76	9.3	6	4.8	17.6	9.6	7	21.7
9	Spain	73.9	6.5	6.4	8.8	15.2	9.8	9.4	17.8
10	Singapore	72.2	3.2	3.6	9	17.2	8.8	8.6	21.8
11	Poland	70.7	6.4	5.6	8.8	16.8	9.8	8.4	14.9
12	Canada	70.4	8.1	6.8	6.2	10.8	10	9.6	18.9
13	Malaysia	59.2	7.1	5.6	5.4	11.4	10	3.8	15.9
14	Mexico	56.4	7.5	4.8	8.6	12.4	9.2	3	10.9
15	Argentina	55.1	5	6	8.2	12.4	4.6	5.8	13.1
16	Russian Federation	52.3	5.4	6.4	6.8	8.4	6.6	5.2	13.5
17	Turkey	52.1	3.5	4	6.4	14	8.6	2.8	12.8
18	South Africa	50.4	2.8	3.2	9.8	13.6	9.8	1.8	9.4
19	India	50	4.1	4.4	7.4	9.2	10	6.4	8.5
20	Indonesia	49.7	4.6	3.2	7	11.2	8.2	5.2	10.3
21	China	47.5	3.5	2	4.6	13.6	7.8	4.8	11.2
22	Thailand	42.6	3.5	1.6	7.4	7.2	8.8	3	11.1
23	Viet Nam	39.5	4.1	2.8	5	9.2	7	1.4	10
24	Brazil	35.1	4.7	3.6	1.6	7.2	3.4	2.2	12.4

Source: Business Software Alliance and Galexia, 2012.

Economy	Data privacy	International connectivity	Data sovereignty	Broadband quality	Government online services and ICT prioritization	Power grid and green policy	Intellectual property protection	Business sophistication	Data centre risk	Freedom of information access	Cloud Readiness Index	Rank
Japan	9.0	10.0	5.6	7.6	7.9	7.8	7.6	8.4	6.0	8.9	78.8	1
Republic of Korea	9.0	8.0	6.2	9.0	9.1	7.1	5.9	6.9	7.4	7.7	76.3	2
Hong Kong, China	7.5	7.4	7.6	7.6	8.4	5.7	7.9	7.1	8.0	8.7	75.9	3
Singapore	4.5	9.2	8.1	6.3	9.5	5.7	8.7	7.3	6.4	7.1	72.8	4
Taiwan Province of China	7.0	7.5	5.9	6.1	8.8	7.1	7.1	7.5	6.5	8.9	72.4	5
New Zealand	9.0	1.3	8.1	5.4	7.8	8.3	8.3	6.6	7.1	8.9	70.8	6
Australia	7.5	2.7	7.3	6.0	8.2	7.5	7.6	6.7	5.6	8.6	67.7	7
Malaysia	7.5	4.6	5.6	3.7	8.2	6.2	7.0	7.1	6.2	6.9	63.0	8
India	6.0	8.4	4.7	2.4	6.3	3.3	5.0	6.1	3.1	7.6	52.7	9
China	4.0	5.0	3.5	3.5	6.6	4.5	5.7	6.2	5.1	7.1	51.2	10
Indonesia	6.0	4.8	2.1	2.2	5.7	4.9	5.1	6.0	3.1	7.2	47.1	11
Philippines	2.5	4.6	4.3	2.3	5.5	5.8	4.0	5.9	3.6	7.5	46.0	12
Thailand	3.0	2.8	1.5	5.9	5.5	4.8	4.4	6.0	3.6	7.4	44.9	13
Viet Nam	5.0	3.2	3.9	2.2	5.9	3.8	3.6	5.3	5.4	6.6	44.9	13

Annex table 3.   Asia Cloud Computing Association Readiness Index, 2012

Source: Asia Cloud Computing Association.

Annex table 4.	Cisco global cloud readiness, 2012						
Top 10 fixed network performing economies				Top 10 mobile network performing economies			
	Download (kbps)	Upload (kbps)	Latency (ms)		Download (kbps)	Upload (kbps)	Latency (ms)
Bulgaria	18 973	12 256	35	Austria	3 671	1 864	107
Hong Kong, China	27 710	22 570	32	Canada	5 824	2 980	128
Japan	20 335	17 326	39	Denmark	3 445	1 316	121
Republic of Korea	23 222	22 682	38	Finland	3 439	1 791	136
Latvia	19 240	14 146	48	Hungary	3 607	1 278	99
Lithuania	26 810	21 308	39	Poland	3 080	1 207	135
Netherlands	22 495	5 822	29	Portugal	2 875	1 561	105
Romania	22 937	11 834	39	Romania	3 133	1 178	115
Singapore	19 399	12 255	38	Sweden	3 377	1 446	110
Sweden	20 835	9 657	53	United Arab Emirates	3 133	1 353	120

Source: http://www.cisco.com/en/US/solutions/collateral/ns341/ns525/ns537/ns705/ns1175/CloudIndex_Supplement.html (accessed 10 October 2013).
Note: Countries are listed in alphabetical order.

Annex table 5.	Key cloud service infrastructure indicators

Economy	Fixed download (kbps)	Fixed upload (kbps)	Fixed latency (ms)	Mobile download (kbps)	Mobile upload (kbps)	Mobile latency (ms)	Co-location data centres, 2013	IXPs, 2013	International Internet bandwidth, 2011 (bps per Internet user)	Secure Internet servers, 2012 (per 1 million people)
Afghanistan				626	413	561				1.0
Albania	2 568	1 051	102	2 843	1 015	197		1	19 038	18.3
Algeria	683	306	144	695	340	253			8 933	1.4
Angola				1 044	498	317		1		3.6
Antigua and Barbuda				2 007	1 462	193			56 545	1 071.2
Argentina	2 959	757	74	2 649	763	205	6	10	25 712	42.3
Armenia	3 059	2 358	88	4 056	2 531	158		1		26.4
Aruba				2 972	554	133				396.0
Australia	7 876	1 261	54	2 894	950	161	73	14	50 396	1 777.5
Austria	9 103	2 141	56	3 671	1 864	107	10	3	81 919	1 147.0
Azerbaijan	2 196	732	96	2 480	1 053	171	1		19 102	6.3
Bahrain	2 229	803	114	1 870	736	132	1	1	14 719	137.6
Bangladesh	739	501	153	642	542	346		2		0.8
Barbados				2 506	756	157			38 177	397.0
Belarus	2 468	1 259	85	2 794	1 187	184	2	1	52 833	18.4
Belgium	16 045	2 024	39	8 484	1 730	94	28	1	131 137	697.3
Belize				594	451	315				286.8
Bermuda				3 083	1 979	128				5 030.1
Bolivia (Plurinational State of)				592	302	641	1		4 162	10.0
Bosnia and Herzegovina	2 879	587	69	3 377	732	106		1	17 767	27.5
Brazil	4 891	975	67	3 187	725	220	22	23	29 041	55.5
Brunei Darussalam	1 699	646	136	1 451	678	211			21 995	116.3
Bulgaria	18 973	12 256	35	8 115	5 869	105	17	2	65 832	167.3
Cambodia	2 194	1 804	78	1 840	1 289	181	3	1	13 530	3.0
Canada	10 215	1 564	59	2 972	1 293	308	86	7	70 150	1 277.2
Cayman Islands				2 187	557	276				2 603.8
Chile	6 080	1 448	66	3 563	999	243	4	1	20 414	82.3
China	5 075	2 960	87	1 499	709	655	17	4	2 692	3.1
Hong Kong	27 710	22 570	32	6 751	5 335	112	26	2	964 616	643.2
Taiwan Province	17 106	2 901	42	2 213	327	180	4	3		..
Colombia	2 631	994	105	2 021	791	218	2	1	16 796	28.0
Costa Rica	1 934	644	145	684	310	134	2		36 216	98.7
Côte d'Ivoire				871	611	415		1	18 044	1.5
Croatia	4 228	707	62	3 038	1 063	145	2	1	19 948	244.8
Cyprus	3 871	733	68				7	1	53 569	969.7
Czech Republic	11 788	5 836	35	6 420	3 499	88	16	3	91 064	510.6

Annex table 5.	Key cloud service infrastructure indicators *(continued)*									
Economy	Fixed download (kbps)	Fixed upload (kbps)	Fixed latency (ms)	Mobile download (kbps)	Mobile upload (kbps)	Mobile latency (ms)	Co-location data centres, 2013	IXPs, 2013	International Internet bandwidth, 2011 (bps per Internet user)	Secure Internet servers, 2012 (per 1 million people)
Denmark	14 268	7 218	44	3 288	1 492	88	28	2	159 511	2 243.0
Dominican Republic	1 561	634	111	1 308	833	198		1	11 205	23.9
Ecuador	2 053	1 903	109	1 834	1 045	286		2	27 742	23.8
Egypt	1 029	330	132				9	2	6 754	3.7
El Salvador	2 128	1 174	113	2 036	774	270			4 176	20.9
Estonia	9 282	3 716	54	4 423	2 187	134	7	3	24 378	653.8
Finland	10 848	3 435	60	3 508	1 453	149	11	4	118 445	1 621.6
France	9 214	1 974	66	2 196	1 050	133	123	19	78 590	424.9
Georgia	4 076	2 784	69	4 891	3 718	136			15 796	27.2
Germany	13 680	2 536	54	2 847	1 144	150	144	14	74 786	1 102.4
Ghana	2 618	984	122	1 592	749	234		1	225	3.1
Greece	5 438	677	69	4 781	810	110	9	1	26 008	169.6
Guatemala	1 916	814	130	1 553	780	287				14.5
Haiti				1 623	918	246		1		1.7
Honduras	2 210	1 351	94	1 679	804	195			4 866	9.5
Hungary	12 325	4 031	43	6 659	2 641	92	8	1	12 245	252.0
Iceland	17 611	11 404	32	7 399	5 373	90	3	1	287 139	3 064.0
India	1 468	907	121	1 246	748	323	69	7	5 423	3.5
Indonesia	1 009	440	139	839	450	336	22	8	7 196	4.0
Iran (Islamic Republic of)	1 031	504	138	206	191	673	5		3 540	1.3
Iraq	1 877	1 464	174	2 046	1 600	190				0.1
Ireland	5 693	1 409	79				15	3	69 031	1 056.9
Israel	8 460	1 060	52	4 032	830	135	5	1	11 335	429.9
Italy	4 393	765	81				37	7	60 820	210.7
Jamaica	2 748	706	122	3 355	975	265			23 077	51.4
Japan	20 335	17 326	39	6 141	3 352	96	36	16	23 111	774.3
Jordan	2 172	660	131	2 338	656	235	3		6 337	29.7
Kazakhstan	4 049	2 736	101	3 331	2 068	224		1	23 590	7.8
Kenya	2 856	1 740	114	2 354	1 118	311	2	2	4 544	4.2
Kuwait	2 467	1 081	123	1 854	761	177	1			202.3
Latvia	19 240	14 146	48	7 487	5 991	110	18	1	44 779	245.2
Lebanon	920	230	263	1 300	344	166	1	1	2 257	51.3
Lithuania	26 810	21 308	39	7 691	6 052	111	6	2	57 571	262.4
Luxembourg	16 706	8 295	66	6 561	2 552	84	12	2	89 564	2 050.0
Malaysia	2 864	2 324	82				26	1	10 651	66.1
Maldives				1 453	807	379		1	30 659	104.8

Annex table 5.   **Key cloud service infrastructure indicators** *(continued)*

Economy	Fixed download (kbps)	Fixed upload (kbps)	Fixed latency (ms)	Mobile download (kbps)	Mobile upload (kbps)	Mobile latency (ms)	Co-location data centres, 2013	IXPs, 2013	International Internet bandwidth, 2011 (bps per Internet user)	Secure Internet servers, 2012 (per 1 million people)
Malta	12 811	1 345	35	6 853	1 153	104	7	1	47 850	1 662.6
Mauritius	1 186	243	97	1 060	278	309	7	1	12 714	132.4
Mexico	3 688	1 204	90				9		8 743	29.7
Moldova	13 567	9 659	56	6 573	5 330	127		1	91 118	27.6
Mongolia	3 263	2 043	92					1	53 576	17.6
Montenegro	3 534	701	75	2 608	608	170				28.4
Morocco	2 139	398	133	1 898	444	201	2		7 558	3.8
Mozambique				797	436	334		1	1 244	1.4
Myanmar				798	715	334			8 180	0.1
Namibia				1 277	445	334			2 349	19.0
Nepal	919	738	127	985	673	293	1	1	1 531	2.2
Netherlands	22 495	5 822	29	2 209	638	215	71	5	162 532	2 880.0
New Caledonia				3 418	1 072	177				208.7
New Zealand	7 024	1 348	65	5 537	1 282	108	10	5	23 706	1 505.2
Nicaragua	1 996	866	99					1	12 857	10.2
Nigeria	1 299	1 005	239	1 106	763	428	1	1	368	1.8
Norway	15 771	7 665	52	6 874	3 846	140	13	7	151 257	1 924.8
Oman	2 674	626	98						11 648	60.6
Pakistan	1 245	511	131				9	1	4 752	1.3
Panama	2 442	968	158	1 637	614	324	3	1	44 121	144.8
Paraguay	1 276	806	184	1 616	687	292		1	9 482	11.4
Peru				1 174	343	615		1	9 319	22.1
Philippines	1 361	470	102	844	237	346		2	12 360	8.8
Poland	8 006	2 297	57				27	5	40 244	309.7
Portugal	17 267	3 047	43	8 379	2 578	87	22	1	135 332	238.1
Puerto Rico	2 685	733	77				1	1		113.0
Qatar	3 001	1 430	85				3		22 333	149.1
Republic of Korea	23 222	22 682	38	8 065	7 852	106	2	4	17 170	2 733.4
Romania	22 937	11 834	39	8 235	4 365	96	32	3	114 451	67.2
Russian Federation	9 172	9 161	62				35	16	31 911	38.6
Samoa				1 522	406	400				27.1
Saudi Arabia	4 030	755	92	2 696	897	159	10	1	32 985	29.9
Senegal				1 216	319	395			2 909	2.2
Serbia	4 167	861	59	3 648	1 013	127	2	1	76 761	27.2
Singapore	19 399	12 255	38	2 132	289	153	14	3	547 064	651.6
Slovakia	10 356	4 298	46	5 088	2 300	113	13	3	12 276	221.0

Annex table 5. Key cloud service infrastructure indicators *(continued)*										
Economy	Fixed download (kbps)	Fixed upload (kbps)	Fixed latency (ms)	Mobile download (kbps)	Mobile upload (kbps)	Mobile latency (ms)	Co-location data centres, 2013	IXPs, 2013	International Internet bandwidth, 2011 (bps per Internet user)	Secure Internet servers, 2012 (per 1 million people)
Slovenia	7 199	4 198	50	5 975	3 301	85	7	1	68 250	567.1
Solomon Islands				6 361	1 996	156			3 893	8.8
South Africa	2 045	764	95	2 069	865	151	17	5	18 874	84.6
Spain	10 203	1 642	69				42	5	64 069	295.9
Sri Lanka	2 193	513	125	1 839	597	278		1	5 224	7.3
Sudan				821	368	633				0.0
Suriname				738	312	183				43.1
Sweden	20 835	9 657	53	2 462	890	150	29	12	244 440	1 535.1
Switzerland	16 864	3 532	41				49	3	167 636	2 379.0
Syrian Arab Republic	725	275	215						3 489	0.3
Tajikistan				1 619	615	221				1.0
Thailand	5 200	965	71	1 626	542	165	8	1	10 622	19.1
The former Yugoslav Republic of Macedonia	5 609	2 139	60	4 699	1 859	114	1	1	17 945	41.1
Trinidad and Tobago	6 184	1 039	109	4 305	1 000	303			19 753	97.7
Tunisia	1 433	626	147	1 565	628	249		1	14 832	13.0
Turkey	4 508	1 121	59				27	1	33 938	125.8
Turkmenistan				472	202	478			1 567	0.2

Annex table 5.   Key cloud service infrastructure indicators *(continued)*

Economy	Fixed download (kbps)	Fixed upload (kbps)	Fixed latency (ms)	Mobile download (kbps)	Mobile upload (kbps)	Mobile latency (ms)	Co-location data centres, 2013	IXPs, 2013	International Internet bandwidth, 2011 (bps per Internet user)	Secure Internet servers, 2012 (per 1 million people)
Uganda				912	422	586		1	1 752	1.5
Ukraine	11 300	8 710	70	6 875	5 334	165	21	8	9 835	23.9
United Arab Emirates	8 002	2 952	51				4	1	27 609	206.8
United Kingdom	11 460	2 173	54	2 480	948	335	191	9	166 073	1 534.1
United Republic of Tanzania				837	519	623		2	902	0.8
United States	10 332	2 956	64	2 366	923	241	1 144	86	47 174	1 501.0
Uruguay	2 392	530	75	2 083	540	158	3		32 078	84.3
Uzbekistan				1 428	659	256			579	0.8
Venezuela (Bolivarian Republic of)	1 153	386	139	836	207	369			8 108	10.9
Viet Nam	5 851	4 133	70	2 009	593	251	5	3	9 998	6.5
Yemen				939	410	348			1 082	0.4
Zambia				786	463	397		1	452	2.4
Zimbabwe				981	502	355		1	1 748	3.2

Sources and notes: Download and upload speeds and latency: Data are sourced from Cisco (based on analysis dated 2012; see http://www.cisco.com/en/US/solutions/collateral/ns341/ns525/ns537/ns705/ns1175/CloudIndex_Supplement. html (accessed 10 October 2013). The performance data are gathered from network tests and represent the average for the economy. Cisco breaks down the performance data by fixed and mobile networks, and business and consumer users. The fixed network data refer to overall consumer and business usage. The mobile network data generally refer to business usage that had the largest data availability. If this data was not available, overall consumer and business usage is used. If there are insufficient test results, data for the country are not included. Co-location data centres: Data are sourced from the database of Data Centre Map (see http://www.datacentermap.com/ datacenters.html (accessed 10 October 2013)). They were extracted in July 2013. Data refer to the number of co-location data centres in the country. A co-location data centre is a facility that provides space for customers to place their data servers. IXPs: Data sourced from Packet Clearing House (see https://prefix.pch.net/applications/ixpdir/summary/ (accessed 10 October 2013)). They were extracted in July 2013. Data refer to the number of IXPs in the economy. An IXP is a facility ISPs exchange Internet traffic. International Internet bandwidth (bps per Internet user): Data are sourced from ITU. See http://www.itu.int/ITU-D/ict/publications/idi/ (accessed 10 October 2013). They refer to 2011. International Internet bandwidth refers to the total used capacity of international Internet bandwidth. It is measured as the sum of used capacity of all Internet exchanges (locations where Internet traffic is exchanged) offering international bandwidth. If capacity is asymmetric (i.e. more incoming (downlink) than outgoing (uplink) capacity), then the incoming (downlink) capacity is used. Secure Internet servers (per 1 million people): Data are sourced from the World Bank (see http://data.worldbank. org/indicator/IT.NET.SECR.P6 (accessed 10 October 2013). They refer to 2012. Secure servers are servers using encryption technology in Internet transactions.

Abbreviations: bps – bit per second, ms – millisecond

GLOSSARY

cloud aggregators, systems integrators and brokers	Sometimes referred to as cloud service partners, they help customers identify the best solutions and integrate services from different cloud service providers (section I.D). They identify the most suitable cloud services, integrate them, manage relationships with cloud providers and, as a result, offer clients a simpler interface for their IT activities (section III.B.1(c)).
cloud computing	A way of delivering applications, services or content remotely to end users, rather than requiring them to hold data, software or applications on their own devices (section I.B.1).
cloud economy ecosystem	The complex set of relationships, synergies and interactions between technology and business, governance and innovation, production and consumption, different businesses and different stakeholders, that contributes to economic and social development. Encompasses the deployment and impacts of cloud computing and cloud services within the wider information economy and thereby for national economic development (section I.D).
cloud service providers	Businesses that own the cloud computing centres and other infrastructure, that form the cloud, and make services, platforms and/or infrastructure available through them to inter-cloud service providers and cloud service customers (section I.D).
cloud services	Services that are provided and used by clients "on demand at any time, through any access network, using any connected devices [that use] cloud computing technologies" (see section I.B.1).
cloud-based services	Cloud services that require software installation to make use of the cloud's resources (section I.B.1).
cloud service customers	Citizens, consumers, enterprises and Governments that procure various kinds of cloud services directly from cloud service providers or inter-cloud service providers (section I.D.).
co-location data centre	A facility that provides space for multiple customers to place their data servers (section II.B.3).
community cloud	A resource/service provided for and shared between a limited range of clients/users from a specific community with common concerns. It can be managed internally or by a third party and hosted internally or externally. It might be considered halfway between public and private cloud provisioning (section I.B.3).
download speed	The time taken to transfer data packets from a server to an end user device. Usually measured in kilobits per second (kbps) or megabits per second (Mbps) (section II.B.5).
hybrid cloud	Expands deployment options for cloud services by mixing, for example, public and private cloud provision (section I.B.3).
infrastructure as a service (IaaS)	Cloud service category. In this mode, the provider's processing, storage, networks and other fundamental computing resources allow the customer to deploy and run software, which can include operating systems and applications. The customer does not manage or control the underlying cloud infrastructure but has control over operating systems, storage, and deployed applications; and possibly limited control of select networking components (for example, host firewalls) (section I.B.1).
inter-cloud service providers	Providers of cloud services that rely on one or more other cloud service provider(s) (section I.D).

Internet exchange point	A facility where Internet service providers (ISPs) exchange Internet traffic (section II.B.3).
jitter	The variation of latency or the variation in time of data packets arriving. Usually measured in milliseconds (ms) (section II.B.5).
latency or round trip time (RTT)	Time taken for a packet to reach the destination server and return to the client (the end-user device). Usually measured in milliseconds (ms) (section II.B.5).
multi-tenancy	Physical and virtual resources are allocated in such a way that multiple tenants and their computations and data are isolated from and inaccessible to one another (section I.B).
packet loss	The share of packets that fail to arrive at the destination server. Usually measured as a percentage of the total number of packets transferred (section II.B.5).
platform as a service (PaaS)	Cloud service category. In this case, the customer deploys its own applications and data on platform tools, including programming tools, belonging to and managed by the cloud provider. The consumer does not manage or control the underlying cloud infrastructure including network, servers, operating systems, or storage, but has control over the deployed applications and possibly configuration settings for the application-hosting environment (section I.B.2).
private cloud	A proprietary resource provided for a single organization (for example a Government or large enterprise). It can be managed internally or by a third party and hosted internally or externally (section I.B.3).
public cloud	An open resource that offers services over a network that is open for public use. Many mass market services widely used by individuals, such as webmail, storage and social media are examples of public cloud services (section I.B.3).
secure Internet servers	Servers using encryption technology in Internet transactions (section II.B.3).
software as a service (SaaS)	Cloud service category. In this case, the customer takes advantage of software running on the provider's cloud infrastructure rather than on its own hardware. The applications required are accessible from various client devices through either a thin client interface, such as a web browser (for example, web-based email), or a program interface. In SaaS services, the customer has no control over the underlying cloud infrastructure, accessing applications through a web browser or separate program interface (section I.B.2).
upload speed	Time taken to transmit data packets from an end user device to a server. Usually measured in kilobits per second (kbps) or Mbps (section II.B.5).
virtualization	Implies the creation of a "virtual version" of a device or resource, such as a server, storage device, network or an operating system where the framework divides the resource into one or more different execution environments (section I.B.1).

LIST OF SELECTED PUBLICATIONS IN THE AREA OF SCIENCE, TECHNOLOGY AND ICT FOR DEVELOPMENT

A. Flagship reports

Information Economy Report 2013: Cloud Computing and Developing Countries. United Nations publication. Sales no. E.13.II.D.6. New York and Geneva.

Information Economy Report 2012: The Software Industry and Developing Countries. United Nations publication. Sales no. E.12.II.D.14. New York and Geneva.

Information Economy Report 2011: ICTs as an Enabler for Private Sector Development. United Nations publication. Sales no. E.11.II.D.6. New York and Geneva.

Technology and Innovation Report 2012: Innovation, Technology and South-South Collaboration. United Nations publication. UNCTAD/TIR/2012. New York and Geneva.

Technology and Innovation Report 2011: Powering Development with Renewable Energy Technologies. United Nations publication. UNCTAD/TIR/2011. New York and Geneva.

Technology and Innovation Report 2010: Enhancing Food Security in Africa through Science, Technology and Innovation. United Nations publication. UNCTAD/TIR/2009. New York and Geneva.

Information Economy Report 2010: ICTs, Enterprises and Poverty Alleviation. United Nations publication. Sales no. E.10.II.D.17. New York and Geneva. October.

Information Economy Report 2009: Trends and Outlook in Turbulent Times. United Nations publication. Sales no. E.09.II.D.18. New York and Geneva. October.

Information Economy Report 2007–2008: Science and Technology for Development – The New Paradigm of ICT. United Nations publication. Sales no. E.07.II.D.13. New York and Geneva.

Information Economy Report 2006: The Development Perspective. United Nations publication. Sales no. E.06.II.D.8. New York and Geneva.

Information Economy Report 2005: E-commerce and Development. United Nations publication. Sales no. E.05.II.D.19. New York and Geneva.

E-Commerce and Development Report 2004. United Nations publication. New York and Geneva.

E-Commerce and Development Report 2003. United Nations publication. Sales no. E.03.II.D.30. New York and Geneva.

E-Commerce and Development Report 2002. United Nations publication. New York and Geneva.

E-Commerce and Development Report 2001. United Nations publication. Sales no. E.01.II.D.30. New York and Geneva.

B. ICT Policy Reviews

ICT Policy Review of Egypt. United Nations publication (2011). New York and Geneva.

C. Science, Technology and Innovation Policy Reviews

Science, Technology & Innovation Policy Review of the Dominican Republic. United Nations publication. UNCTAD/DTL/STICT/2012/1. New York and Geneva.

A Framework for Science, Technology and Innovation Policy Reviews. United Nations publication. UNCTAD/DTL/STICT/2011/7. New York and Geneva.

Science, Technology & Innovation Policy Review of El Salvador. United Nations publication. UNCTAD/DTL/STICT/2011/4. New York and Geneva.

Science, Technology and Innovation Policy Review of Peru. United Nations publication. UNCTAD/DTL/STICT/2010/2. New York and Geneva.

Science, Technology and Innovation Policy Review of Ghana. United Nations publication. UNCTAD/DTL/STICT/2009/8. New York and Geneva.

Science, Technology and Innovation Policy Review of Lesotho. United Nations publication. UNCTAD/DTL/STICT/2009/7. New York and Geneva.

Science, Technology and Innovation Policy Review of Mauritania. United Nations publication. UNCTAD/DTL/STICT/2009/6. New York and Geneva.

Science, Technology and Innovation Policy Review of Angola. United Nations publication. UNCTAD/SDTE/STICT/2008/1. New York and Geneva.

Science, Technology and Innovation Policy Review: the Islamic Republic of Iran. United Nations publication. UNCTAD/ITE/IPC/2005/7. New York and Geneva.

Investment and Innovation Policy Review of Ethiopia. United Nations publication. UNCTAD/ITE/IPC/Misc.4. New York and Geneva.

Science, Technology and Innovation Policy Review: Colombia. United Nations publication. Sales no. E.99.II.D.13. New York and Geneva.

Science, Technology and Innovation Policy Review: Jamaica. United Nations publication. Sales no. E.98.II.D.7. New York and Geneva.

D. Other publications

Review of E-commerce Legislation Harmonization in the Association of Southeast Asian Nations. UNCTAD/DTL/STICT/2013/1. United Nations publication. New York and Geneva.

Mobile Money for Business Development in the East African Community: A Comparative Study of Existing Platforms and Regulations. UNCTAD/DTL/STICT/2012/2. United Nations publication. New York and Geneva.

UNCTAD Current Studies on Geospatial Science and Technology for Development. United Nations Commission on Science and Technology for Development. United Nations publication. UNCTAD/DTL/STICT/2012/3. New York and Geneva.

Promoting Local IT Sector Development through Public Procurement. UNCTAD/DTL/STICT/2012/5. United Nations Publication. New York and Geneva.

UNCTAD Current Studies on Applying a Gender Lens to Science, Technology and Innovation. United Nations Commission on Science and Technology for Development. United Nations publication. UNCTAD/DTL/STICT/2011/5. New York and Geneva.

UNCTAD Current Studies on Implementing WSIS Outcomes: Experience to Date and Prospects for the Future. United Nations Commission on Science and Technology for Development. United Nations publication. UNCTAD/DTL/STICT/2011/3. New York and Geneva.

UNCTAD Current Studies on Water for Food: Innovative Water Management Technologies for Food Security and Poverty Alleviation. UNCTAD Current Studies on Science, Technology and Innovation. United Nations publication. UNCTAD/DTL/STICT/2011/2. New York and Geneva.

UNCTAD Current Studies on Measuring the Impacts of Information and Communication Technology for Development. UNCTAD Current Studies on Science, Technology and Innovation. United Nations publication. UNCTAD/DTL/STICT/2011/1. New York and Geneva.

UNCTAD Current Studies on Financing Mechanisms for Information and Communication Technologies for Development. UNCTAD Current Studies on Science, Technology and Innovation. United Nations publication. UNCTAD/DTL/STICT/2009/5. New York and Geneva.

UNCTAD Current Studies on Green and Renewable Energy Technologies for Rural Development. UNCTAD Current Studies on Science, Technology and Innovation. United Nations publication. UNCTAD/DTL/STICT/2009/4. New York and Geneva.

Study on Prospects for Harmonizing Cyberlegislation in Central America and the Caribbean. UNCTAD/DTL/STICT/2009/3. New York and Geneva. (In English and Spanish)

Study on Prospects for Harmonizing Cyberlegislation in Latin America. UNCTAD publication. UNCTAD/DTL/STICT/2009/1. New York and Geneva. (In English and Spanish.)

Manual for the Production of Statistics on the Information Economy 2009 Revised Edition. United Nations publication. UNCTAD/SDTE/ECB/2007/2/REV.1. New York and Geneva.

WSIS Follow-up Report 2008. United Nations publication. UNCTAD/DTL/STICT/2008/1. New York and Geneva.

Measuring the Impact of ICT Use in Business: the Case of Manufacturing in Thailand. United Nations publication. Sales no. E.08.II.D.13. New York and Geneva.

World Information Society Report 2007: Beyond WSIS. United Nations and ITU publication. Geneva.

World Information Society Report 2006. United Nations and ITU publication. Geneva.

The Digital Divide: ICT Diffusion Index 2005. United Nations publication. New York and Geneva.

The Digital Divide: ICT Development Indices 2004. United Nations publication. New York and Geneva.

Africa's Technology Gap: Case Studies on Kenya, Ghana, Tanzania and Uganda. United Nations publication. UNCTAD/ITE/IPC/Misc.13. New York and Geneva.

The Biotechnology Promise: Capacity-Building for Participation of Developing Countries in the Bioeconomy. United Nations publication. UNCTAD/ITE/IPC/2004/2. New York and Geneva.

Information and Communication Technology Development Indices. United Nations publication. Sales no. E.03.II.D.14. New York and Geneva.

Investment and Technology Policies for Competitiveness: Review of Successful Country Experiences. United Nations publication. UNCTAD/ITE/IPC/2003/2. New York and Geneva.

Electronic Commerce and Music Business Development in Jamaica: A Portal to the New Economy? United Nations publication. Sales no. E.02.II.D.17. New York and Geneva.

Changing Dynamics of Global Computer Software and Services Industry: Implications for Developing Countries. United Nations publication. Sales no. E.02.II.D.3. New York and Geneva.

Partnerships and Networking in Science and Technology for Development. United Nations publication. Sales no. E.02.II.D.5. New York and Geneva.

Transfer of Technology for Successful Integration into the Global Economy: A Case Study of Embraer in Brazil. United Nations publication. UNCTAD/ITE/IPC/Misc.20. New York and Geneva.

Transfer of Technology for Successful Integration into the Global Economy: A Case Study of the South African Automotive Industry. United Nations publication. UNCTAD/ITE/IPC/Misc.21. New York and Geneva.

Transfer of Technology for the Successful Integration into the Global Economy: A Case Study of the Pharmaceutical Industry in India. United Nations publication. UNCTAD/ITE/IPC/Misc.22. New York and Geneva.

Coalition of Resources for Information and Communication Technologies. United Nations publication. UNCTAD/ITE/TEB/13. New York and Geneva.

Key Issues in Biotechnology. United Nations publication. UNCTAD/ITE/TEB/10. New York and Geneva.

An Assault on Poverty: Basic Human Needs, Science and Technology. Joint publication with IDRC. ISBN 0-88936-800-7.

Compendium of International Arrangements on Transfer of Technology: Selected Instruments. United Nations publication. Sales no. E.01.II.D.28. New York and Geneva.

E. Publications by the Partnership on Measuring ICT for Development

Measuring the WSIS Targets - A statistical framework. ITU. Geneva.

Core ICT Indicators 2010. ITU. Geneva.

The Global Information Society: A Statistical View 2008. United Nations publication. Santiago.

Measuring ICT: The Global Status of ICT Indicators. Partnership on Measuring ICT for Development. United Nations ICT Task Force. New York.

READERSHIP SURVEY

Information Economy Report 2013: The Cloud Economy and Developing Countries

In order to improve the quality of this report and other publications of the Science, Technology and ICT Branch of UNCTAD, we welcome the views of our readers on this publication. It would be greatly appreciated if you would complete the following questionnaire and return it to:

ICT Analysis Section, Office E-7075

Science, Technology and ICT Branch

Division on Technology and Logistics

United Nations

Palais des Nations,

CH-1211, Geneva, Switzerland

Fax: 41 22 917 00 50

ICT4D@unctad.org

1. Name and address of respondent (optional)

....

....

....

2. Which of the following best describes your area of work?

Government ministry (please specify)	❏	Not-for-profit organization	❏
National statistics office	❏	Public enterprise	❏
Telecommunication regulatory authority	❏	Academic or research institution	❏
Private enterprise	❏	Media	❏
International organization	❏	Other (please specify)	❏

3. In which country do you work? ....

4. What is your assessment of the contents of this publication?

Excellent ❏

Good ❏

Adequate ❏

Poor ❏

5. How useful is this publication to your work?

              Very useful   ❑

     Somewhat useful   ❑

              Irrelevant   ❑

6. Please indicate the three things you liked best about this publication.

a) ....

b) ....

c) ....

7. Please indicate the three things you liked least about this publication.

a) ....

b) ....

c) ....

8. What additional aspects would you like future editions of this report to cover:

....

....

....

9. Other comments:

....

....

....